Practical Knots
and Ropework

Practical Knots and Ropework

Percy W. Blandford

Dover Publications, Inc.
Mineola, New York

623.8882

Preface

Man has made ropes and tied knots in them from the earliest days. Until very recently, all ropemaking materials were natural products, but now nearly all ropes are made of synthetic materials and some of these require knots to be made in different ways, all of which are described in this book. Older books that were only concerned with natural fiber ropes may be unsatisfactory guides today.

Of the very large number of knots that have been devised over the thousands of years of man's use of ropes, by far the largest number have been associated with the sailing ships that reached their peak a century ago. So many knots had special applications that no longer exist. Those knots that may have modern uses have been included in this book, but anyone interested in the historical aspects of knotting will find guidance in some of the books listed in the Bibliography. Similarly, decorative ropework is such a vast subject that it can only be dealt with briefly in a book devoted mainly to practical knotting and splicing. More information can be found in one of the specialized books listed.

There are many names for some knots, but those used here are believed to be the most usual ones. Some authorities say the word *knot* should only be applied to something worked in a single rope, that joining knots are *bends* and that *hitches* are used to join ropes to solid objects. These would be very useful classifications, but there are far too many exceptions in recognized names. In this book the terms bends and hitches are used where they have been accepted for particular applications, but there has to be a collective word and that word is knots. Similarly, there have been certain specialized terms, often with seafaring connotations, that appear in some knotting instructions. There are occasions when these are especially applicable, but in general, everyday language is more suitable and that is used in most places in this book. An oldtime seaman might have *bent* two ropes together, but we *tie* them. He might *cast off* a knot. We would *undo* it. There may be some satisfaction to be obtained out of using language appropriate to an activity, but this is not a book especially for seamen. It is hoped that it will be of use to all users of rope, so the terms given are those expected to be most easily understood.

One of the most difficult things to do is to tell someone in print how to make a knot without using diagrams. Consequently, about half of this book is made up of drawings. These, combined with the text, show how every knot is made, but for convenience and following knotting jargon, there are a few points to be noted in the drawing. When it is necessary to show the end of a piece of rope, it is drawn as if whipped (A), but if the direction the end is to take is shown, without the whole length of rope involved being drawn, there is an arrow (B). Where the end has not been taken through,

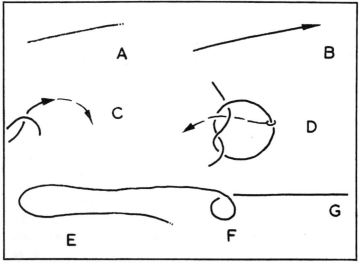

In the following pages of this book the end of a rope (A) will be shown, continuing rope with an arrow (B) and further movements with broken lines (C and D). A bight is turned back (E), an eye is a full circle (F) and the remainder of the rope is the standing part (G).

but where it is to go has to be shown, there is a broken line and arrow (C). If it is a part of the rope away from the end that has to be moved, a similar broken line and arrow is shown with a ring around the rope (D).

A *bight* is formed if a rope is doubled back on itself (E). There is an *eye* if the rope is twisted into a small ring (F). A *loop* is what the word signifies and is not normally part of a knot. To distinguish the main part of a rope from the end, it is called the *standing part* (G). In many knots it is the long part which takes the load and the knot is formed by working the end around it.

The coming of synthetic braided rope brought a need for new thinking on ways of splicing, and I am glad to be able to include information on ways of splicing braided cordage supplied by the Samson Cordage Company of Boston, Massachusetts.

Information on such a subject as knotting can only be an accumulation of the findings and methods of earlier workers in rope. To all those earlier makers of knots and splicers of rope, I am grateful that they allowed their ideas to be set down for the benefit of those of us who follow on with similar interests.

There is a fascination about working in cordage, whether the material is fine thread or massive ropes. I hope the reader will find clear information in this book to enable him to find his own interest in the subject, whether it is for practical purposes, as a means of keeping alive an old craft or just as an engrossing hobby.

Percy W. Blandford

Contents

Cordage  1

The first ropes were probably natural creepers, fronds and climbing plants found in the jungle, but ropes made of twisted fibers were believed to have been made in about the year 3000 BC by the Ancient Egyptians. They used papyrus leaves and fibers from hemp, flax, alfalfa grass and date palms. In the thousands of years since then, all kinds of fiber and other natural products have been used, even human hairs.

In more recent years the natural materials have been superseded by synthetic materials and nearly all cordage in the future, from fine string to the largest ropes, will be made of man-made filaments instead of the natural fibers which have been the mainstay of the ropemaker's art for nearly five thousand years.

NATURAL FIBERS

Some of the natural fibers that were used up to the coming of man-made materials may still be found and used, so anyone interested in knotting should be aware of them. These include *hemp*, which makes a strong rather rough rope, and *flax*, which was sometimes mixed with it, but not used alone.

Italian Hemp. Italian hemp was considered the strongest, being smoother and easier to handle. Until the coming of synthetics, this was the first choice for heavily-loaded and frequently handled ropes.

Manila. Manila looks like Italian hemp and is of about the same strength and smoothness, but it is made from the fiber from plantain leaves.

Cotton. Cotton was used where supplies were plentiful to make a smooth easy-running rope with a white appearance when new, although it soon darkened with dirt.

Sisal. Sisal became more generally used towards the end of the use of natural fiber in ropemaking as it was cheaper. This came from the fiber of aloe leaves. It is almost as strong as hemp, with a light brown color and a rather rough surface. It may still be used for string as well as occasional ropes.

Coir. Coir rope was made from the fibers of coconuts and was sometimes described as *grass rope*. Coir ropes are only about one-quarter the strength of the same size hemp rope, but coir will float, where all other natural fiber ropes soon sink. It is also more elastic, so coir ropes of considerable size were used afloat for mooring lines and towing.

Synthetic fiber ropes were developed during World War II and their development continues with new materials and new ways of forming them into ropes being discovered. All these ropes have a chemical base and some have extremely ponderous chemical names, so it is more likely that rope making materials will be described by trade names. This is satisfactory, except that it may not be immediately obvious that two very different trade names indicate the same materials by different rope makers. The technical literature of the makers will usually give the chemical name.

One of the best known names is *nylon*, which is a polyamide polymer. Of the synthetic ropes, this is the material with the greatest stretch. It is a very elastic, so it cannot be used where something has to be pulled tight. Of the synthetics, it is the only one that will absorb water, although this is only to a small extent and much less than any of the natural fibers.

The synthetic ropes that have taken over from hemp and manila, with strength at least twice as great are *polyethylene terephtalate*. Some of the trade names are Dacron and Terylene.

A lighter rope that will float is made from *polypropylene*. This is stronger than any natural fiber rope, but its ability to float makes it the modern alternative to coir.

SYNTHETIC FIBERS

All of the synthetic rope materials have much better resistance to abrasion than natural fibers. Their strength and resistance to water absorption make them much better for use afloat, as they can be stored wet without risk of rot. Natural fiber ropes were treated with proofing solutions or tarred, but many ropes were weakened by rot before they wore out. Natural ropes are weaker when wet. Synthetic ropes do not have their strength affected by moisture.

Natural fibers are short. This means that a rope of any size is made up of a large number of short pieces and their ends project to give the hairy feel that became associated with rope. Synthetic ropes are made from continuous filaments, which may go the whole length of a rope, meaning that it can be made absolutely smooth. Much synthetic rope is smooth, except for the very occasional broken filament. Some users prefer rope with the hairy traditional surface and synthetic ropes can be made to have this sort of exterior.

Traditionally rope was made three stranded. In a section containing three round strands, each strand touches the other two and the section cannot go out of shape (Fig. 1-1A). With a greater number of round strands this condition does not apply again until seven strands are used (Fig. 1-1B). The seven-strand formation is used for wire ropes, but it is unlikely to be met in fiber ropes, although some French rope is made this way. There have been four-strand ropes, but to keep their shape there is a smaller straight central strand (Fig. 1-1C).

Nearly all traditional three-strand rope is laid up right-handed and may be called *hawser-laid*. If you look along the rope, the strands twist away from you towards the right (Fig. 1-1D). Rope may be laid up left-handed for special purposes. Slings for lifting a load may have opposite ropes twisted in opposite ways, as there is then less risk of them twisting around each other at the crane hook.

Four-stranded rope may be described as *shroud-laid* and is normally laid up right-handed, but this formation is now rare.

With the need for bigger diameter ropes, there is a limit to what can conveniently be made three-stranded. *Cable-laid* ropes were made with three ropes laid up right-handed and twisted together left-handed (Fig. 1-1E). This kept the value of the retention of the cross-sectional shape due to the three formation—in effect a nine-strand rope.

In a rope the fibers or filaments are twisted together to form yarns (Fig. 1-1F). The yarns are twisted together to form strands (Fig. 1-1G), then the strands are twisted together to make the rope. At each stage the twist is to tighten the previous stage, and so the rope retains its construction.

For many thousands of years ropes were made by hand. There were simple contrivances to guide the rope and to apply the twist, but the work was done by a man walking backwards and adding fibers to build up the rope. Although some of the completed rope might be rolled, the method of construction really dictated a very long straight ropewalk, and the presence of these may be located by the lanes and districts that have retained the name. Later rope was made mechanically and even more modern machinery producing three-strand rope uses similar techniques to the hand ropemaker.

Mechanical methods have brought other rope formations. In particular there are braided or plaited ropes, in which the outer casing has yarns woven across each other diagonally, so there is a pattern of yarns spirally around in both directions. This makes a smooth flexible rope. The heart may be made up of many yarns laid lengthwise, although some braided rope is made around a three-stranded rope heart. Another type has one braided casing around another. There may be single yarns interlaced, but it is more usual for groups of yarns to be taken around together (Fig. 1-1H).

Traditionally rope has been described by its circumference. This has meant the need for anyone only occasionally using rope to visualize this in relation to its thickness. The diameter is slightly less than one-third of the circumference, so a 1-1½ inch circumference rope is not quite ½ inch thick.

With a move towards metrication, a tendency has also come to describe a rope size by its diameter. Fortunately there is a convenient relationship between circumference in fractions of an inch and diameter in millimeters. If a circumference is expressed in one-eighths of an inch, that is the same number as the diameter in millimeters. For instance, a 2 inch circumference is 16 x ⅛-inch, so the diameter is actually 16 millimeters. Or 1⅛-inch circumference (9 x ⅛ is millimeters. The traditional measurement of length was the fathom (6 feet), but it is now more common to measure in feet or meters.

The strength of the rope is greatest when it is pulled straight. If it is taken around a sheave or pulley, some strength is lost. The larger the diameter of the pulley, the less will be the loss of strength. There is obviously a practical limit to the size a pulley can be, particularly if it is part of the rigging of a sailing boat, but taking the rope around a small curve should be avoided if a larger curve can be substituted.

There is similar reasoning in the formation of a knot. If the rope is tightly kinked to make a particular knot, it will be weakened more

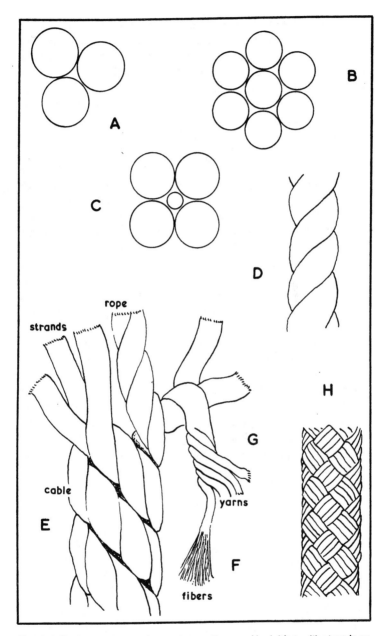

Fig. 1-1. Rope may have various cross-sections and be laid up with strands or be braided: (A) each strand touches the other two; (B) seven strands; (C) central strand; (D) strands twist to right; (E) cable laid; (F) yarns; (G) strands; and (H) groups of yarn are taken around together.

than if a knot with easier curves is used. However, knotting is a compromise. If the knot is not to slip, there have to be some tight turns, but sometimes there can be a knot with many moderate turns as a stronger alternative to one with fewer sharply bent turns. In any case, whatever is done, the knot will always be weaker than the body of the rope. If tested to destruction, the break often comes where the rope enters the knot.

Another knotting problem with modern synthetic ropes is the smoothness compared with the natural fiber ropes. The many thousands of knots developed over centuries have been intended for the hairy type of natural fiber ropes. Some knots that depended on that friction are less successful with smooth newer ropes. In some cases older knots have had to be discarded and replaced with new ones. In other cases older knots have been modified with extra turns to provide grip.

There have been some excellent knotting and ropework books produced, mainly from the days of square-rigged sail when there were miles of ropes on a ship and a great many situations needing special knots, splices and other treatments. Although these books can provide plenty of interest and are good sources of information for anyone with some knowledge of the subject, it would be unwise to take some of those knots and try to apply then today. They were all intended for natural fiber ropes, and many of these ropes on board ship were very coarse and rough, so they provided plenty of friction in a knot. If some of them were used on synthetic cordage, they would probably be unsafe. Modern knotting needs are not as extensive. The utility knotting requirements of the average person may be few, but many of the older knots and other rope treatments can be adapted to modern needs, either for practical purposes or as a form of decoration.

The End of a Rope

Because of its method of construction, a rope laid up in three strands may start to unlay into its separate strands, yarns and fibers if nothing is done to a cut end. The effect may not be as serious with braided rope, but that will also start to separate. This tendency is much greater with synthetic ropes than natural fiber ones. Some synthetic ropes will unlay for a considerable length if released after cutting, and it is almost impossible to lay them up again satisfactorily by hand, so a piece of *cow's tail* may have to be cut off and wasted.

All of the common synthetic materials used for ropes will melt if heated. They will burn eventually if heating with a flame is continued for too long, but the first effect of heat is to melt the filaments. This can be a disadvantage in some circumstances as friction may generate heat across a rope to soften and melt it to a dangerous state. The ability to melt and fuse the filaments together by applying heat can be used to seal the ends of synthetic ropes. It may also serve as a test if you are uncertain about whether a piece of rope is synthetic or made from natural fibers. A flame applied to the end will char natural fibers, but synthetic fibers will melt.

Few tools are needed for knotting and general ropework, but a sharp knife is important. For fine line, such as thread and cord, a pair of scissors can be used, but for the majority of ropes, a knife is the usual cutter. Almost any knife will do, but riggers, sailors and others who work with rope prefer a thin-bladed type of knife with a handle made from a piece of wood on each side of the blade extension.

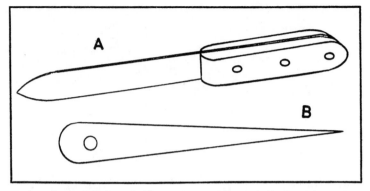

Fig. 2-1. The only tool needed for most ropework are a knife (A) and a marline spike (B).

These types are very similar to the knives used by a butcher. A thin blade about 5 inches long with a good edge will deal with most ropework (Fig. 2-1A). It is also useful to have a spike for picking knots open, getting fancywork into shape and tucking splices. This may be a plain tapered *marline spike* (Fig. 2-1B), and a rigger often has his knife and spike in the same sheath, which hangs low in his belt (Fig. 2-2). The spike and the knife may have holes so lanyards can be attached as precautions when working aloft. With a light cord lanyard around the neck there is no risk of dropping the tools which could be lethal to anyone below.

Some other spikes are described later, but there is no need to buy a special spike for most knotting because any pointed tool can be used. It is convenient to have a handle on the spike and one sold as an awl or icepick may be used.

A ropeworker or sailmaker may call a finer pointed tool a pricker or a stabber. Any of these may be useful in knotting. Some clasp knives have a spike folded on the back. This is safe stowage and convenient for carrying in a pocket. At one time wood and bone were used for spikes as these were considered less hard on rope fibers, but it is common now to only find wood used for very large splicing spikes called *fids*.

Those concerned with ropework frequently may have an electrically heated knife for cutting and sealing synthetic ropes in one action. It may be a tool something like a soldering iron, but with a knife instead of a bit, or a static bench unit through which the rope is passed and the cut made by pulling a handle. If rope is being taken off a reel, this seals what is left as well as the piece being cut off, but most of these tools leave a rough end as the melted material

18

hardens. There will have to be some other treatment before putting the rope into use, particularly if the rope has to pass through a hole or a pulley block.

It is possible to heat any knife and use it for cutting and sealing, but there is always the danger of overheating, which will draw the temper of the steel. If an old knife can be kept for the purpose, the risk of the steel being softened may not matter, but once the temper of a blade has been drawn, it will not keep its edge when used for ordinary purposes.

Most users of rope will find it more convenient to cut and seal in two stages. Most ropes can be cut by slicing with a knife. Very hard, tightly-laid ropes can be cut with a fine metalworking hacksaw if a knife will not work. Very thick ropes were cut with a hatchet, but for most ropes in normal use it is unlikely that the user will have to resort to this method.

If synthetic rope is to be cut, it is advisable to put on a stopping. This temporary whipping may be adhesive tape or a turn or two of thread or any light line on each side of the intended cut (Fig. 2-3A) to prevent unlaying. Sealing is often done with a match flame. This is convenient, but it is a dirty flame that will blacken the rope end. The flame from a cigarette lighter is cleaner and burns longer. For normal use, hold the end of the rope over the flame and turn it to

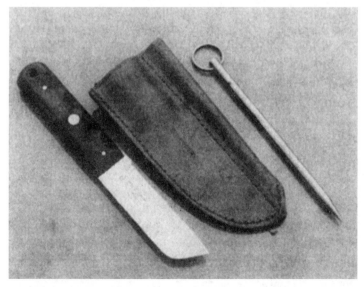

Fig. 2-2. A knife and spike are the only tools needed for most ropework. The same sheath will hold both tools.

evenly heat the extreme end (Fig. 2-3B). Quite a brief heating will usually be enough, but make sure there are no stray filaments that have curled away from the flame.

Remove the flame and moisten the first finger and thumb of the other hand, then quickly roll the end of the rope between finger and thumb (Fig. 2-3C). With a little practice, a rounded end with a slight taper can be produced. This method is used for laid or braided rope. Moistening your finger and thumb prevents burning yourself and stops the softened filaments from sticking to your skin. Be ready to lick your fingers a second time. If the end is not to your satisfaction, it can be heated and rolled again. Be careful not to heat the rope further along, or you may get fibers set rigidly fused together where you wanted the rope to remain flexible. You cannot undo the effect of heating and fusing.

WHIPPING

Heating and fusing the ends of synthetic rope may be all the protection needed in many cases, but for rope that is to be used quite often, there is a risk of at least part of the end becoming loose and unlaying. As natural fiber rope cannot be sealed in this way, it needs a different treatment. Traditionally this was by whipping. It is common when working with synthetic ropes to whip them as well as heat-seal them. The whipping then backs up the sealing and provides a second line of defense in case the sealing ever fails. Of course, a whipping alone could be used, but sealing as well is usually worthwhile, if only to keep the filaments under control while applying the whipping.

A whipping is a tight binding of light line around the rope. There has been an enormous number of whippings devised. Some seem needlessly complicated and others are purely decorative. Both of these types were probably invented by sailors of sailing ship days, looking for something to combat boredom with the few materials readily at hand.

Within reason, the thinner the whipping line in relation to the thickness of the rope, the more secure will be the whipping. A common fault is to put on a whipping with a too thick line. For most of the rope in common use, the material sold as sail twine is suitable. This is a stout thread intended for hand-sewing sails of medium-weight cloth. For the smaller ropes domestic sewing thread may be more suitable. It is also possible to buy hanks or reels of special whipping twine.

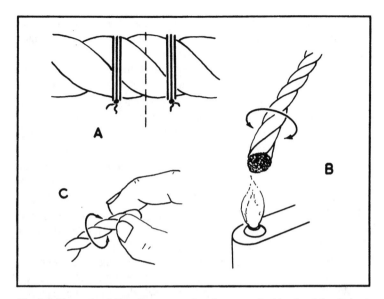

Fig. 2-3. There should be a temporary stopping on each side of an intended cut (A), then the end of a synthetic rope can be sealed by softening in a flame (B) and rolling between finger and thumb (C).

Some whipping line is made from natural fibers and may be supplied already treated with oil or wax. An advantage of this is the greater ease with which a tight secure whipping can be applied. The wax or oil preserves the fibers and makes the line stay put as it is wound around the rope, but there is a risk that wear will cause the preserving qualities to disappear and the line may rot and come away.

Synthetic sail twine or thread is probably a better choice. This may be supplied already waxed for convenience in putting on the whipping. If the wax wears away after that, it does not matter because the synthetic line cannot rot.

Another common fault among beginners is to make the whipping too long. It is a safe rule to never make a whipping longer than the diameter of the rope (Fig. 2-4A). It is really the number of turns that matter, and these have to be found by experience with particular materials. Keeping the complete length of the whipping about the same as the diameter is reasonable up to about ⅝-inch diameter. Above that the length need not be as much—20 turns is about the maximum to put on larger ropes.

How far to keep the whipping back from the end of the rope is a matter of experience. With the usual heat-sealed end, the whipping may finish between ¼ inch and ½ inch from the end (Fig. 2-4B). With an unsealed end, the distance can be about the same on smaller ropes. It may be more on thicker ropes, but loose fibers at the end will tend to spread out. This may not matter for normal usage, but if the thicker rope has to pass through a hole, the whipping can be closer to the end to prevent it from spreading.

It is possible to get colored line. Some of it is sold for sewing carpets. This might be used for the identification of ropes, just as when similar ropes are together in the running rigging of a yacht.

One alternative to a whipping is a shrink-fit plastic sleeve. This is a short piece of soft plastic tube that will slide over the rope. The application of a little heat will then cause it to shrink and tightly grip the rope. This is quite effective, but serious users of rope still prefer a conventional whipping. A tight binding with self-adhesive electricians tape may serve as a temporary whipping.

Putting on a successful whipping is made easier if the whipping line is waxed, preferably just before use, even if it is bought already waxed, or oiled. Almost any hard wax will do. A piece of candle is often used. The line is drawn across the wax tightly several times, so it picks up a coating of wax.

Oldtime knotting instructions always say a whipping should be applied against the lay (Fig. 2-4C). This follows the reasoning in the design of rope, where fibers, yarns and strands are twisted in opposite ways, so any tendency of one to loosen tightens the next. In practice it does not seem to matter which way the turns are made and it is actually easier to get a whipping really tight, as it should be if it is to do its job, by putting it on in the same direction as the lay of the rope (Fig. 2-4D). With ropes that are braided or made in any other way, there is no lay, so the whipping can go on either way. If

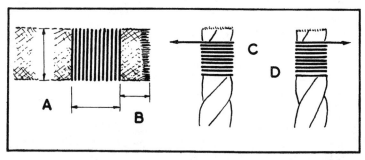

Fig. 2-4. A whipping should be about as long as the diameter of the rope; (A) and a short distance from its end; (B). Some whippings are made against the lay; (C) and others with it; (D).

whipping is tight, it does not matter which way around it was made, so please yourself. A whipping that is not tight is a waste of time.

COMMON WHIPPING

There are other names for this type of whipping, but it is the most used whipping, although not necessarily the best. There are some variations, but the results are very similar. These whippings are worth learning, but once experience has been gained with some of the other whippings, most users would prefer them for many whipping needs.

In the first method the starting end is laid along the rope towards the end, then tight turns put on over it (Fig. 2-5A). After going more than half the length the whipping is to be, the first end is turned back to leave a loop (Fig. 2-5B) and turns on over this. After three or four turns the working end is passed through the loop (Fig. 2-5C). If the end projecting from further back in the whipping is pulled (Fig. 2-5D), the working end will be drawn back under the turns, so both ends project and can be cut off to complete the whipping (Fig. 2-5E).

Another way to arrange to haul back the working end is to have a separate loop, which is not inserted until the point where the first part would be doubled back in the first example (Fig. 2-5F). After pulling back the working end, this separate piece is discarded.

Possibly a tighter way of locking the two ends is to double back the first part before putting on the turns (Fig. 2-5G), then pass the working end through this loop after all the turns have been applied. The first part has to be pulled until the linked loops are halfway (Fig. 2-5H), then the ends are cut off. It is important to judge the amount of pulling so the link is central, otherwise one end of the whipping may loosen.

One variation gets a similar result without using a loop. This variation is probably the most used whipping by seafarers. The first end is put along the rope and about half the whipping turns put over it, then it is allowed to project (Fig. 2-5J). After a few more turns, the working end is laid back along the rope and more turns put on with the resulting loop (Fig. 2-5K). When sufficient turns have been put on, pulling the working end will draw back what is left of the loop. Pull both projecting ends tight and cut them off. Sometimes both ends are arranged to project from the same space and are joined together with a reef knot before cutting off.

Yet another way of drawing back the working end uses a needle. At the point where a loop would be made in the first method,

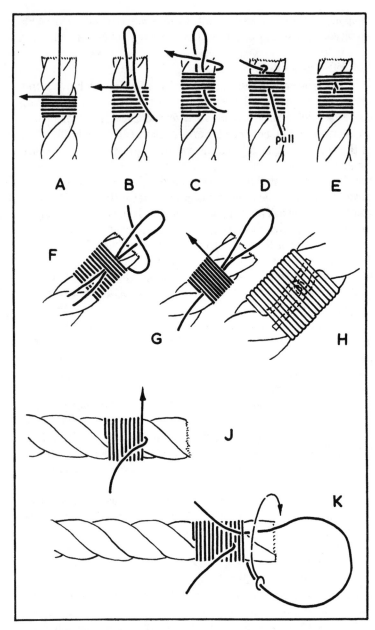

Fig. 2-5. In the various versions of the common whipping, (A) final turns missing part; (B) loops; (C) working end passes through loop; (D) pulled end; (E) completed whipping; (F) separate loop; (G) double back; (H) linked loops; (J) projected end; and (K) resulting loop.

a needle is laid along the rope with its eye projecting past the end of the rope. After sufficient turns, the working end is put through the eye of the needle, which is pulled back. Pliers will probably be needed. They are useful for pulling ends tight, in any case.

There are two contradictory snags with all of the variations of the common whipping. If the final turns are slack enough to allow the end to be pulled back, the completed whipping will not be as tight as it should be. If the whipping is made very tight, it may not be possible to pull the end back without breaking the line. Another problem comes if one turn is cut or worn through. The whole whipping will come away. This does not happen with some of the other whippings. There is also the problem of working tightly. If one turn is made loosely, this loosens the whole whipping. In some of the other whippings, each turn is separately locked.

FRENCH WHIPPING

This type may be called a half-hitch whipping. It is made like a common whipping, but each turn is locked, so getting everything tight is simpler and there is less risk of the whipping coming adrift if part of it is chafed.

Instead of putting on simple turns, pass the end under at each turn to make half hitches (Fig. 2-6A) or lift a loop over the end of the rope (Fig. 2-6B). If the work is done in the direction of the lay the crossings of the half hitches will follow the lay of the rope (Fig. 2-6C). Deal with the ends in any of the ways described for the common whipping.

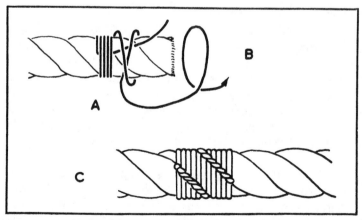

Fig. 2-6. In French whipping every turn is a half hitch; (A) pass the end; (B) lift a loop; and (C) crossing.

WEST COUNTRY WHIPPING

The name comes from the southwestern part of England where so many of the famous voyages started from, including the Pilgrim Fathers. The group of counties west of Bristol are collectively called the West Country. This whipping can be used on any type of rope and is at least as easy to apply as a common whipping. Tightness in making and security in use are obtained by locking each turn. The heavy drawing lines needed to show construction make it appear clumsy, but in whipping line the crossings are almost invisible.

Cut a suitable length of line and put its middle behind the rope. At the front twist the two parts together in an overhand knot (Fig. 2-7A). Pull this as tight as possible. With waxed line, the knot will not slip. Take the line to the back of the rope and do the same (Fig. 2-7B). Come to the front and do it again close to the first knot. Continue in this way until a sufficient length has been done. Do all knots the same way so they fit against each other. Pull every knot very tight and keep all turns as close together as possible. Make the final knot into a reef knot by making another twist the other way (Fig. 2-7C), then cut off the ends.

The West Country and the common whippings can be used away from an end as well as at an end. This allows them to be used as markers along a rope. Sometimes a second whipping can be put a short distance from an end whipping as a back-up in case that one fails, but with a heat-sealed synthetic rope this seems unnecessary.

PALM AND NEEDLE WHIPPING

The greatest strength in a whipping should come if some turns go through the rope as well as around it. This can be done by using a needle on the whipping twine. Any needle that will take the line could be used, but the best type is a sail needle, which is triangular behind the point and reduces to round at the eye end (Fig. 2-8A). Sail needles are described by a gauge number and a size around 16 should suit many lines and ropes. A palm is a device worn on the hand to thrust the needle through sail cloth. It is not essential for whipping.

To start the whipping pass the needle through a strand or a part of a braided rope, probably twice, so the starting end of the whipping line is sewn in. The remainder of the end can be covered by the whipping turns. Put on sufficient turns and take the needle through a strand.

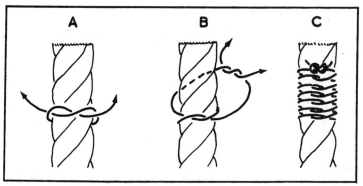

Fig. 2-7. The West Country whipping is made by knotting alternately in back and front of the rope and finishing with a reef knot; (A) overhand knot; (B) take line to the back of rope; and (C) cut off the ends.

The round turns have to covered by *worming turns*, which go around the rope over the spaces between the strands of a laid rope, or straight along a braided rope. How this is done depends on the tightness of the construction of the rope. If it is possible to pass the needle diagonally through the rope for the length of the whipping, take it from the top to the bottom, so it emerges from a space, then up the outside (Fig. 2-8B) and down through the center to another space. In this way a worming turn follows outside over each space between strands. These turns can be followed again, so there is a double line in each position, then the needle is thrust through once more and the line cut off (Fig. 2-8C).

Much synthetic rope is too tight for a needle to go through in this way. Instead of going through the rope inside the whipping to get from one space to the next, it can be taken through or around a strand at the end of the whipping (Fig. 2-8D).

An interesting variation of this is made on stranded rope without using a needle. This sailmaker's whipping can only be near the end of the rope. The finished whipping shows single worming turns and should be as secure as a whipping made with a needle.

With synthetic rope seal the ends of the strands separately, not the rope as a whole. After whipping, the heat-sealed strands can be fused together by a further heating. Be careful that the rope does not unlay itself unintentionally. A few turns of adhesive tape near what will be the bottom of the whipping will prevent unlaying. In any case, unlay for a length of about three times the diameter of the rope in readiness for whipping. Natural fiber rope will probably not be as troublesome and some may be whipped without any precautions.

27

Turn back the whipping line into a loop with long and short ends. The short end may be about 6 inches, so it is long enough to grip. The long end should be enough to put on the whipping turns, with a little to spare. Put this line into the opened rope, so the loop loosely encircles one strand and the two ends project from the opposite space (Fig. 2-8E). Lay up the strands again and hold the loop and the short end down the rope out of the way while turns are put on with the long part (Fig. 2-8F). It will help to pull the lay of the rope tight if the turns are put on in the direction of the lay.

When sufficient turns have been made, hold them tight and lift the loop over the top of the strand it already encircles (Fig. 2-8G). Pull the short end and make sure the loop beds down into the center of the end of the rope. The two sides of the loop will form two worming turns and leave the short end projecting from the only space between strands that is not covered with a worming turn.

Take the short end over the outside of the whipping to form the third worming turn, then into the center of the rope, where it is tied tightly with a reef knot to the remains of the long end. Cut off the surplus.

The sailmaker's whipping can also be used on four-stranded rope by adapting the way the line is first laid into the opened rope. Have short and long ends, but arrange the line so it loops around the opposite strands (Fig. 2-8H).

Put on the whipping turns, then lift the loops over the end strands. To tighten them the loop that is connected to the short end should be left until last. The side of this loop can be pulled to tighten the other, then the end pulled to tighten that loop before taking the short end over the outside to tie to the long end in the center of the end of the rope. This results in single worming turns over three spaces and double turns over the fourth.

SNAKING

Putting decorative snaking turns outside a whipping is a way of decorating the end of a rope. Snaking does not contribute to the strength of a whipping, except possible on a really large rope.

The basic whipping is any of the types that does not have worming turns. A common whipping is normally used. The end of the whipping line or a new piece of similar line makes the snaking. It could be in a different color.

In the simplest snaking the line loops around the end turns of the whipping to make a simple pattern (Fig. 2-9A). There could be a half hitch at each crossing (Fig. 2-9B). This is probably as far as any

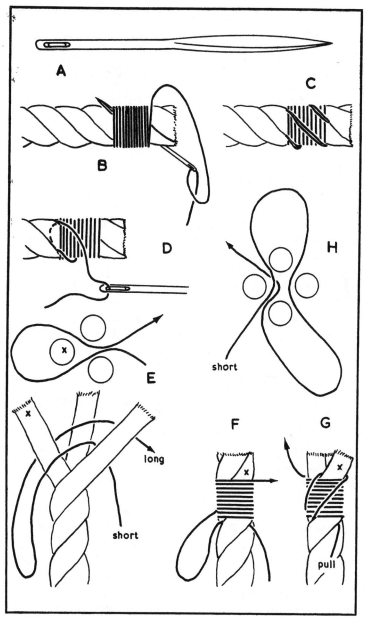

Fig. 2-8. A strong whipping is made by taking the line through the rope, as well as around it, in the palm and needle and sailmaker's whippings; (A) eye end; (B) pass the needle up the outside; (C) cut off line; (D) end of whipping; (E) opposite space; (F) turns on the long part; (G) lift the loop over the top of the strand; and (H) line loops around opposite strands.

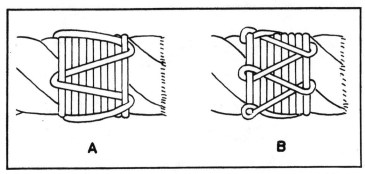

Fig. 2-9. A whipping can be decorated by putting snaking turns outside the ordinary turns; (A) simple pattern and; (B) half hitch each crossing.

complication should go as finer work is unlikely to be seen, but other variations can take in two end turns each time, go around twice at each end, put two opposing hitches there or use any of the appropriate bends described later in the book.

Some oldtime instructions say that a whipping, like a splice, should be rolled underfoot to give it an even shape. This may have been satisfactory on a clean deck under a clean foot, but it would be unwise on the ground under a shoe ashore. If there seems to be a need to true the shape of a whipping, roll it between two boards.

SEIZINGS AND STOPPINGS

The terms seizing and stopping are sometimes used for the same things. They are like whippings, but used around two wire or fiber ropes to draw them together or to stop one from sliding over the other. Two parts of the same rope may draw together around a thimble or other solid object. If there is any distinction, a stopping may be intended as a temporary fastening, while a seizing is more permanent.

When two ropes are drawn together in this way, one is said to be *stopped* to the other. Putting on a seizing may be said to *clap on* a seizing. Besides turns around, like whipping, there may be turns over them lengthwise. These are *frapping turns*. In some seizings there is a second set of turns over the first called *riding turns*.

As the ropes being seized often have to be pulled together by the first turns of the seizing, a start like a whipping is impractical. It is common to have a slip knot. If a stranded line is being used an eye can be tucked (Fig. 2-10A). The projecting end should be covered by adjoining turns for extra strength. If it is not stranded line, there could be a figure-eight slip knot, but it is better to use a timber hitch

(Fig. 2-10B). As with the tucked eye, cover the end with following turns.

ROUND SEIZING

The most commonly used arrangement is a round seizing. It is used in any situation where two ropes have to be held alongside each other. Pass the end through the eye and draw the line tight (Fig. 2-11A). Put on a number of turns. The number depends on the circumstances, but eight or nine turns are common (Fig. 2-11B). It is important to put on all the tension that can be managed. As the line is quite thin and difficult to grip, it is best to provide some sort of handle and this is conveniently done with a marline spike, passed through an overhand knot to form a *marline spike hitch*. With a little experience this can be done almost in one continuous action. Put the spike over the line (Fig. 2-11C) and twist an eye in it (Fig. 2-11D). Carry on twisting to fold the eye over the standing part (Fig. 2-11E). The spike and line are gripped to pull and the knot is instantly released by withdrawing the spike.

Lock those seizing turns by making a half hitch of the last one. Have the crossing over one rope, not across the space between ropes (Fig. 2-11F) where it might slip. Put on riding turns over the first layer, covering each space between turns, but not forcing so tightly as to push the first turns apart. There will then be one less riding turn than the first number of turns. As the end returns to the

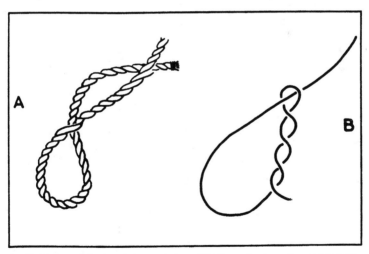

Fig. 2-10. If a seizing has to be made by pulling through a loop, the end may be tucked back (A) or made into a timber hitch (B).

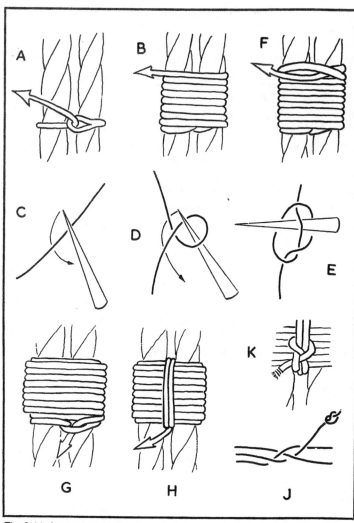

Fig. 2-11. A round seizing holds ropes together. The line may be pulled with the aid of a marline spike hitch and the turns tightened with frapping turns : (A) draw the line tight; (B) put on eight or nine turns; (C) spike over the line; (D) eye; (E) standing part; (F) space between ropes; (G) small starting eye; (H) two to three flapping turns; (J) three plait and (K) heavy line.

start, take it down through the small starting eye, if possible (Fig. 2-11G).

Put on frapping turns between the ropes. Pull each half turn tight as it is made. Two or three frapping turns will be the most that can be gotten in (Fig. 2-11H).

32

There are several possible ways of finishing the seizing. The frapping turns can be crossed and the end taken through as if working a three plait (Fig. 2-11J). An overhand knot in the end will prevent it from pulling back, probably the best way for very fine line. Another way, more suitable for heavy line, takes the end around the turns, over itself and under the opposite turn (Fig. 2-11K). This procedure should be done close to where the end comes from between the ropes so it is prevented from pulling back.

FLAT SEIZING

Flat seizing may also be called an *ordinary stopping,* but that is really a simplified version for very temporary use. A flat seizing may be the same as a round seizing, without the riding turns. It can be completed in the same way, but an alternative construction is shown in Fig. 2-12.

The slip knot is put in place and sufficient turns taken, but all quite loosely at this stage. Then the end is passed down through the turns and out through the small eye (Fig. 2-12A). This is the full construction of the turns, but tightening has to be done progressively, a turn at a time from the slip knot. When all of the turns are as tight as possible, the end is pulled to draw through the surplus line and the end continues to put on tight frapping turns and is finished in the same way as a round seizing.

A temporary stopping can be put on without the slip knot start. Instead, a long part of the starting end is laid along the two ropes and

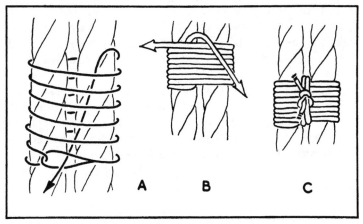

Fig. 2-12. A flat seizing is simpler than a round seizing for the same purpose and may finish with the end tucked through or frapped around (A) small eye; (B) turns; and (C) reef knot.

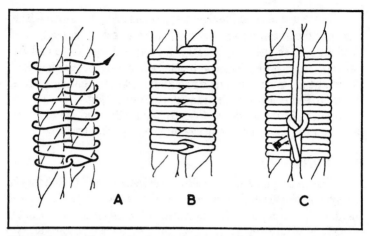

Fig. 2-13. A racking seizing has the turns in a figure-eight form to resist movement of the ropes: (A) cross the turns; (B) fill the gaps; and (C) complete the seizing with frapping turns.

turns are put over it tightly (Fig. 2-12B). The working end puts on the frapping turns, or there could be one frapping turn put on with the starting end and the working end taken around the other way to meet it, giving a total of two or three turns. The ends are then joined with a reef knot (Fig. 2-12C).

RACKING SEIZING

When considerable strain is expected that may cause one rope to try to move in relation to the other, the turns are put on with a figure-eight form to give increased friction on the rope surfaces. This may be particularly important with wire rope where the smooth surface gives little grip to the turns compared with fiber rope.

Start as if for a round seizing, but cross the turns between the ropes (Fig. 2-13A). Pull each turn tight and continue for 10 or more turns to get maximum friction. Because of the crossing action the turns will not come close around each rope. Go back over the seizing with riding turns, but let them fill the gaps in the first turns (Fig. 2-13B). Complete the seizing with frapping turns in the usual way (Fig. 2-13C).

THROAT SEIZING

Throat seizing is not so much a different seizing as a different application of a round seizing without frapping turns. It is used where a rope is turned into a small loop with the parts crossing alongside each other (Fig. 2-14A). This is seen in a clinch to stop the rope pulling through a block or hole, but traditionally it was used around the wooden blocks with holes through and called *deadeyes*.

The usual turns of a round seizing are put on, then riding turns to bring the end back to the start. In small stuff the end could be doubled back under the last few riding turns (Fig. 2-14B). With stouter line it would be better to knot the end into the starting eye.

MOUSING A HOOK

Mousing is an application of the round seizing. It is used across a hook to prevent a sling or other load from coming off the hook. It may be in stouter line than would be used for seizing. Mousing is done with both ends used equally, so what is judged to be sufficient line has to be started with its middle behind the hook.

Put on three or four complete turns, using both ends in opposite directions, then cross the ends (Fig. 2-14C). Put on

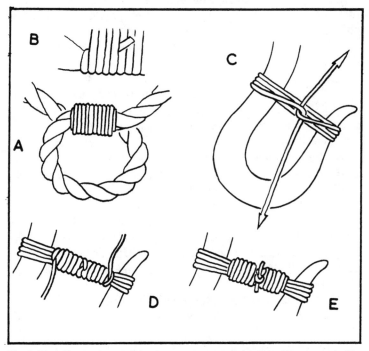

Fig. 2-14. A throat seizing holds a loop of rope in a clinch. A hook is moused with turns of line to prevent a sling from coming out: (A) parts cross; (B) end is doubled back; (C) cross the ends; (D) half hitches; and (E) reef knot.

enought turns each way to reach the sides of the hook and make the last turns into half hitches (Fig. 2-14D). Go back over these first turns with riding turns toward the center. When the center is reached, join the ends with a reef knot (Fig. 2-14E).

Make sure that a mousing is put on across the narrowest part of the hook. In a standard hook there is a hollowing on both sides and the mousing should be fitted into these so there is no risk of it slipping from a wider to a narrower part and becoming loose.

Although a mousing must be tight enough to stay in place under all circumstances, there should be no need for the extreme tensioning of a seizing on rope. It will be necessary to cast off and replace a mousing, so it is better to use line that can be tied and untied than to use thin line that has to be cut.

SERVING

In the days of large sailing ships with fiber rope rigging there was a constant fight against the elements to protect the large ropes, particularly against chafe and the entry of water which would cause rot. The complete process was *worm, parcel and serve*. There is little need for this complete treatment today, but a knowledge of what is involved will show where a whole or partial treatment might be used.

Rope to be treated has to be supported at about waist height and pulled taut. With three or four-stranded rope the first treatment is worming. This treatment is the filling of the spaces between the strands so the exterior becomes a reasonably smooth cylinder. Small lines of a suitable diameter to fill the gaps are temporarily seized beyond where one end of the worming is to come and then laid around the gaps between the strands with a moderate tension. The other ends are then seized (Fig. 2-15A).

Parcelling is done with strips of canvas which have been proofed or tarred. Narrow strips are used and wound around like a bandage in the same direction as the lay (Fig. 2-15B). To help keep the parcelling in place, it can be *marled over*. This process involves a series of half hitches made in sail twine or other quite light line (Fig. 2-15C).

Over this goes the serving and this is really an extra long whipping put on against the lay. Old time seamen were fond of quoting:

Worm and parcel with the lay,
Turn and serve the other way.

The important thing about the serving is that it must be tight. There has to be some assistance in levering the turns tight. This assistance is provided by a *serving mallet* or *serving board*. The board is a simplified version, with a groove across its end (Fig. 2-15D). It is more common today to use a serving mallet. It is called that because it looks like a mallet with a groove in the head (Fig. 2-15E), but it is not used for hitting.

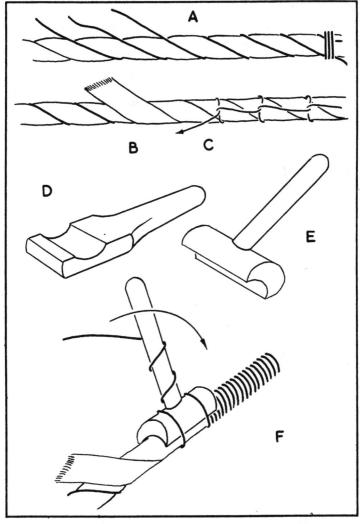

Fig. 2-15. As a protective treatment, three-strand rope may have the spaces brought level by worming, then cloth parcels the rope ready for serving: (A) seized ends; (B) lay; (C) light line; (D) groove; (E) groove in the head; and (F) turns taken around the head and the handle.

Serving is started with one end of the line turned under along the rope, in the same way as starting one type of whipping. The first few turns are put over this by hand. After that the serving mallet is put with its groove around the rope and a few turns taken around the head and the handle (Fig. 2-15F). From here on the hand on the handle also controls the run of the line as the mallet is turned around the rope. By regulating how the line runs out, tension can be adjusted and maximum tightening can be applied as each turn is made. Experience shows the limits. It is possible to put on so much tension that the line breaks.

For a long piece of serving there has to be a considerable length of line. There can be joins, but it is better to put on as much as possible in one length. This means that the traditional marline or spun yarn was in a ball and it was necessary to have an assistant passing the ball around the rope as the work progressed. Serving mallets equipped with reels have been devised so the work can be done single-handedly now. The end of the serving is finished like a whipping, with the end of the line drawn back under the last few turns.

Basic Knots  3

Although there are thousands of different knots and certain groups of special knots used in particular activities, there are a few knots which have proven their worth as the ones most generally useful. Between them they serve the majority of everyday needs and are the ones on which some of the other knots are based. Many special knots will be found to have developed from one or more of this group.

Although many other knots may be of occasional or specialized interest, it is worthwhile learning the basic knots thoroughly. They should become things that the user of ropes can tackle almost instinctively under many circumstances. It should be possible to get them right the first time and not have to untwist ends so they can be put together the other way. Knotting often has to be tackled in difficult situations. It should be possible to make these knots in the dark, behind the back and even by one hand.

It is also important to know the application of each knot. It is very easy to acquire skill at knotting and not be able to say what a particular knot is used for. It is no use being able to tie a knot and then try to use it in the wrong circumstances. There is something to be said for starting with usage and learning the appropriate knot before bothering with its name, but that makes classification difficult and the name comes first in this book.

Knotting should be learned and practiced with rope, unless it is a knot particularly intended for string or fishing line. Even then it is

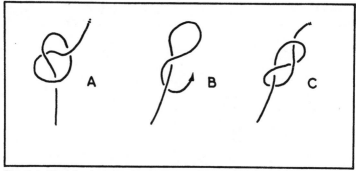

Fig. 3-1. The simplest stopper knots are the overhand and figure-eight: (A) simple twist; (B) end is taken to the other side; and (C) loop.

easier to see the formation in the thicker rope. It need not be very thick rope, but a supple piece about ¼ inch thick (¾ inch circumference) and 6 feet long can be carried in the pocket or kept in a desk drawer and it is large enough to see details of a knot. Better still, have two pieces of rope. If a knot is for joining two pieces of rope, you can do that, instead of getting confused in joining the two ends of the same rope. If the ropes are different colors, the parts of a complicated knot are better seen. Some knots are used between ropes of different thicknesses, so it is helpful to have one rope very different in thickness from another so there is no doubt which is which.

OVERHAND KNOT

The first need in ropework is often a stopper knot to prevent a rope from slipping through the hand or back through a hole. In sailing, the ends of sheets are knotted to prevent them from running back through fairleads or blocks.

The simplest knot for this purpose is made by a simple twist (Fig. 3-1A). We are calling it an overhand knot, but it may be a *thumb knot* or a dozen different names. If the bulk produced by this knot is sufficient, there is no need to use anything more complicated.

FIGURE-EIGHT KNOT

A slightly more bulky knot and one less likely to slip or loosen in smooth rope is made by starting as for an overhand knot, but the end is taken around to the other side (Fig. 3-1B) and into the loop that way (Fig. 3-1C). The figure-eight knot does not keep that shape once it is loaded, but bunches up to make a good stopper that is bigger than an overhand knot. If that is not bulky enough, there are other larger stopper knots described later in the book.

COMMON BEND

The common bend should be the general-purpose joining knot. The term *bend* is supposed to mean a joining knot, but there are a great many exceptions. It can be used between ropes of the same size or of different sizes. Some rope users would say the reef knot is the general-purpose knot, but that has limitations, as noted in the next entry. The common bend is sometimes called a *sheet bend*, from its use in joining a sheet (controlling rope) to a cringle (rope eye) spliced into the corner of a sail, but as its applications are much wider than that, it is better to call it a common bend. If ropes have to be joined end to end, in most circumstances it is the knot to use.

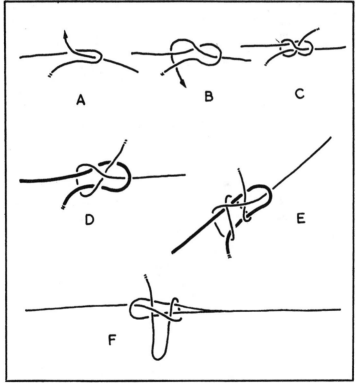

Fig. 3-2. The common or sheet bend is simple joining knot for ropes of the same or different thicknesses: (A) rope goes up through the bight; (B) around the back of it; (C) under itself; (D) thinner rope is worked around the bight; (E) normal single knot; and (F) double back end.

41

Fig. 3-3. Double sheet of common bend between ropes of different thicknesses.

To form a common bend, turn back a bight (loop) on the end of one rope. Take the end of the other rope up through it (Fig. 3-2A), around the back of it (Fig. 3-2B), then across the front of it and under itself (Fig. 3-2C). Draw the knot tight by holding the sides of the bight in one hand and pulling the standing part (loaded part) of the other in line with the other hand.

There are two ways that the working end could go around the bight. Tests have shown that there is really little difference in strength whichever way is used. Opinion seems to be slightly in favor of finishing the knot with the ends on opposite sides, as in the example, but going the other way around is not necessarily wrong.

If the ropes are of different thicknesses, the thicker rope is the one bent into a bight and the thinner one is worked around it (Fig. 3-2D). If there is a considerable difference in thickness or the ropes are slippery due to being wet, it is better to use a *double sheet bend* (Fig. 3-3), This is started in exactly the same way, with enough length of end of the thinner rope to go around again after completing the normal single knot (Fig. 3-2E). If there is even more difference in rope thickness, stronger variations are described later in the book.

Either the single or double bend can be used to join a rope to a loop, such as an eye spliced in the end of a rope, with the loop taking the place of the part bent into a bight. The knot can be made slip or quick-release if the final tuck is made with a doubled-back end (Fig. 3-2F). A pull on the loose end then releases the knot.

REEF KNOT

A reef knot is also called a *square knot* and other names, but *reef* seems most generally used, although *square* may be more familiar in some areas. It is the knot which many people proudly claim to know as the only knot that they use for everything—which is all wrong. Some who claim to know it get it wrong and produce a *granny knot* which is of no use for anything. The term granny may be found used for other knots wrongly formed, but it particularly applies to what was supposed to be a reef.

A reef knot is a joining knot for ropes of the same thickness, when it will be bearing against something. It is not safe if the ropes will be in mid-air or any where else that keeps the knot away from

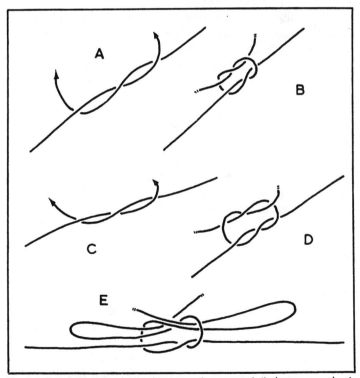

Fig. 3-4. The reef knot is a joining knot sometimes wrongly tied as a granny knot. It can be made a slip or bow knot by using bights: (A) two ends are twisted; (B) ends are pulled tight; (C) first twist; (D) ends finish across the knots; and (E) ends are turned back.

solid support. In those circumstances the knot should be a common bend. The name reef comes from the use of the knot in joining the ends of reef points on a sail under the boom or under the gathered-in canvas when the sail is shortened by reefing. The knot is then bearing against something. This also applies to bandaging—the knot comes against part of the body.

To make a reef knot, the two ends are twisted together one way (Fig. 3-4A), then the other way (Fig. 3-4B) and pulled tight. At both sides of the knot the ends should come alongside the standing parts. One way of learning is to say "right over left, then left over right," but it is probably better to watch the twisting action and do it the other way in the second move.

The granny knot is made by making both twists the same way. After the first twist (Fig. 3-4C), exactly the same action is done again and the result brings the ends finishing across the knot (Fig. 3-4D), with the ends on the opposite sides of the two bights to the nearby standing parts. Quite often a moderate pull on the standing parts will cause the ropes to slide in the knot. It is a treacherous knot and should never be used.

A *reef bow* is sometimes made for decoration, but it is more often used as a knot that can be cast off by pulling an end. The first part is made like an ordinary reef knot, but for the second twisting, one or both ends are turned back (Fig. 3-4E) and the knot completed with them. Pulling an end releases the knot. This is the bow knot that should be used on laced shoes or boots. If your bow rests across your foot, that is a correctly-made reef bow. If the loops of the bow are in line with your foot or ankle, you made the second twist the same way as the first and have a *granny bow*. For that application it may not matter, but if you hope to regard yourself as a keen knot-tier, you will not use a granny under any circumstances and will change the bow so it shows you understand the correct knot to use there.

BOWLINE

This is the knot for putting a loop in the end of a rope (Fig. 3-5). It is sometimes described as the perfect example of a knot as it does its job correctly, it is easy to make, keeps its shape and is easy to cast off (undo), even after it has been under load.

There are several ways of making the bowline, but the result is the same. For a first attempt take sufficient length to make the loop. Let it be a large loop, then there should be no confusion when making the knot. Twist a small eye where the top of the loop is to be

Fig. 3-5. The bowline is the knot for making a non-slip loop in the end of a rope.

(Fig. 3-6A). Arrange this so the part that continues into the loop is on top of the standing part, as shown. The knot can be made with the twist of the eye the other way, but that would confuse instructions for subsequent actions which would also be the other way, so in the first instance, make the eye as shown.

Bring the end up through the eye (Fig. 3-6B), but only pull through enough to form the knot. Hold the crossing of the eye to keep its shape until tucking has been completed. Take the end around the standing part (Fig. 2-6C). Note the direction. Pass the end down through the eye so it is between the sides of the loop (Fig. 3-6D). If it had gone around the standing part the other way, it would have finished outside the loop, and that is wrong.

Keep the bowline in this formation when tightening it. Do not let the eye fall out of shape. Pull the standing part upwards while coaxing the sides of the loop and the hanging end between them downward. If there is just a pull without holding the knot formation in shape, the part around the standing part may drop behind the loop and a loose knot that started correct will finish out of shape and useless. If a correctly formed bowline is examined, the part at the crossing will be seen to have the same formation as a common bend (Fig. 3-6E).

If what you need is a loop in the end of a rope, that is the way to make a bowline. If you want to make the bowline around your waist there is a quick method, but it is no use learning that as the only

45

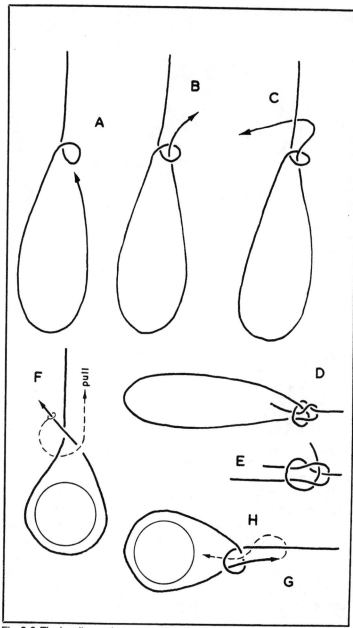

Fig. 3-6. The bowline makes a non-slip eye in the end of a rope: (A) twist a small eye; (B) bring end up through the eyes; ( ) take the end around the standing part; (D) pass the end through the eye; (E) same formation as common bend; (F) standing part; (G) working ends; and (H) complete the knot.

method. You can look rather silly if you need a loop in the end of a rope as a sling, or even to put around someone else's waist, and the only way you can make it is around your own waist and take it off to use elsewhere. However, if you want the bowline around your waist quickly, as you might if thrown the rope in a rescue, this special method is worth knowing.

Pass the rope around yourself with enough end to work with. Hold the end pointing up as the standing part (Fig. 3-6F). Pass it over the standing part and push it straight away from you. This will force the eye into the standing part and leave the working end already through it (Fig. 3-6G), ready to go around and down through the eye to complete the knot (Fig. 3-6H). It is the action with the end over the standing part that is special. There must be some slackness in the standing part to allow the eye to be formed. Your other hand may pull on it to gain some slack. The hand holding the end can actually go with it to lever the standing part into the eye without bending the end.

There are many variations of bowline described later, but in nearly every case where a loop is wanted, the plain bowline is the answer and can only be bettered by an eye splice.

CLOVE HITCH

If a rope has to be attached to something solid, such as an iron ring or a wooden post, the term *hitch* is used for the knot, although

Fig. 3-7. The clove hitch is the basic hitch for joining a rope to a spar.

there are some exceptions. The same hitches can be used when a light rope is to be attached to a larger rope already secured at its ends. The most common of these hitches is the clove hitch (Fig. 3-7), although in practice one of its variations may be preferred.

The clove hitch is a jamming form of two half hitches. A half hitch is made when the working end is taken around something and across its own standing part. This is done twice in a clove hitch, but half hitches are part of the formation of many other knots. A clove hitch is more secure if there is a load on both ends and can then be regarded as a permanent fastening. If it is used so only one end takes a load and the other end hangs loose, it makes a good temporary fastening, as when a boat is moored to a post briefly, but for a more permanent end hitch, another knot should be chosen.

The basic way to make a clove hitch is to put enough of the working end over the solid object and completely encircle it so the end goes over the standing part (Fig. 3-8A). This is the first half hitch. Continue around the same way. If there is space, it is easier to see what is happening and avoid confusion if the end goes around some way from the first half hitch. Encircle the object again and pass the end under its own standing part (Fig. 3-8B). Draw the two half hitches together (Fig. 3-8C) to complete the clove hitch.

If the end of the post or other solid object is accessible, there is another way of making a clove hitch without using the end of the rope. Twist a loop into the rope with the end part under the standing part (Fig. 3-8D). Hold this in shape and do the same above it (Fig. 3-8E). You are then holding a clove hitch in your hand ready to drop over the post. If the rope is under strain, as it might be if a boat is pulling on its mooring rope, the first half hitch can be dropped over the post or bollard so you can hold against the strain while forming the second half hitch and pulling tight.

A common mistake is to change direction after making the first half hitch, so the second half hitch goes around the object the other way (Fig. 3-8F), forming a *cow hitch* (Fig. 3-8G). There are a few uses for a cow hitch, but it is suitable as an alternative to a clove hitch. The name is supposed to come from its use for tethering a cow to an upright post so it may graze within a circle.

ROUND TURN AND TWO HALF HITCHES

This knot is used for attaching the end of a rope to something solid, such as a ring or post. It has not acquired any generally-acceptable more compact name, although some of its variations have. The name describes its formation.

48

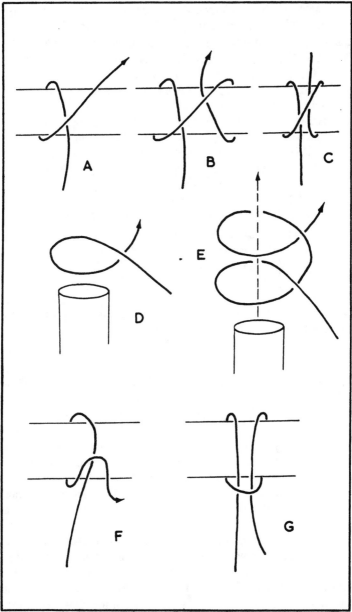

Fig. 3-8. The clove hitch is formed of two half hitches around a spar. If the second turn is reversed, it becomes a cow hitch: (A) first half hitch; (B) pass the end under its own standing part; (C) draw two half hitches together; (D) twist a loop; (E) twist a second loop; (F) second half hitch goes around the other way; and (G) cow hitch.

Enough of the working end is used to completely encircle the object. This is the round turn (Fig. 3-9A). The two half hitches in the title are actually formed like a clove hitch around the standing part. Keep the standing part straight. Do not bend or kink it in forming the rest of the knot so what you are doing with the working end does not become confusing. Treat the standing part as if it is a rigid post on which a clove hitch is to be made.

Bring the end to the standing part and under its own part on the side nearest the round turn (Fig. 3-9B). Draw this close to the round turn and continue around the standing part the same way to make the second half hitch (Fig. 3-9C). As with the ordinary clove hitch, be careful not to change direction and make the second half hitch the other way. Allow the knot under load to pull the two half hitches close up (Fig. 3-9D). See that the two half hitches are tight and there is enough free end hanging for there to be no risk of it pulling back and releasing the second half hitch.

One way to visualize the different uses of the clove hitch and round turn and two half hitches is to consider a rope between a number of posts. All intermediate points could be clove hitches, as both parts are under load. The ends are then attached with round turns and two half hitches (Fig. 3-9E).

PACKER'S KNOT

A packer's knot is for drawing string or cord tight and then locking it. It is not a knot for rope. It has a great many different names as almost all shopkeepers and others who have to tie parcels name it as their own. Pulling string tight around a parcel is the main use, but this knot is also one to use for gathering loose things together or anywhere that it is necessary to tighten light line so there is enough friction in the knot to hold the strain while the locking turn is made and the ends cut off. There are a few minor variations, but basically this is a slip knot which can be locked with a half hitch.

After the string has been put around the parcel, the end is taken around the standing part (Fig. 3-10A) and back around itself to form a figure-eight knot (Fig. 3-10B). This should be made so the end stands up alongside the standing part. Making the first twist of the figure-eight the other way would leave it pointing downward, and this would not do.

Instead of a figure-eight knot, some users form a simpler overhand knot, again with the end standing up alongside the standing part (Fig. 3-10C). This may be satisfactory in hairy natural fiber

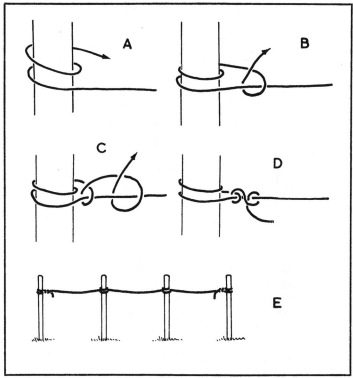

Fig. 3-9. For the end of a rope to be attached to a pole, the knot is a round turn and two half hitches, but a clove hitch can be used intermediately: (A) round turn; (B) bring end to standing part; (C) second half hitch; (D) pull the two half hitches; and (E) ends are attached.

string, but in the more slippery synthetic strings, the extra turn of a figure-eight knot is better able to grip.

If the standing part is pulled, the string will tighten around the parcel and there should be enough friction in the knot to prevent it from loosening during the brief period while the knot is finished. The usual way to lock the knot is to make a half hitch, like part of the second method of forming a clove hitch, and drop this over the standing end (Fig. 2-10). Pull it tight and cut off both ends.

To allow the string to be undone later, there are two ways of making it quick-release. The end standing up can be turned back and the half hitch put over the bight (Fig. 3-10E). Pulling the end from the bight will release the lock so the knot can be drawn apart. Another way is to make the locking half hitch with a bight of the standing part (Fig. 3-10F). The first method should be more satisfactory.

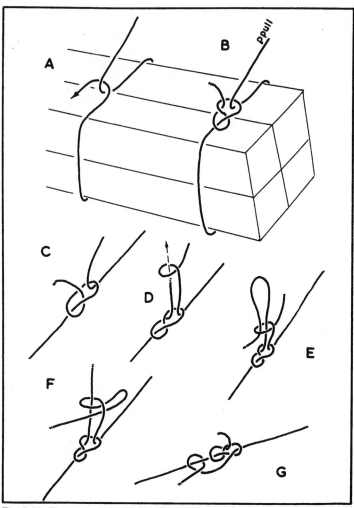

Fig. 3-10. The packer's knot is used to tighten a line around a parcel, then it is locked with a half hitch: (A) the end is taken around the standing part; (B) figure-eight knot; (C) overhand knot; (D) drop clove hitch over standing ends; (E) half hitch over the bight; (F) locking half hitch; and (G) cut-off standing part.

If the string is coming from a reel or ball, it does not have to be cut off until the knot is locked, so there is no waste. Another method of locking necessitates cutting before making the half hitch, but probably provides the greatest security. Instead of making half hitch around the standing end, the cut-off standing part is taken over the knot and half hitched behind it (Fig. 3-10G). There could be a second half hitch, but that should be unnecessary.

Single-Strand Knots

The overhand and figure-eight knots (Fig. 3-1) are the basic stopper knots, but there are a great many more, some of them merely elaborations on these examples. Usually the knots are put on the end of a rope to prevent it from slipping through the hand or a pulley block, but they may be arranged in the length of the rope to mark distances, provide foot holds or offer a grip. There are other knots made in a single piece of rope or cord that are quite elaborate and their purpose is often more decorative than practical. There is no clear cut dividing line, but the knots described in this chapter are those that are primarily practical. The decorative ones are described later.

Although a knot may be used to prevent a rope from unlaying or fraying, that should only be regarded as a temporary measure. A whipping is the correct treatment then. An exception may be twine or thread, which obviously cannot be whipped. A knot may then be used to prevent the thread from pulling through when sewing, but for much sewing a knot in the end is considered incorrect. Instead a short part of the end is laid along the seam and sewn over.

BLOOD KNOT

A blood knot is an overhand knot with the end taken around a second time. It is sometimes called a *double overhand knot* (Fig. 4-1A). When pulled tight it makes a round hard knot (Fig. 4-1B). It was used in the ends of the strands of a cat-o'-nine-tails or a whip

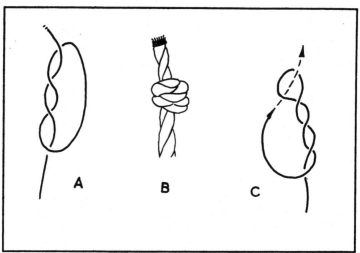

Fig. 4-1. A blood knot is a larger stopper made by putting extra turns into an overhand knot A and B. A stevedore's knot, (C) makes another large stopper that is easily released.

lash. It can be trebled or taken even further, but with extra turns it has to be manipulated into shape. A variation is the *French knot* used in embroidery. The multiple turns are taken over the needle, which is then pulled through.

STEVEDORE'S KNOT

When a stevedore has to let go of a rope while working on a ship's cargo, he ties a temporary knot to prevent the rope from running away through a pulley block. As the space may be large, he needs a bulky knot and his variation is on the figure-eight knot. A start is made as if to make a figure-eight knot with a fairly long loop. Instead of going in with the end, the loop is given two complete twists before tucking it (Fig. 4-1C). When pulled tight, the lump formed is quite large, but the knot is easily undone later.

SLIP KNOT

An overhand knot can have its end doubled back so a bight is tucked (Fig. 4-2A) and a figure-eight can be treated in the same way (Fig. 4-2B). In both cases the knot closes up under strain so it is slightly bulkier than the plain knot (Fig. 4-2C) and it can be released by pulling the end. A generally similar appearance, but with more bulk and without the easy release advantage, is obtained by doubling back a long bight of line and tying either knot with it (Fig. 4-2D).

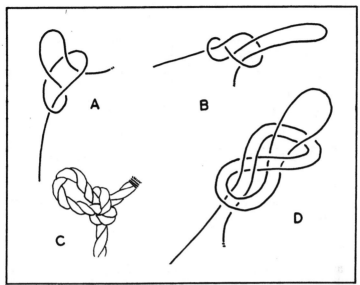

Fig. 4-2. Tucking a bight makes an overhand knot (A) or a figure-eight knot (B) into a slip knot (C). Making it completely with a bight puts an eye in the end of the line (D).

OYSTERMAN'S STOPPER

This knot is a larger stopper knot than most of the others and has the advantage of being symmetrical when drawn tight. Many of the others have a one-sided appearance when tightened. A start is made with an overhand slip knot, but it is a loop of the standing part, and not the end that is pulled through. The working end is then brought through the bight (Fig. 4-3A). These are all the tucks, but

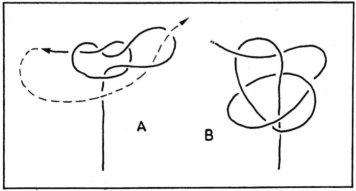

Fig. 4-3. An oysterman's stopper knot closes symmetrically: (A) working end and (B) symmetrical parts.

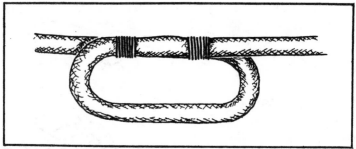

Fig. 4-4. A clinch made by seizing the parts of a loop forms a stopper.

before pulling tight, get the parts even and symmetrical (Fig. 4-3B). The knot should close up with the standing part coming out of its center.

CLINCH

If there has to be a stopper with the minimum weakening of the rope, yet the stopper is needed for some time, any of the common knots are best avoided, as some weakening occurs. A clinch is the alternative. It may not strictly be a knot, but it serves the purpose of one. A small loop of the rope is secured with two seizings (Fig. 4-4). They could be put on in the same way as West Country whippings. A clinch has several other names including *throat seizing, pigtail* and *seized round turn.*

HEAVING LINE KNOT

Besides stopping the end of a rope, a single-strand terminal knot may also use its bulk to provide weight in a heaving line. Some heaving lines are provided with a small bag of sand to concentrate weight at the end, but it is more common among seamen to make a weighted end from the rope itself. There are a great many variations because it is possible to gather up enough of the rope to provide the weight and seize the parts together by knotting around in many ways. The better heaving line knots are symmetrical, without protuberances and with the end coming out alongside the standing part.

A popular version is based on the *hangman's knot.* A sufficient length at the end is bent into a long S-shape (Fig. 4-5A). The end is passed through the bight and around it (Fig. 4-5B) before being wrapped around the whole knot on its way back to the start (Fig. 4-5C) where it goes through its own bight. If the top loop is first pulled and then the standing part, the turns tighten and the knot closes to a symmetrical cylinder (Fig. 4-5D). For a hanging it was the bight opposite the standing part that went around the neck and the long part was arranged behind one ear.

MONKEY'S FIST

This makes more of a knob than a long cylinder. It is probably the most used of the heaving line knots. The knot itself may have sufficient weight, but it is possible to make it around a small metal ball or a rounded pebble to get extra weight. The knot is actually several turns taken around each other in three directions. For clarity, it is shown with two turns each way, but there could be more to hold larger objects or to provide more weight in itself.

Experiment with the amount of slackness needed in making the knot. There has to be some freedom to allow the turns to be made, but an excessive amount makes tightening tedious. With the usual size of heaving line, turns can be looped around one hand while working with the other. Put on two complete round turns, then change direction and put two turns around them (Fig. 4-6A). Hold those turns in place and put two more turns around them, but inside

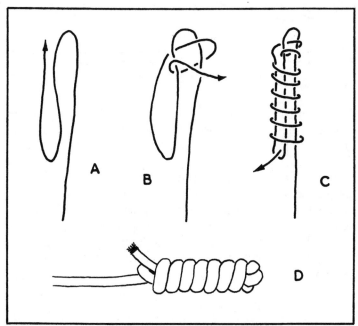

Fig. 4-5. A heaving line knot to put a weight in the end of a line is based on the hangman's knot: (A) s-shape; (B) end is passed through the bights; (C) end is wrapped around whole knot; and (D) symmetrical cylinder.

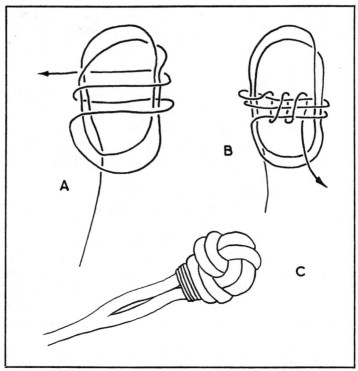

Fig. 4-6. A monkey's fist knot is made by coiling in three directions to form a heavy knob on the end of a heaving line: (A) turns; (B) two more turns; and (C) splice the end.

the first turns (Fig. 4-6B). If a more bulky version is being made, make the same chosen number of turns each way to get a balanced knot. Work through the slack until the knot is tight and a foot or so of the end is alongside the standing part. The end of a marline spike or other pointed tool will be needed to work around the turns finally and pull the whole thing really tight. It is common to seize under the knot and splice the end into the standing part (Fig. 4-6C), but they could be joined with a bowline if the knot is only for temporary use.

With more turns, particularly if enclosing a weight, manipulate the turns so they lie alongside each other and do not ride up so you get a neat final appearance.

Joining Knots  **5**

To the casual user, the mention of knotting is likely to conjure up a picture of joints between two lines which may be anything from sewing thread to hawsers, depending on the person's activities. It is true that much knotting is concerned with joining lines together, but as can be seen by the rest of this book, there are large numbers of knots for other purposes as well.

A seaman may talk of bending two ropes together. This has been accepted nautical jargon, in the same way that the majority of knots intended for the purpose afloat have been described as *bends*, but there are so many exceptions and it would be pedantic and rather foolish to talk of bending fishing line or sewing thread together. It is more usual to *tie* knots ashore and this is a safe word to use in relation to any knots, even if an enthusiastic amateur boatman prefers to bend his lines together.

There are an enormous number of joining bends or knots. Many of them were devised for special needs and it is advisable to keep them for these purposes. In particular, those intended for large ropes are mostly unsuitable for twine and other small stuff, and the same applies the other way around. In some cases, particular users have adopted certain knots, yet the general user may be able to see no good reason for not using a more common knot. However, tradition must have shown the value of the chosen knots. It is easy to learn a large variety of knots, but with joining knots, more than some of the others, it is also important to learn uses so knots are not wrongly applied.

The basic joining knots are the common or sheet bend (Fig. 3-2) and the reef knot (Fig. 3-4). In the large number of situations where there is no clear reason for using any other knot, one of these knots or a variation of it, should be satisfactory.

Another consideration is the intended permanence of the knot. If it is temporary and will have to be cast off or undone, it must not be a type that jams, but if the knot is in string that will be discarded, it does not matter if it pulls into a form that defies separating. A spike may have to be used to open a knot, but it is very easy to damage and weaken fibers with this, so its use should be kept to a minimum. A knot between ropes will be weaker than the ropes. For a permanent joint between ropes it would be stronger to splice them.

OVERHAND BEND

Users of sewing cotton and thread often tie ends together by forming an overhand knot in the two ends held together (Fig. 5-1A). It is satisfactory for this purpose, but when the two standing parts are drawn in opposite directions, the bending of the lines entering the knot is tightly curved and this weakens them. Because of this it is not a bend to use between larger lines. It is also possible to use a figure-eight knot instead of the overhand knot, but there is the same weakening fault under strain.

FLEMISH BEND AND RING KNOT

Another way of using a figure-eight knot for joining is to make it loosely in one end, then bring the other line in where the end comes out and follow around to double the knot (Fig. 5-1B). A simpler version uses the thumb knot and is probably equally as strong and less bulky. This may be called a *ring knot*, but it is also described as a *water knot,* although that name has also been used for some other knots. A ring knot can be made by forming a thumb knot in one end and following back around with the other piece (Fig. 5-1C) or the two ends twisted together and the ends taken back alongside their standing parts (Fig. 5-1D). These are all knots for thin line, not rope. Izaac Walton in his early writings on fishing describes the ring knot as a water knot. Although these knots were suitable for traditional fishing line materials, they are less satisfactory for the modern more slippery synthetic lines.

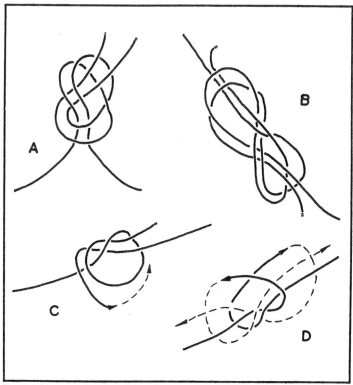

Fig. 5-1. Lines can be joined by making overhang or figure-eight knots between them: (A) overhang knot; (B) double the knot; (C) thumb knot; and (D) ends taken alongside standing parts.

FISHERMAN'S KNOT

There are a large number of knots used by anglers and fishermen, but the name has been commonly applied to a jamming form of two thumb knots. This is another knot also called a *water knot* and it may be described as a *waterman's knot*, an *Englishman's knot* and even a *true lover's knot*. There are even many more names for this knot. The standard version is good on string, twine and any natural thin line, but it does not have enough turns to be secure in smooth synthetic line.

A thumb knot is tied in one end, either around the meeting piece or that end is thrust through it after making it (Fig. 5-2A). The second end is worked into a thumb knot around the first piece (Fig. 5-2B). Both knots are tightened and the standing parts pulled to close the knots together. It is important for a neat finish that both knots are made by twisting the same way with the ends alongside

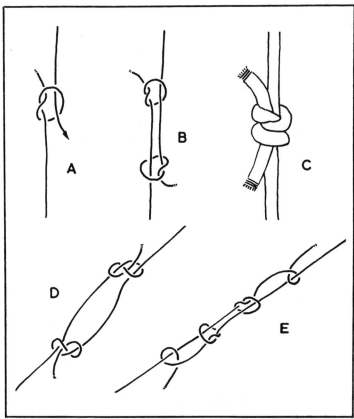

Fig. 5-2. The fisherman's knot is suitable for thin lines and is made with turns around the opposite lines: (A) thumb knot at end; (B) thumb at other end; (C) twisting the knots: (D) figure-eight knots: and (E) half hitch around standing parts.

the opposite standing parts, so they fit into each other (Fig. 5-2C). If the twist of the second thumb knot is made the opposite way to the first, the parts will not mate. Using figure-eight knots may be slightly stronger for slippery line (Fig. 5-2D).

In slippery line a fisherman's knot, made with thumb or figure-eight knots can be given extra security if ends are left long enough to each put a half hitch around the standing parts after the first tightening (Fig. 5-2E).

BARREL KNOT

For the same purpose as the fisherman's knot, but claimed to be more secure in thin slippery line, the overlapped ends are each twisted around the other part and the end brought through between the lines (Fig. 5-3A). Perform the actions in exactly the same way at each end of the knot so the ends are passed through the same way. The parts pull tight in a similar way to the fisherman's knot. When drawn up tight it is possible to cut the ends off quite close—without fear of the knot parting, so there is not much projecting to catch if the knot is drawn through a hole or ring or wound on to a reel. More turns are sometimes added, but they increase the bulk and may not be stronger.

A knot that looks very similar on paper is a *wire knot*. It might have uses in fiber cord, but its particular use is in joining stiff wire, such as may be used for fences, which has to be manipulated with pliers and could not be twisted into ordinary knots by hand. The wires are overlapped and each is brought around the other so it can be twisted back on itself several times (Fig. 5-3B). This can be done with a long overlap at first, so there is space to use pliers and get the twists close to their loop, then the whole thing is pulled tight and the twisted parts jam close.

BLOOD KNOT

The names *blood* and *barrel* are sometimes transposed. As described here, a blood knot is similar to a fisherman's knot, but for increased grip on slippery line there is an extra turn put in before tucking each thumb knot (Fig. 5-4A) so the end passes through two loops (Fig. 5-4B).

A recent fisherman's joining knot is also called a *blood knot*, but it has been devised for slippery synthetic lines. Hold the overlapping

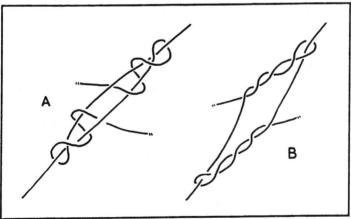

Fig. 5-3. The barrel knot is particularly suitable for thin slippery lines: (A) the end is brought through the lines and (B) overlapped wires.

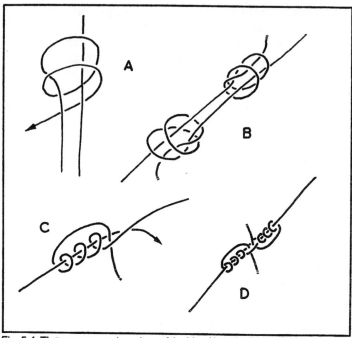

Fig. 5-4. There are several versions of the blood knot for joining fishing lines: (A) tucking each thumb knot; (B) end passes through two loops; ( ) wrap the end; and (D) wrap the other end.

lines at what will be the center of the knot, then wrap one end three times around the other piece, back towards the center (Fig. 5-4C). Still holding the center and those first wraps, do the same with the other end (Fig. 5-4D). Make sure the twists on both sides are made in the same direction. Draw up carefully and tightly before cutting off.

WEAVER'S KNOT

A weaver has to join lines which are usually little more than threads and he often has to do this quickly without stopping his loom. Some of the knots are the same as those used in other places, but he has a special way of tying to get quick results. Some weaver's knots may not be very strong and would be unsuitable for use elsewhere, but in weaving a piece of cloth the close over-and-under arrangement of the warp and weft provide support to the knot and great strength in it is unimportant.

One of the best knots used by the weaver would be called a common or sheet bend elsewhere, but it differs in the way it is made. The method is worth knowing for application in places other than weaving cloth.

The ends are held crossing with the left thumb and forefinger (Fig. 5-5A). Take a bight of the standing part of the piece underneath and lift it over its own end (Fig. 5-5B). Take the other end down through the bight (Fig. 5-5C) and pull tight to form a common bend with the ends on the same side of the knot (Fig. 5-5D).

LEFT-HANDED WEAVER'S KNOT

Whether the two ends finish on the same side or on opposite sides probably does not matter, either for strength or for satisfactory running in the loom, but some weavers prefer to make the knot

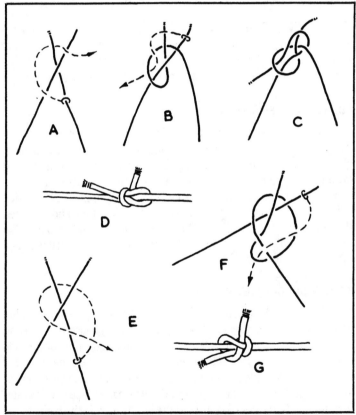

Fig. 5-5. A weaver uses knots which finish with a sheet bend form, but they are made in a different way: (A) crossing ends; (B) bight of second part; (C) end goes through the bight; (D) common bends; (E) bight is lifted over both ends: (F) straight end is turned; and (G) keeping the knot in shape.

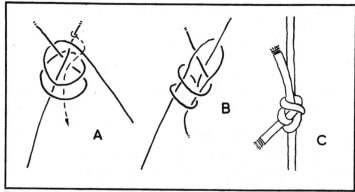

Fig. 5-6. A double weaver's knot includes extra turns: (A) encircle the end: (B) end is turned through two loops; and (C) result is same as double sheet bend.

the other way. The ends are held together in the left hand in the same way as for the first example, but the bight is lifted over both ends (Fig. 5-5E). The straight end is turned down with it (Fig. 5-5F) and the knot pulled tight, taking care to keep it in shape (Fig. 5-5G).

DOUBLE WEAVER'S KNOT

A weaver also uses what is in effect a double sheet bend, but as with the basic weaver's knot, he has a special way of making it quickly. The two ends are held crossing between the left thumb and forefinger and a bight of the under piece lifted over its end as for a basic weaver's knot, then it is done again to encircle the end twice (Fig. 5-6A). Hold these parts in place while the other end is turned down through the two loops alongside its own standing part (Fig. 5-6B). The result is the same as a double sheet bend and it is pulled up in the same way (Fig. 5-6C).

SECOND DOUBLE WEAVER'S KNOT

This knot has some of the virtues of the previous double weaver's knot. It may not be quite as strong, although strong enough for its purpose in cloth, but it pulls tight with both ends pointing the same way. If both ends are trailing when the thread is drawn through the loom reed or any other hole, there is less risk of snagging and less risk that the thread will be caught and break again. The two ends are held together in the left hand, and the bight of the working part is lifted as in the previous examples, but this time it encircles its own end (Fig. 5-7A). The straight end is then taken down through the loop (Fig. 5-7B). Hold that end down alongside its standing part while tightening by pulling the standing parts in opposite directions (Fig. 5-7C).

TUCKED SHEET BEND

As in the double weaver's knot, there is always an advantage in having both ends the same way if the knot is liable to foul anything up when it is dragged along or pulled through a confined space. This applies to larger ropes as well as to weaving thread. When dealing with a common or sheet bend one way to get the ends the same way without weakening the knot is to complete the bend in the ordinary way (Fig. 5-8A), but with enough of the tucked end left to turn it back through its own loop (Fig. 5-8B). Tighten in the usual way and be careful that the turns do not upset, then the two ends should finish in the same direction on each side of the standing part (Fig. 5-8C).

BINDER TURN

A simpler version of the common bend with its ends in the same direction is used to join binder twine in a hay baling machine. That gives it its name, but it could be used anywhere else that its advantages outweigh its disadvantages. It has minimum bulk and its ends trail together so it has the least possibility of catching anywhere when being drawn through a machine. Against that it is not quite as strong as the ordinary common bend or the tucked sheet bend. It could be used for a temporary light line that is to pull a heavier one, such as a mooring line for a ship through the water, but

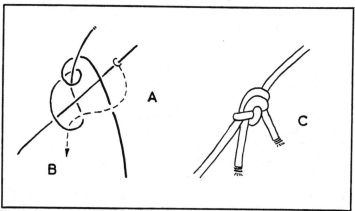

Fig. 5-7. Another version of the double weaver's knot gets its extra turns in a different way: (A) bight encircles its own end; (B) straight end is taken through the loop; and (C) pull standing parts in opposite directions.

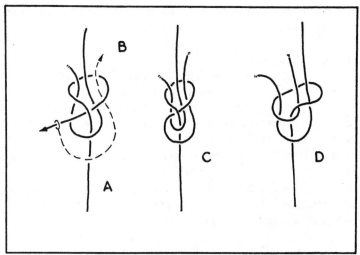

Fig. 5-8. A tucked sheet bend has the ends adapted to both point the same way. A binder turn also brings the ends the same way: (A) complete the bend in ordinary ways; (B) turn tucked end back through its own loop; (C) two ends finish in same direction; and (D) end goes under its own part.

if there is very much difference in the sizes of the ropes there are other better knots.

To make a binder turn, turn back a bight in one rope (the thicker one if they are different thicknesses) and work the other end through it exactly as if making a common bend, except for the final tuck, when the end goes under its own part the other way (Fig. 5-8D). Manipulate the knot carefully into shape as it is drawn tight.

HARNESS BEND

If two pieces of flat leather strap have to be knotted together, ordinary knots are awkward and the resulting twisting puts kinks into the straps. A harness bend is a means of joining flat straps without much risk of them becoming twisted or damaged. The knot can be used with rope that is fairly stiff, but it tends to slip in soft flexible line.

The strap ends are laid so they overlap, then each is worked around the other as shown in Fig. 5-9A. It is possible to let each loop be a simple half hitch, but getting in the extra movement is slightly more secure. When the knot is drawn tight, the two ends finish alongside each other, but pointing in opposite directions (Fig. 5-9B). There will be some slipping when the knot tightens under strain so do not have the projecting ends too short.

DOUBLE HARNESS BEND

This bend differs from the harness bend in the way the two ends are finally tucked. As the two parts are tightened by sliding towards each other, the ends are crossed (Fig. 5-9C) so they are interlocked and there is less risk of the two ropes or straps sliding apart if strain on the knot is released.

MACHINE SHEET BEND

There have been several attempts to devise knots that could be tied down by machine. The under and over formation of most of them make mechanical knotting difficult, but a machine to make a variation of the sheet bend was patented by G.H. Lind in 1942. This knot is generally similar to the sheet bend, except for the final turn (Fig. 5-10) and its strength should be comparable, whether made by machine or hand.

TOGGLED SHEET BENDS

A piece of wood may be put through a knot for various reasons. It could be a marline spike or fid in a temporary situation, a tapered peg or just any piece of wood that could be picked up. Sometimes the toggle is there to keep the knot in shape under load and prevent it from spilling to an unsafe shape. Sometimes it is used to allow quick release after the knot has served its purpose.

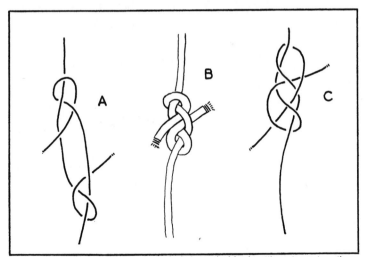

Fig. 5-9. Harness bends are particularly intended for knotting straps together: (A) overlapped ends; (B) ends point in opposite directions; and (C) ends are crossed.

69

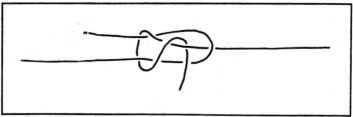

Fig. 5-10. This version of the sheet bend was devised by machine.

A simple sheet bend may be toggled (Fig. 5-11A) when it is to come under heavy load. The toggle then prevents the knot from pulling out of shape and it also prevents the parts from jamming, so they are easily cast off when the knot is no longer required, although there is no quick-release action.

For a quick-release arrangement there is a version of the double sheet bend, in which the working part is not passed through the bight of the other part. Instead, the double turns are made around the upper part of the bight (Fig. 5-11B), with the standing part on top of the turn of the bight. This is dipped through the bight and held with the toggle (Fig. 5-11C).

ROPE YARN KNOT

This knot may not have many modern applications, but its particular use is for joining the ends of yarns when serving a rope. Its particular value is in having the minimum bulk. It finishes thinner than any of the common joining knots, although it may not be as strong. In serving (like a long whipping), the load is not finally as great as if the joint was between two free parts.

Yarns are mostly two parts, laid up by twisting together. In line with other numbers of parts, the parts have to be re-grouped and laid into two. The unlaid ends are brought together (Fig. 5-12A). One pair of these is not used, but the other pair goes around and is twisted together above them in the same way as if completing a reef knot (Fig. 5-12B). The knot is neater and more compact if the tucked ends and the final twist are with the lay of the yarn.

TUCKED ENDS

With stranded rope, whether two-strand yarn or stouter three-strand cord or rope, it is possible to push the ends between the strands. In splicing, the tucking strands are separated, but in knotting, the whole thickness of the end goes through. This is

70

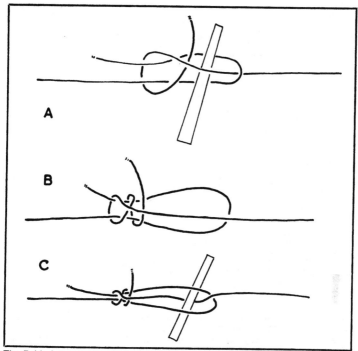

Fig. 5-11. A toggle through a sheet bend prevents it from jamming or it can be used in another version for a quick release: (A) toggled sheet bends; (B) double turns at upper part of bight; and (C) turns held with the toggle.

sometimes done with a reef knot if it is used for uniting ropes when the knot does not bear against something. It is not the correct knot for this purpose, but if it is used, it can be strengthened if the ends are passed through the rope outside the knot (Fig. 5-13A). This can

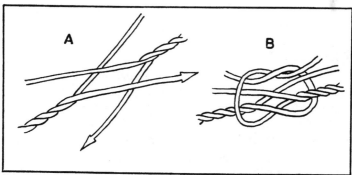

Fig. 5-12. Rope yarns can be joined by interlocking and knotting with a rope yarn knot: (A) unlaid ends are brought together and (B) similar to completing a reef knot.

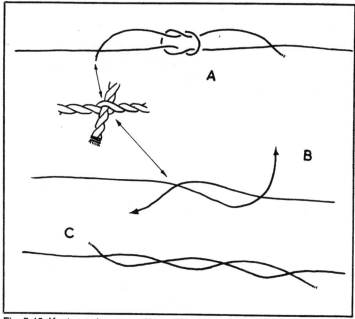

Fig. 5-13. Knots can be secured by tucking the ends through the rope, or small lines may be joined only by tucking: (A) ends passed through rope outside the knot; (B) tucked overlapping ends; and (C) ends are tucked again.

be done with the ends outside other knots. Strain tightens the grip on the tucked ends.

Carried to a logical conclusion, lines are joined by tucking only. This might not be very satisfactory for ropes, but for small laid line, such as is used for serving, tucking without using knots will produce satisfactory joints of little bulk. The overlapping ends are each tucked into the other (Fig. 5-13B), then the ends are taken further along and tucked again (Fig. 5-13C).

SURGEON'S KNOT

When a surgeon ties stitches in a wound he uses a smooth gut and has to work with tweezers. He may use a reef knot, or even a granny knot, but there is a special surgeon's knot that holds better on the slippery material. It could have other uses when dealing with modern smooth synthetic cords and ropes.

In the standard surgeon's knot, a start is made as if tying a reef knot, then an extra turn taken (Fig. 5-14A). This gives enough friction for the knot, at this stage, to be pulled tight and hold while the second part is made. Completion is in the same way as a reef knot (Fig. 5-14B). In another version, there is a double twist included at the second stage (Fig. 5-14C). Yet another version is completed in the first way, but the ends are again twisted together so the result is like a reef knot above the first twisting (Fig. 5-14D). In surgery there may be a need to consider bulk because of the need to leave the knot to be absorbed in the tissues. Both of the later versions are bulky. For slippery lines elsewhere than in gut in the body, bulk may not matter and they may be preferred.

THIEF KNOT

Another variation on the reef knot is more of a trick than a serious knot. It can be shown to a casual observer who will say it is a reef knot, which they will say does not slip, but you pull the ends and it does. The story that goes with the thief knot is of a seaman who suspected his chest was being burglarized. When he roped it, he joined the ends with a thief knot instead of his usual reef knot. The burglar used a reef knot to re-tie the chest so the owner knew he had been burglarized, hence the name of the knot. What use that knowledge was to him is debatable!

The thief knot has the reef knot formation, but the ends finish on the opposite sides (Fig. 5-15A) instead of the same sides of the standing parts. It cannot be made by twisting parts together. Instead, one end has to be taken through the bight of the other, in much the same way as for making a sheet bend, but it goes down through the bight (Fig. 5-15B) instead of across it.

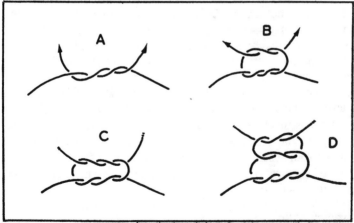

Fig. 5-14. A surgeon's knot is an adaption of a reef knot with extra turns applied in various ways: (A) extra turn; (B) complete as if a reef knot; (C) double twist; and (D) ends twisted together.

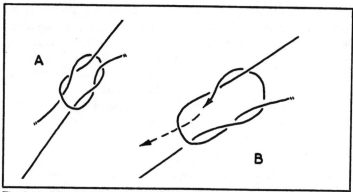

Fig. 5-15. A thief knot is a trick knot that looks like a reef knot, but has ends on opposite sides: (A) ends finish on opposite sides and (B) end goes down through the bight.

HEAVING LINE BENDS

If a thin rope has to be attached to a thick rope, a sheet bend can be used if the differences in thickness are not very great. If there is more difference or the ropes are slippery or wet, a double sheet bend is preferable. In both cases it is the thicker rope that is doubled back into a bight and the thinner rope worked through it.

There comes a stage where the difference in rope sizes is so great that these knots are not practical. An example is a light heaving line thrown between a ship and the shore that has to be used to haul a very large hawser through the water.

Sometimes the sheet bend is trebled (Fig. 5-16A) or taken even further, but a stout hawser doubled back is stiff and resists bending so it may open. A seizing has to be used as well, which may be a nuisance for a temporary purpose. Although if there is already an eye spliced in the hawser, this seizing does have possibilities.

The more common heaving line bend, sometimes called a *racking bend,* takes the line into the bight, around one side of it, then in an over-and-under action around the two sides (Fig. 5-16B). How many times this is done depends on the difference in sizes of the ropes, but there should be at least four crossings. The knot is finished with a half hitch around one side of the bight (Fig. 5-16C). The racking turns pull the sides of the bight together and there is no need for a seizing.

CARRICK BEND

A problem with such thick ropes as hawsers and cable is their stiffness which prevents them from taking the loops and bends of many knots suitable for smaller line. There may also be the problems associated with a man's strength in dealing with them. Knotting has to be within his limits and not require mechanical assistance. This applies both to making the knot and in casting it off after it has been under load. If there has to be much hitting and levering, the rope fibers may be damaged and the rope weakened.

The best known joining knot for hawsers and cables is the carrick bend. The pattern of its over-and-under formation also makes it the start of some forms of fancy ropework. It may also be considered sufficiently decorative in itself for such purposes as joining the ends of tasseled cords around drapes.

A great many variations of the carrick bend have been published, but many that vary from the accepted way of tucking depend on the ends being seized outside the knot and any strength comes from the seizings in most cases. Without the seizings these knots would slip. The standard carrick bend is often seized, but even without the seizings it will hold after the initial slip as the knot closes up.

To make a carrick bend, the end of one rope is turned back into a loop with the end under the standing part (Fig. 5-17A). The end of

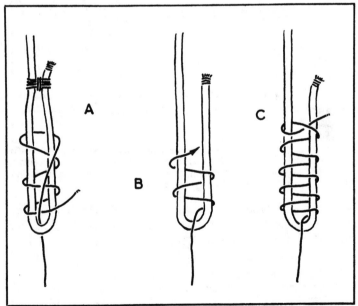

Fig. 5-16. Heaving line bends are used when a thick rope has to be pulled by a much lighter line and are developments of the sheet bend: (A) trebled sheet bend; (B) over-and-under action; and (C) half hitch around one side of the bight.

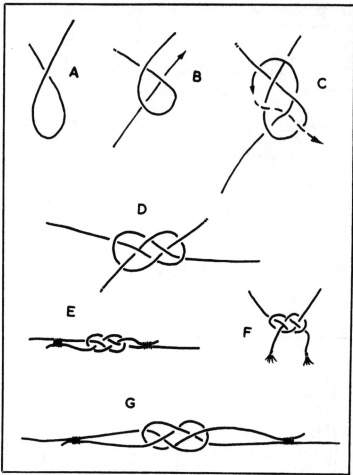

Fig. 5-17. The carrick bend is particularly suitable for joining very thick ropes: (A) end under standing parts: (B) other rope brought towards it; (C) similar loop with its own standing part; (D) even pattern; (E) seized ends; (F) ends on same side of the knot; and (G) parts go through the loops.

the other rope is brought towards it with its end under (Fig. 5-17B) to make a similar loop with its own standing part (Fig. 5-17C). The ends come out on opposite sides and there is an even pattern (Fig. 5-17D). No part should go through a loop, nor over or under more than one other part at any place.

The ends may be brought alongside their standing parts and seized (Fig. 5-17E). It is possible to take the working end around the other way and get exactly the same pattern, but with the ends on the same side of the knot (Fig. 5-17F). Tests have shown that this is not as strong as having the ends on opposite sides, but it is the way to tie the knot if its purpose is decoration and not strength.

Under load the carrick bends pulls to a flat pattern. It is reasonably flexible if it has to follow the cable around a drum, but possibly the only advantages of some of the other versions is in their better section if they have to follow tight curves.

If the parts go through the loops (Fig. 5-17G), instead of being woven across them, the knot pulls into a more rounded shape. The formation is actually that of a granny knot, so if the advantage of its flexibility is wanted, there have to be good seizings because any strength will be mainly due to them.

Carrick bends were more frequently used in the days of large sailing ships. Seamanship manuals published over the last two or more centuries have described a great many carrick bends, but none of them have the strength of the standard version (Fig. 5-17D).

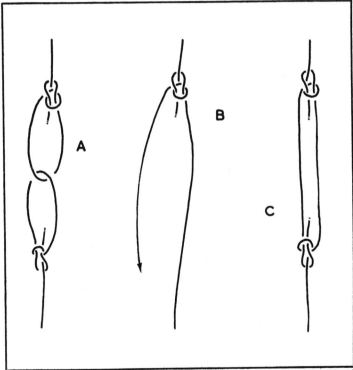

Fig. 5-18. Bowlines can be interlocked or the overlapping ends can be joined into each other in the same fashion as making bowlines: (A) joined loops; join each line to the other; (B) and (C) two parts must be of equal length.

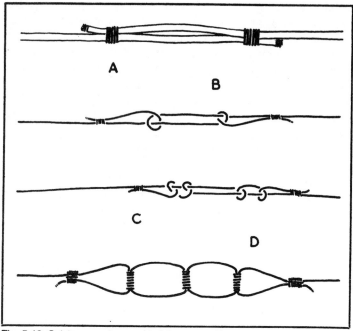

Fig. 5-19. Seizings can be used to join ropes, either alone or with turns in the ropes: (A) two seizings; (B) half-hitched ends; (C) clove hitches; and (D) round seizings.

BOWLINE BEND

There are not many alternatives to carrick bend for large ropes, but bowlines can be linked. Each is made in the normal way (Fig. 3-6), but their loops are joined (Fig. 5-18A). A bowline should never be difficult to cast off after it has been under load. It is a knot with one of the best strength characteristics. A bowline bend satisfies the main rope-joining requirements.

TWIN BOWLINE BEND

Another way of using the bowline knot formation (it could be described as the sheet bend formation) is to overlap the two lines to be joined, then join each to the other so it is done as if completing a bowline (Fig. 5-18B). It is important to see that the two parts are of equal length so they share the strain (Fig. 5-18C).

SEIZED BENDS

If two large ropes have to be joined so they will follow through a hole or hawse pipe, bulk has to be kept to a minimum. Carrick bends and bowline bends may be too thick. To get less bulk there has to be a sacrifice of strength, but if all that is required is that one rope should follow another, this is not important.

The two ropes may be overlapped and joined with two (Fig. 5-19A) or four seizings. Any strength is then only that of the seizings. If more strength than this is required, the ends can be half-hitched around the other standing parts before seizing (Fig. 5-19B). There could be a second half-hitch in each direction so the pairs form clove hitches (Fig. 5-19C). In both forms this may be called a *reeving-line bend*.

Older manuals from sailing ship days show a variety of ways of joining hawsers with seizings. One such *hawser bend* has the two ropes crossing at three places with throat seizings, then the ends are brought alongside the standing parts with round seizings (Fig. 5-19D). Opposite parts should have matching lengths. As security depends on the seizings, they should be examined while the ropes are in use.

HUNTER'S BEND

It is not often that a knot is claimed to be new and original, with the thousands of knots that have been described in books, there would not seem to be room for another, but this joining knot is

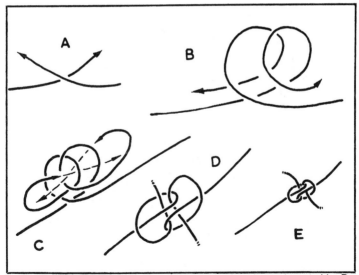

Fig. 5-20. This knot is claimed to be the newest knot. It was invented by Dr. Edward Hunter in 1978: (A) overlap the ends; (B) turn both ends into eyes; (C) each end goes around the eyes; (D) overhand knot; and (E) complete the knot.

claimed to have never appeared before. The fact was noted in the prestigious English 'Times' newspaper in 1978. The inventor was Dr. Edward Hunter, a retired physician and a knotting enthusiast.

The knot is suitable for joining ropes of any thickness as an alternative to the sheet bend. It is slightly more bulky and not as simple to tie, but the extra crossings should make it stronger in smooth synthetic fiber materials.

Overlap the ends of the pieces (Fig. 5-20A) and turn both ends into eyes on the same side as the other piece (Fig. 5-20B). Take each end around the eyes and through them from opposite sides (Fig. 5-20C). Each will have made an overhand knot linked with the other (Fig. 5-20D). Work the parts tight to complete the knot (Fig. 5-20E).

Fixed End Loops  6

When a fixed loop is needed in the end of a rope, the bowline is the normal choice. In most circumstances, the only better way of making a loop is by eye-splicing. However there are other loops and many ways of making a bowline, as well as a long list of bowlines without names. The standard bowline (Fig. 3-6) will serve most needs and usually it can be made best in one of the ways described in Chapter 3. Some other ways of getting the same result are given below.

If an overhand knot is tied (Fig. 6-1A) and this is upset by pulling the end up alongside the standing part (Fig. 6-2B), the small loop is formed and the end is ready for tucking (Fig. 6-1C). This is supposed to be a method favored by climbers for putting a loop around their waist.

In another method, the end is brought around the standing part by using a loop instead of working it around. Take up enough for the loop and make the small eye (Fig. 6-2A). Pass a bight of the standing part through the eye, far enough for the end to be put in (Fig. 6-2B). Pull the two sides of the part that has been knotted so the bight is drawn straight. This will straighten the standing part and pull the end to a loop around it in the normal bowline form (Fig. 6-2C).

A bowline can be attached to a ring without actually passing the end of the rope through the ring, although it is necessary to pass the standing part through the knot. Put a small bight through the ring (Fig. 6-3A). Put a half hitch over it with the standing part (Fig.

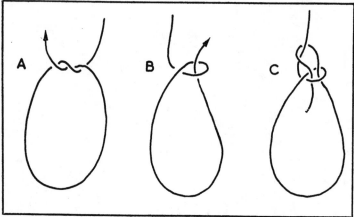

Fig. 6-1. An overhand knot can be twisted to make the start of a bowline: (A) overhand knot is tied; (B) pull end alongside the standing part; and (C) end is ready for tucking.

6-3B). Lead the standing part through the end of the bight (Fig. 6-3C) to complete the bowline.

WATER BOWLINE

Although the bowline is supposed to be easy to undo at all times, if it is to be immersed in water, there is a special version in which there is an extra half hitch included (Fig. 6-4) to prevent it from seizing tight.

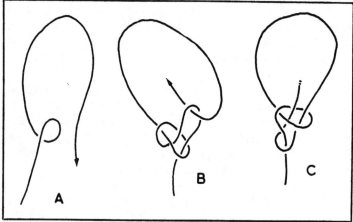

Fig. 6-2. A bowline can be made by pulling the end with a bight through an overhand knot: (A) small eye; (B) pass bight through the eye; and (C) normal bowline form.

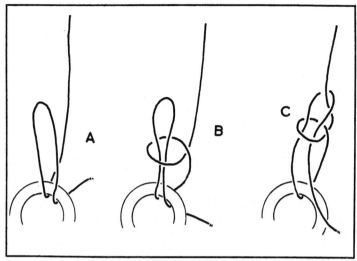

Fig. 6-3. A bowline can be formed from a half hitch over a bight: (A) put small bight through the ring: (B) half hitch; and (C) complete the bowline.

DOUBLE BOWLINE

If stiff rope has to be made into a bowline there is a risk of the knot becoming upset. To reduce this risk the eye is made into a complete round turn and the bowline completed in the usual way (Fig. 6-5).

BOWLINE WITH A BIGHT

The name distinguishes this knot from the bowline on a bight, which follows. If a rope's end is to support the hook of a tackle or any other metal object, it is considered better for there to be two parts of the rope in contact with the metal. The knot to use for this purpose is a bowline with a bight.

A start is made to form a bowline with a loop of the required size, but instead of the end being passed up through the eye a long bight is taken (Fig. 6-6A). The bight continues around the standing

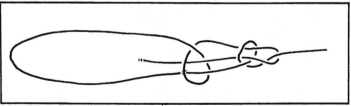

Fig. 6-4. The extra half hitch in a water bowline helps to make it easy to undo after immersion.

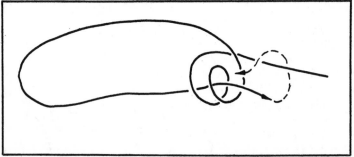

Fig. 6-5. The extra turn in a double bowline helps the knot to keep its shape in stiff rope.

part and is taken down far enough for it to match the size of the main loop (Fig. 6-6B). Adjust the knot as it is tightened so the two loops will share the load equally.

BOWLINE ON A BIGHT

This bowline is one of the knots for making a double loop. As the name indicates, it is made on the bight of a rope. It can be formed completely without using the ends of the rope. It could be used near the end of a rope, but its main use is for a completely doubled rope, as would be used for slinging a load or for sitting in.

Use the bight to start as if it was a single line making an ordinary bowline. The end of the bight is passed up through the doubled eye (Fig. 6-7A). The end of the bight has to loop around the

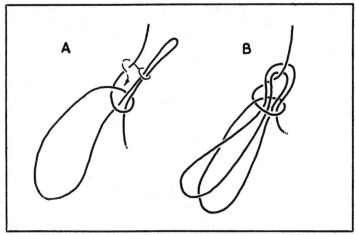

Fig. 6-6. In a bowline with a bight the working end is tucked as a bight to make a second loop: (A) long bight and (B) bight matches size of main loop.

84

doubled standing part. This could be done by going to the ends of the rope, but the standard method gets the same results without using the ends.

Hold the eye in shape and keep the double loop to its size, except for enough of the end of the bight to double back and pass over it (Fig. 6-7B). Without disturbing the other parts, lift this until it is behind the standing parts (Fig. 6-7C). Work the knot tight carefully so it does not lose shape.

PORTUGESE BOWLINE

This bowline provides one way of putting a double loop in the end of a line. It is less commonly called a *French bowline*. Enough line is taken in a round turn to make loops of the required size, with a little extra for tucking (Fig. 6-8A). An eye can be made in the standing part and the end passed through it so as to trap the extra turn (Fig. 6-8B). The same result can be obtained by passing the end over and up through the loops and pulling it straight to force a turn in the standing part (Fig. 6-8C). From this stage it is passed

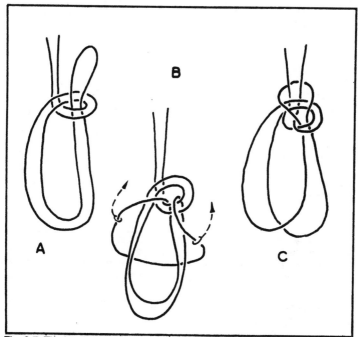

Fig. 6-7. The bowline on a bight is made completely from a bight to produce a double loop: (A) end is passed up through the doubled eye; (B) end of bight doubles back; and (C) lift until behind the standing parts.

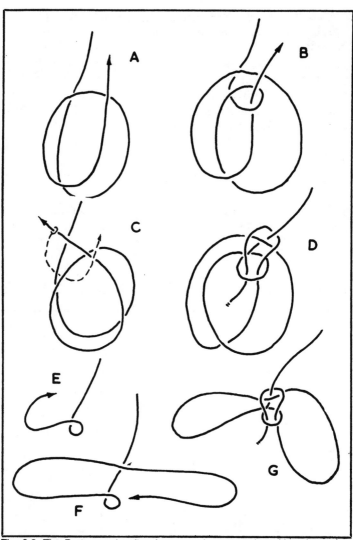

Fig. 6-8. The Portugese bowline forms two loops together although another version has them on opposite sides: (A) tucking the line; (B) trap the extra turn; (C) force a turn in the standing part; (D) complete the knot; (E) one loop at the side; (F) second loop at opposite side; and (G) pass the end up through the eye.

around the standing part and down through the eye in the usual way to complete the knot (Fig. 6-8D).

As the link between the two loops passes across the knot without turns, it is possible to adjust the sizes of the loops by pulling through before fully tightening. They can be adapted to different sizes to suit the load. However, both loops must be under load, or strain on one will close the other.

The normal Portugese bowline has the two loops together and this should suit most needs, but there is a variation that finishes with the loops on opposite sides of the knot. Form the small eye at a point that leaves enough to form the two loops. From this make one loop at the side (Fig. 6-8E) and go across to make the second loop at the opposite side (Fig. 6-8F). Hold the eye in shape and the loops to size, then pass the end up through the eye and around the standing part in the usual way (Fig. 6-8G), trapping the crossing between the

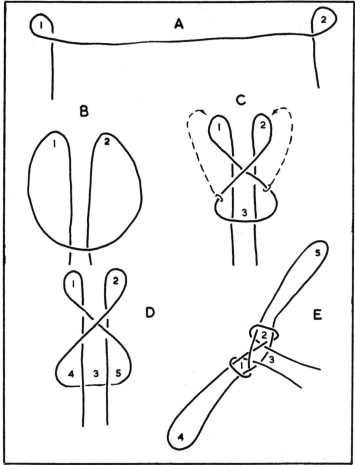

Fig. 6-9. The Spanish bowline is made without using the ends and makes a pair of loops on opposite sides of the knot: (A) twist two eyes; (B) pull the eyes together; (C) twist; (D) crossing in front; and (E) extend the loops.

loops as in the first version. Keep the parts in shape as the knot is tightened.

SPANISH BOWLINE

The Spanish bowline is another bowline worked on a bight without using the ends of the rope. When completed, it has the two loops projecting from opposite sides of the knot and it is convenient for a man to sit with a leg in each loop. It can also be used as a sling for lifting a load.

Take enough rope to make the two loops and at this limit twist in two eyes (Fig. 6-9A). Bring the eyes close together so the standing parts hang parallel and the rope for the loops hangs in front (Fig. 6-9B). Put a twist in this without disturbing the eyes (Fig. 6-9C) and lift this part over the top so it hangs behind, leaving the crossing in front (Fig. 6-9D). At the same time, lift the sides of this loop and pass them through their own eyes, pulling outward to extend the loops (Fig. 6-9E). Draw the whole thing tight to complete the knot.

BOWLINE ON BOWLINE

If any of the bowlines made with a bight of rope will have the load taken entirely by both parts there is no need to do anything further. But if the bight is being used so the bowline will have two loops, and the load will only be taken by one standing part, some-

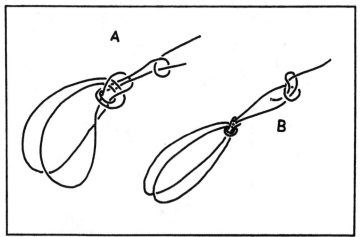

Fig. 6-10. When any double bowline is to have the load taken on only one standing part, the other can be knotted into it like a second bowline: (A) pass the end through the eye and (B) both parts should take an equal load.

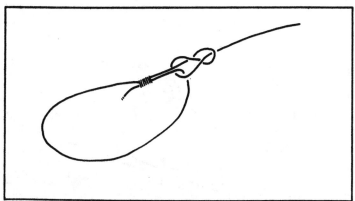

Fig. 6-11. This true bowline is claimed to be the original version used on the bow line of a sailing ship.

thing has to be done with the end so the load within the knot is shared.

The end has to be knotted into the standing part above the bowline and the best way to do this is to treat it as another bowline. Whatever the main bowline, go a short distance above it, form the usual eye and pass the end through it (Fig. 6-10A). Go around the standing part and down through the eye, but adjust the knot as you tighten so both parts will take an equal load (Fig. 6-10B).

MULTIPLE BOWLINES

If more than two loops are wanted it is possible to work a bowline on a bight so the bight is folded in two and the resulting knot has four loops. It is also possible with some of the bowlines to use the bowline with a bight idea, using a turned-back end instead of a plain end so it forms an additional loop. This is convenient if an odd number of loops are needed. The Portugese bowline can be formed with any number of loops, but too great a number makes a knot, which could be insecure if carried too far.

TRUE BOWLINE

For historical interest, the true bowline is claimed to be the earliest knot called a bowline. The bowline proper was a main forward support for a sailing ship mast and what we now call a bowline was then called a bowline knot. As the rope is no longer in use, the name has been shortened to just bowline. It seems likely that the true bowline was used at the bow until it was superseded by the knot we now know.

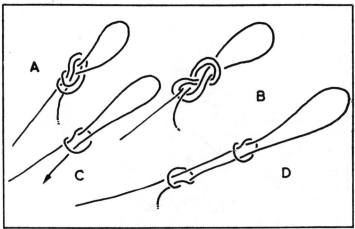

Fig. 6-12. Loops in fishing line are made with bights in various ways: (A) overhand knot in a bight; (B) figure-eight loop; (C) pull end back through overhand knot; and (D) overhand knot around the first part.

The true bowline is made with a figure-eight knot in the standing part, then the end is taken down through it towards the loop, where it is seized to the side of the loop (Fig. 6-11). Strength has to be provided by the sqeeze of the figure-eight and the grip of the seizing. Because of the direction of tucking the end, the loop may have a more round form than the other bowlines.

FISHERMAN'S LOOPS

The bowline is not so easily made nor as satisfactory in very small line, particularly down to the sizes used for angling. A fisherman often ties an overhand knot in a bight (Fig. 6-12A) or gives an extra turn to make a *figure-eight loop* (Fig. 6-12B). For many purposes either is satisfactory.

A stronger loop is made in the same form as a *fisherman's knot* (Fig. 5-2) for joining lines, but here it is made on one piece by turning it back. The best way with fishing line is to make one overhand knot with the end back through it (Fig. 6-12C) and use that to make an overhand knot around the first part (Fig. 6-12D). Make sure the second knot is twisted so its end comes out alongside the standing part and the two knots bed properly together when tightened.

This knot has a large number of alternative names, including *true-lover's knot, Waterman's knot, Englishman's loop,* and *angler's loop.* Another use is suggested by yet another name, *middleman's knot.* It can be tied without using the ends of the line. This means that if a loop is needed, possible for getting a shoulder in to assist pulling a heavy load, and both ends are already tied, this knot can be used to make the loop. It was supposed to be used by climbers for a third man to get into a line already tied at the ends to other climbers, but there are better knots for this. There would be a risk of the middleman's knot slipping and tightening around the waist if loaded in one direction only.

To make the knot without using the ends, whether using fishing line or large ropes, either in the body of the rope or using a bight near the end, throw back the middle of the bight over the standing parts (Fig. 6-13A). Cross the two loops that this forms

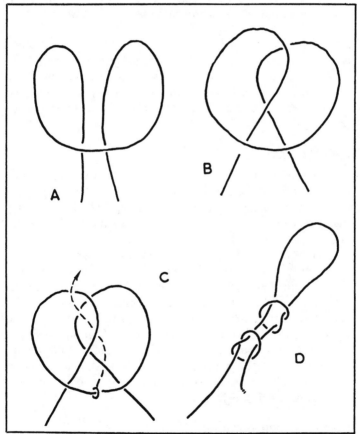

Fig. 6-13. A loop made without using an end and finishing like a fisherman's knot may also be called a middleman's knot: (A) throw middle of bight over standing parts; (B) cross two loops; (C) grasp middle of bight; and (D) draw the knot into shape.

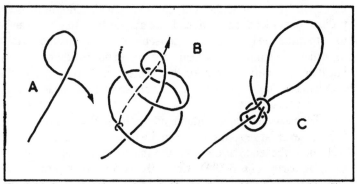

Fig. 6-14. An angler's loop is intended for thin line and finishes something like a bowline: (A) twist a small eye: (B) hold the crossing; and (C) draw the knot tight.

(Fig. 6-13B). It does not matter which piece goes over the other. Reach down through the crossing space and grasp the middle of the bight, so it can be pulled up through (Fig. 6-13C). This is the complete action, but the two overhand knots may be one on top of the other. Shake or pull them apart and draw the knot into shape (Fig. 6-13D).

ANGLER'S LOOP

The angler's loop is another fisherman's loop without a particular name, but it is especially suitable for the very thin slippery line used by river anglers. It has a good strong form, but it jams so tightly that it cannot be undone. This makes it unsuitable for larger cords and ropes that may have to be undone.

There is a likeness to a bowline, but there are more crossings of line in the knot to provide more friction and prevent slipping. Twist a small eye with enough of the working end under the standing part (Fig. 6-14A). Hold the crossing while taking the end around and back across the front (Fig. 6-14B). It is the size of this loop that settles the final size of the end loop. While still holding the crossing of the eye and the end part above it, tuck the loop through the eye (Fig. 6-14C) and draw the knot tight. There can be some adjustment of the size of the loop by drawing through or letting out the end before final tightening.

OVERHAND LOOP KNOTS

The fisherman knot uses two thumb or overhand knots and there are several others that use only one of these. If an overhand knot is made with one part turned back, the resulting loop can be adjusted, then another knot in the projecting end will prevent the line from pulling through (Fig. 6-15A).

Another way of stopping the loop from pulling through is to half-hitch the end around the standing part. It is stronger than the first example. It is yet another knot that is sometimes described as a *weaver's knot*. It is also an *Eskimo bowstring knot*. The half-hitch is made so it beds against the overhand knot when pulled tight (Fig. 6-15B). If it is expected that the loop will have to be released or adjusted the half-hitch can be made with a bight (Fig. 6-15C).

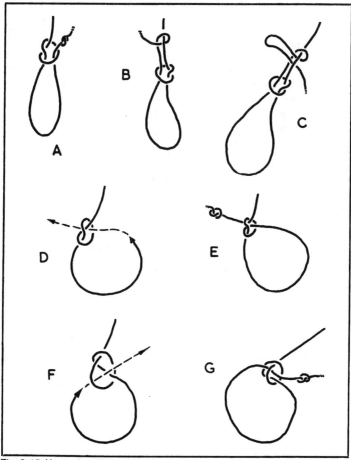

Fig. 6-15. Knotted ends through other knots are used to stop slipping in several methods of forming loops: (A) knot in projecting end; (B) half-hitch beds against overhand knot; (C) half-hitch with a bight; (D) end is passed through in direction across the knots; (E) knot in the end; (F) end is against the other two parts; and (G) knot in the end.

If the end goes into the knot alongside the other part of the loop, the loop is extended long and narrow. For some purposes it would be better to have a rounder loop. One of these is a *halter loop* used for a rope around an animal's neck. An overhand knot is made and the end is passed through in the direction across the knot (Fig. 6-15D). A knot in the end stops it from pulling through (Fig. 6-15E).

Another knot that makes a round loop is very similar, but the end goes across the standing part and is against the other two parts (Fig. 6-15F). A knot in the end stops it after adjusting to size (Fig. 6-15G). This is a *honda knot* when used for a lariat, but it has been used in many parts of the world for bowstring and other purposes.

FIGURE-EIGHT LOOPS

Some of the knots based on the overhand knot can be made with a figure-eight knot. The extra turn provides more strength in slippery line. One knot very much like the ordinary figure-eight loop (Fig. 6-12B) is called a *rover knot*. But it is without the complete bight and it isn't possible to adjust it before final tightening. The end is taken up through the figure-eight knot and the loop is adjusted (Fig. 6-16A). It then goes around the standing part and in alongside the upper part of the knot (Fig. 6-16B).

BELLRINGER'S LOOP

This loop is based on the knot used by bellringers to gather up the slack of a bell rope when it is out of use. A half-hitch is made and

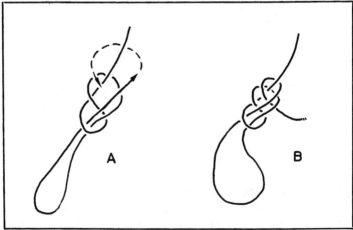

Fig. 6-16. In a rover knot a figure-eight slip knot is locked with a turn of the end: (A) loop is adjusted and (B) end goes alongside the upper part of the knot.

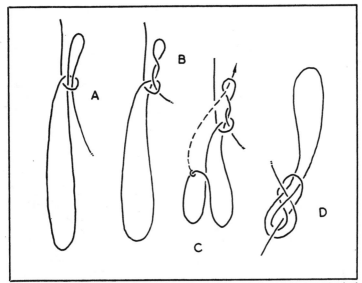

Fig. 6-17. A bellringer's loop develops the bellringer's knot into a method of forming a loop in the end of a thin line: (A) bight of the standing part is passed through; (B) bight is given a full twist; (C) hanging loop is pushed through the end of the bight; and (D) keep the knot in shape.

the bight of the standing part is passed through it (Fig. 6-17A). The bight is given a full twist (Fig. 6-17B) and the hanging loop is pushed through the end of the bight (Fig. 6-17C). Keep the knot in shape as the parts are drawn tight (Fig. 6-17D). The result is very similar to the angler's loop and the rover knot, but there are more crossings within the knot.

Running Loops  7

There are many uses for slip knots, nooses and other adjustable loops. Most fixed end loops can be made into nooses by passing the standing part through the loop or making the loop around it. In many cases the name of the resulting knot is the original name with *running* in front of it, thus a bowline with the standing part through the loop is a *running bowline* (Fig. 7-1).

Besides the running loops made from fixed loops, there are some that are for special purposes. They are broadly divided into slip knots that are used to pull a line tight around something and may then be locked with a half hitch or in some other way, and others that remain running. An example of the former is the *packer's knot* (Figs. 3-10 and 7-8A). An example of a permanently running loop is a lariat.

A lasso or lariat may have a *honda knot* (Fig. 6-15G). Rope for a lariat is often four stranded as this is more flexible than the usual three-stranded rope. An alternative way of making the eye is to pass the end through the rope, dividing the strands. The end is knotted to prevent it from pulling back and there are seizings on each side of the gap (Fig. 7-2A). These could be West Country whippings. Besides preventing the gap from widening in use, they keep the tucked end square across the rope and the eye circular.

A lariat may have a metal eye or thimble. The best way to attach the rope would be with a splice, but when that is not done, the next best close attachment is a seized eye (Fig. 7-2B).

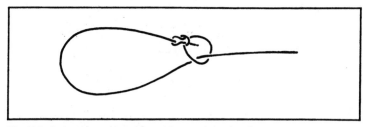

Fig. 7-1. A simple noose is formed by running a bowline.

CLINCHES

At one time seamen preferred clinches to ordinary knots for running loops. Clinches are still preferred in very large lines that would be difficult to knot. In the days of large sailing ships a clinch could be expected to stand up to the constant slatting of ropes and sails better than a knot.

An inside clinch is more secure than an outside clinch because it becomes trapped when the loop is drawn tight. The outside clinch was used at sea when there was a possibility of the loop having to be cast off quickly. The seizings could be cut and the clinch would come away without damage to the rope.

To make a clinch, take the end around the standing part into a fairly close eye and seize it back on itself (Fig. 7-2C). Go around once more and seize again (Fig. 7-2D). That completes an inside clinch. An outside clinch is made in a similar way, but the turns come outside the loop (Fig. 7-2E).

The *hangman's knot* has already been described as a way of putting a heavy end in a heaving line (Fig. 4-5). That is its only real use today, but for the record, in its intended use it is made in the following way. A quantity of the end of the rope is made into a long S-shape, then the end is taken around these parts many times (Fig. 7-3A). Authorities have different ideas about the number of turns. Eight or nine seem usual. After these turns the end goes through the upper bight (Fig. 7-3B) and the lower bight is drawn down to tighten on it and make the noose (Fig. 7-3C). Adjusting the noose around a neck with the long knot behind the left ear was supposed to break the neck during the drop.

Although that is the generally accepted knot for a hanging, there were many others, but they all formed the long part in different ways to have the same effect. None of them appear to have uses as ordinary slip knots that would be better than those formed from the more common knots.

TAG KNOT

The tag knot is a running *lark's head* knot made with a bight that pulls up securely, but there has to be a load on both ends. It would not do if there was one standing part and the other end hung loose.

It can be made in the bight without using the ends. The end of the bight is lifted back so as to encircle its sides (Fig. 7-4A). The upper part is then put down through the loop this forms (Fig. 7-4B) and the parts are adjusted to the final shape (Fig. 7-4C).

CRABBER'S KNOT

The tag knot may also be called a crabber's knot for use around crab and lobster pots, but there is another knot for this purpose which may also be called a *crossed running knot*. In its first form it is a running loop, but when adjusted it can have its form altered to lock it without the addition of the half-hitch required with most other running loops.

The end is used to make an overhand knot around the standing part in a way that traps it between the central crossing part from the side of the loop and the two sides of the knot (Fig. 7-5A). In this

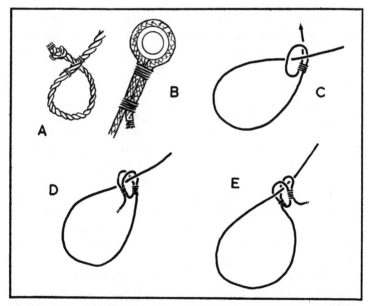

Fig. 7-2. Nooses can be made with clinches formed in various ways: (A) knotted end; (B) seized eye; (C) seize the end back on itself; (D) seize again; and (E) outside clinch.

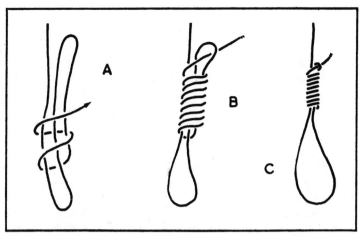

Fig. 7-3. The hangman's knot is a special running noose: (A) end is taken around the s-shape; (B) end goes through the upper bight; and (C) make the noose.

form the knot can slide along the standing part to alter the size of the loop.

If the side of the loop and the end are pulled in opposite directions (Fig. 7-5B), the construction of the knot alters until it looks like a bowline on its side (Fig. 7-5C). This may not be as

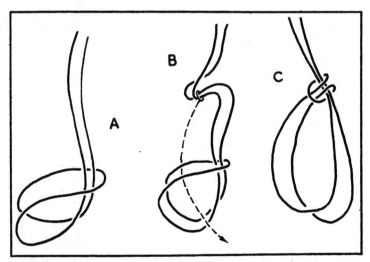

Fig. 7-4. A tag knot is a running noose on the bight of a rope: (A) bight is lefted back; (B) upper part is put down through the loop; and (C) parts are adjusted to the final shape.

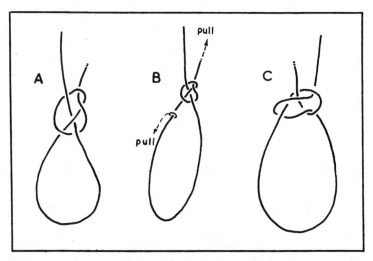

Fig. 7-5. The crabber's knot is a running knot that can have its shape altered to lock it: (A) end makes an overhand knot; (B) side and end are pulled in opposite directions; and (C) looks like a bowline on its side.

strong as an ordinary bowline, but it is satisfactory for many purposes.

CAPSTAN KNOT

The capstan knot is another knot with a similar function to the crabber's knot. It can slide and then be locked by distorting the parts. It is started by following a figure-eight path with the end tucked back around the standing part (Fig. 7-6A). Then the end goes through what will be the noose and back alongside itself to make a turn around the side of the noose (Fig. 7-6B). The knot can then be moved along the standing part to adjust the size of the loop, although not as freely as in the crabber's knot. The end and the side of the noose below can be pulled in opposite directions (Fig. 7-6C) so the standing part is curved and the knot takes a different locked shape (Fig. 7-6D).

DOUBLE OVERHAND NOOSE

In something like a lariat the freedom of movement of the noose is important and the knot used has to allow sliding over the standing part as easily as possible. There are other circumstances where it is necessary for there to be some sliding so the loop can be adjusted, but there should be enough friction for the knot to stay in

100

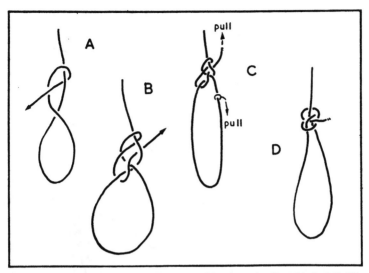

Fig. 7-6. The capstan knot will also run until its shape is altered to lock it: (A) tucked end; (B) end goes through the noose; (C) end and side are pulled in opposite directions; and (D) locked shape.

place when it is left unattended. Slip knots based on overhand and figure-eight knots usually have some of the properties needed, but this is a neat frictional knot that also has the advantage of the end being out of the way alongside the standing part.

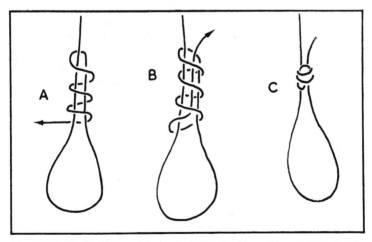

Fig. 7-7. A double overhand noose is preferable where it has to stay as set, instead of pulling up like most nooses: (A) encircle both sides of the loop twice; (B) pass the end up through the knot; and (C) turn turns provide friction.

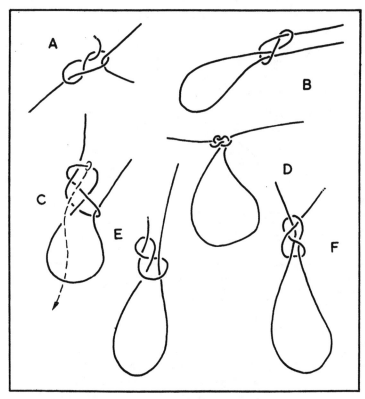

Fig. 7-8. Slip knots based on the figure-eight knot can be locked when set to size with extra turns: (A) packer's knot; (B) noose is last part of the knot; (C) slip loop; (D) farmer's loop; (E) unloaded end; and (F) end crosses.

Turn back enough of the end to go around the standing part and completely encircle both sides of the loop twice (Fig. 7-7A). Pass the end up through the knot beside the standing part (Fig. 7-7B). Then pull tight so there are two turns providing friction (Fig. 7-7C).

FIGURE-EIGHT NOOSES

The packer's knot would seem to be the obvious adaption of a figure-eight knot to a running noose (Fig. 7-8A). With its half hitch on the end it fulfills all the requirements of a noose that has to be locked after adjusting, but some variations have their uses.

For a slip knot at the end of a bight, when both parts will be sharing a load, a figure-eight is made with the bight and the noose becomes the last part of the knot (Fig. 7-8B). This knot can be converted to a fixed loop by passing the upper turn through the *slip loop* (Fig. 7-8C) and the result is a version of the *farmer's loop* (Fig. 7-8D).

The figure-eight formation allows the standing part to pass through in ways other than in the packer's knot. The slip knot on a bight is an example, but with the end unloaded (Fig. 7-8E) it is not a good formation. A stronger arrangement that is still able to slide for adjustment is made so the standing part passes through the upper part of the knot and the end crosses it (Fig. 7-8F).

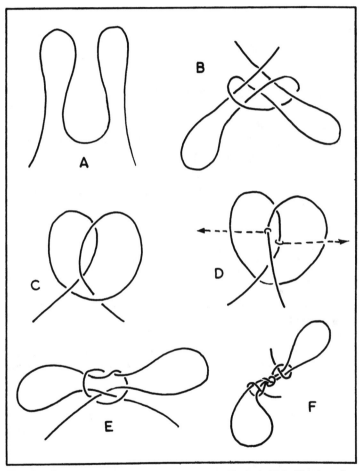

Fig. 7-9. Opposing slip knot loops can be made and locked with half hitches after adjusting in the handcuff and Tom Fool's knot: (A) two opposing loops; (B) each loop goes through the other; (D) crossing ends; (D) pull overlapping parts through the opposite loops; (E) final shale; and (F) each end is half-hitched around the opposing loop.

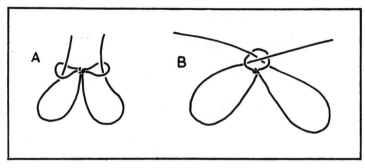

Fig. 7-10. Double bowlines or other loops can be made running by passing the ends through the loops: (A) double nooses and (B) two ends can be taken through single loop.

Many of the foregoing knots differ from nooses by being slip knots that have to be around something. In those conditions they are satisfactory, but if the loop is not around something solid and the standing part is pulled, the knot will completely upset and come apart. If such a slip knot has to be removed from a bundle or package and kept for a further load, there should be a piece of scrap wood or other solid material put through the loop. It is then drawn tight on it to prevent the knot from coming apart.

HANDCUFF KNOT

This knot is a double noose. The simplest version is also called a *Tom Fool's knot.* Two opposing loops are formed (Fig. 7-9A) and crossed so each loop goes through the other (Fig. 7-9B).

A better version is stronger because of an overhand knot formation at the center. Two half-hitch loops are made, one over the other and with the ends crossing (Fig. 7-9C). This is the same formation as would be used to drop a *clove hitch* over a post. Pull the overlapping parts through the opposite loops (Fig. 7-9D) to get the final shape (Fig. 7-9E).

For use as a handcuff, the wrists go through the loops and the ends are pulled to tighten them. Then each end is half hitched around the opposing loop (Fig. 7-9F). The ends can then be knotted together.

Any of the double loops can be made running by taking the ends through the loops. The Spanish bowline is an example—the double nooses (Fig. 7-10A) could go around an animal's legs. With only a single loop in the body of the rope, the two ends could be taken through for a similar use (Fig. 7-10B).

Multiple Loops  8

Some loops with two or more parts have already been described, particularly the variations on the bowline in Chapter 6, but there are others for particular purposes and some which have no connection with any basic single loops. There are other loops with more than one part, which come in the body of the rope, and these are described in Chapter 9. Most of the multiple loops described in this chapter are made at the end of a rope, although some can be formed away from the ends.

DOUBLE BOW STRING KNOTS

The end of a bow string may be attached to the bow with a single bow string knot, but for extra friction around the wood it may be doubled. An overhand knot is made and the end passed through it to make the single knot (Fig. 8-1A), then the end continues around to go through a second time (Fig. 8-1B). There may be sufficient friction in the knot to prevent slipping, but an overhand knot in the projecting end will make sure it cannot pull back (Fig. 8-1C).

A different and practical knot is a clove hitch around the bow with two half hitches around the string. Two half hitches are made and slipped over the end of the bow (Fig. 8-1D) so they jam against each other. The end is then taken around the standing part with two half hitches (Fig. 8-1E) that are really another clove hitch.

DOUBLE ANGLER'S LOOP

The double angler's loop is a knot for fishing line and other fine material. It is not satisfactory in rope or cord. It is made in a similar

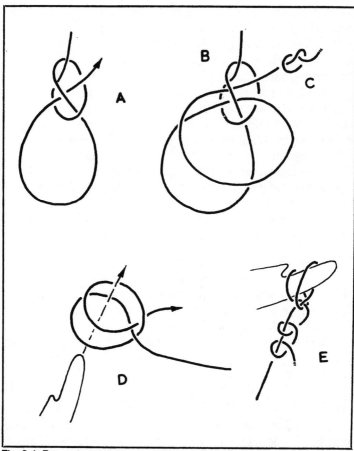

Fig. 8-1. Bow strings are attached with special knots: (A) single knot; (B) end goes through second time; (C) overhand knot in projecting end; (D) two half hitches; and (E) clove hitch.

way to the angler's loop, but two turns of a suitable size for the loops are formed while the crossing is held (Fig. 8-2A), then both loops are thrust through the eye and the knot is tightened (Fig. 8-2B).

FORKED LOOPS

Loops may be needed on opposite sides of the knot instead of together projecting from it. One version comparable with the bow string knots has an overhand knot tied in the line far enough from the end to allow enough material for both loops (Fig. 8-3A), then a bight of this piece is thrust across the knot (Fig. 8-3B), but not pulled right through. Instead, the end of the bight and what is left of the bight on the other side are adjusted and the knot is tightened over them (Fig. 8-3C). Like the double bow string knot, there is a possibility of the end pulling through under load. It could be knotted in the end, or the end could be half hitched above the knot around the standing part (Fig. 8-3D).

Another knot with the same name, although the loops are alongside each other and not on opposite sides, starts with a simple noose or slip knot (Fig. 8-3E), but has a long end projecting from the bight. That end then goes around the back of the standing part and a second bight in it is pushed down through the knot (Fig. 8-3F). When the loops have been adjusted, the end is taken across the first knot behind the parts of the loops (Fig. 8-3G) to lock the parts together.

These knots are intended for small lines. For ropes and heavier cordage it would be better to use one of the double bowlines.

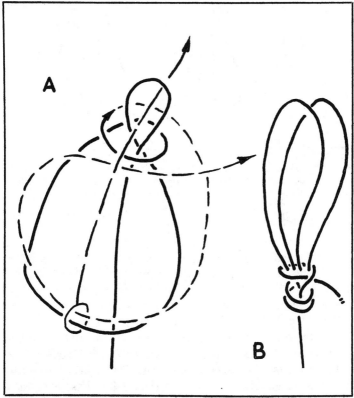

Fig. 8-2. A angler's loop can be doubled by thrusting two loops through the eye: (A) crossing and (B) knot is tightened.

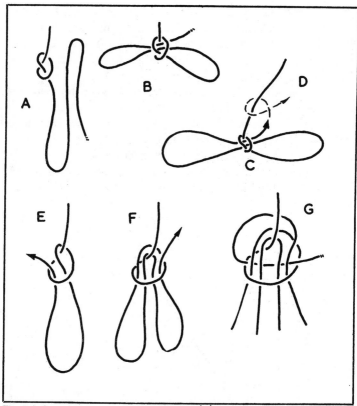

Fig. 8-3. Some double loops can be made in ways other than using the bowline: (A) overhand knot; (B) bight is thrust across the knot; (C) knot is tightened; (D) half hitch above the standing part; (E) slip knot; (F) second bight; and (G) lock parts together.

COILED LOOPS

If a large number of loops are needed at the end of a rope, they may be for individual use or they may be a way of gathering up surplus line. It may happen when a halliard is used to hoist a sail, then there is a considerable amount of free line left after the rope has been secured to a cleat. This may also be used as a way of securing a coil of rope that is to be stored or carried.

In the first method, gather up the rope into coils of the size wanted in the final knot. Lift the coil over a bight of the standing part so the end of its bight projects (Fig. 8-4A). This bight is the last part that was coiled. Give it a half turn (Fig. 8-4B). Pass everything through the twisted bight. Make sure the hanging end as well as the coils go through (Fig. 8-4C). Draw the half hitch that has been

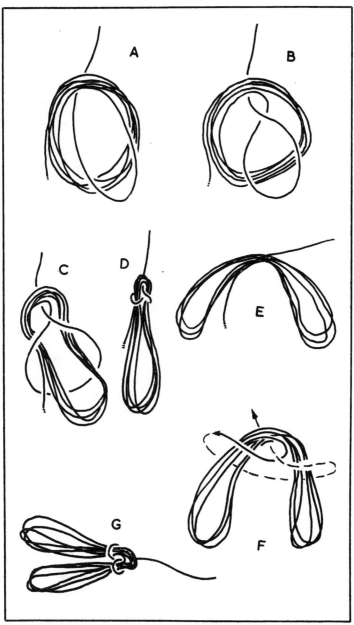

Fig. 8-4. Multiple loops of any number of turns can be made in a similar way to some ways of securing coiled rope: (A) projecting end of bight; (B) half turn; (C) hanging end and coils; (D) drawn half hitch; (E) bend coils; (F) twisted eye in front of center of bundle; and back crossing.

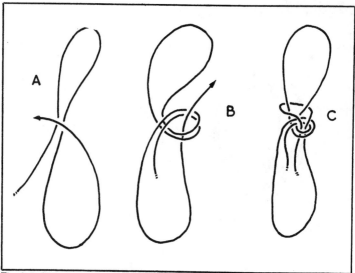

Fig. 8-5. Sister loops are a pair of loops made where there is no requirement for an end to go elsewhere: (A) take end over parts of the bights; (B) form an eye; and (C) continue around the top loop and down through the eye.

formed close up to where the standing part comes through (Fig. 8-4D).

If it is more convenient, the rope can be gathered into coils twice the size wanted in the final assembly. The whole bundle of coils is then bent at the middle (Fig. 8-4E). Twist an eye in the standing part in front of the center of the bundle (Fig. 8-4F) and take the standing part around the back of the bundle to go through the eye and under the center of the loops above its own crossing at the back (Fig. 8-4G). As making this knot involves passing the standing part through, it cannot be used where the end of the standing part is unavailable, as in a halliard. In any case, the first method is preferable and stronger for taking a load on the loops or for gathering up slack rope.

SISTER LOOPS

If a pair of loops are needed there are several ways of making adjustable loops that can then be secured. Sister loops are a pair of firm loops made where there is no requirement for the rope to continue elsewhere. The two loops are self-contained.

Gather up enough rope for the two loops and turn back one end more than one loop is to be. If this is thought of as the standing part for a bowline, further actions are obvious. Take the other end over the parts of this bight (Fig. 8-5A) and form an eye as for a bowline (Fig. 8-5B). Continue around the top loop and down through the eye (Fig. 8-5C). When the knot is pulled tight, both loops will be locked and surplus ends can be cut off.

TOWING HITCHES

If a rope has to be attached to a vehicle that has to be towed and there is no hook or ring, the rope has to be taken underneath to the

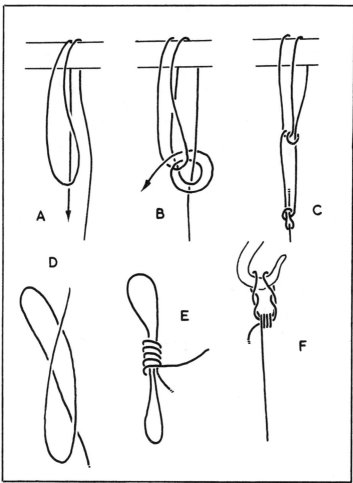

Fig. 8-6. The axle hitch is used for towing when the attachment point is awkwardly situated. The catspaw is used for the end of a line to a towing hook: (A) bight around strong part; (B) end goes through bight; (C) bowline; (D) standing part overlaps: (E) four turns; and (F) twist in opposite directions.

axle or other strong point. The other end of the rope may have to be attached to a hook on the towing vehicle.

It may be difficult or impossible to get underneath and knot the rope to the axle. A hitch is needed that keeps the working parts of the rope outside where the forming of the knot can be seen and checked for security.

The *axle hitch* is made by first passing a bight around the strong point (Fig. 8-6A). The end of the bight is brought out to where the knot is to be made. The end goes around the standing part and through the bight twice (Fig. 8-6B) and further up the standing part where it is joined in with a bowline (Fig. 8-6C).

At the other end of the rope there could be an eye splice to put over the hook, but the more common knot is a single *catspaw*. It has two loops to bring together and put over the hook. Its advantage over other double loop knots for this purpose is that it does not include tucks and crossings that would seize tight under load and be difficult or impossible to undo. The single catspaw can be merely unrolled when taken from the hook.

The rope is gathered into a loop with the end and standing part overlapping (Fig. 8-6D). Further work is done with the standing part, so only a short part of the end needs to extend. Wrap the standing part around the center of the loop. The number of turns depends on the rope, but make at least four turns (Fig. 8-6E). The two extensions of the loop can be brought together and put over the hook as they are, but it is better to twist them in opposite directions before doing this (Fig. 8-6F).

STRAP DOUBLE LOOP

A leather strap or thong can have its end slit and made into a double loop by a method similar to making a bowline on a bight. Enough of the end of the strap is left solid to provide enough strength, then a cut is made with a knife for as far as the loops are intended to be. At the limit of the cut make an eye (Fig. 8-7A). Pass the end through this (Fig. 8-7B) and use the end of the slot to go back over the double loop (Fig. 8-7C) and up to the back of the standing part of the strap (Fig. 8-7D). These actions will probably bring in some unwanted twists to the cut parts of the strap and it will be necessary to work back from the end untwisting until the solid part of the strap is reached.

CLIMBER'S RESCUE KNOT

The climber's rescue knot is a knot with three loops. It is intended for lowering a person safely without a risk of turning over,

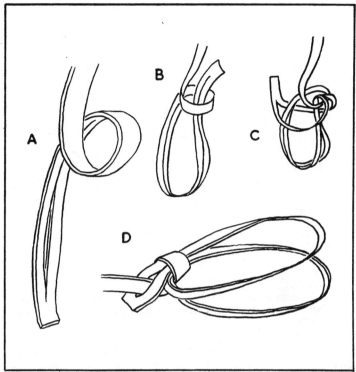

Fig. 8-7. A slit leather thong can be made into a loop in a manner similar to forming a bowline on a bight: (A) eye; (B) pass the end through the eye; (C) double loops; and (D) standing part of the strap.

even if he is unconscious. The loops are arranged so two go around the thighs and the other is over a shoulder and under the other armpit. The knot part is arranged to come in front fairly over the chest so the person being rescued does not become top-heavy (Fig. 8-8A). The loop sizes have to be adjusted before tightening to get them so loads they take are correctly proportioned.

The knot will be seen to be a bowline with a bight, tied with a doubled rope. Turn back enough to make the three loops into a long bight and join the end into the standing part, preferably with a bowline. Extend the long loop and treat its extremity as the working end.

Make the usual bowline small eye in the doubled line and pass the end of the loop up through it (Fig. 8-8B), taking enough through to make the third loop and leaving the other two loops below the eye. Take the working end of the loop around the doubled standing part and down through the eye to make the third loop (Fig. 8-8C).

113

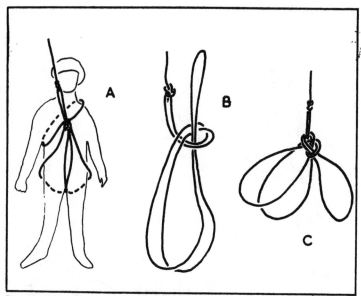

Fig. 8-8. A climber's rescue knot has three loops that can be adjusted to suit the person to be lowered: (A) rope arrangement on body; (B) bowline small eye; and (C) third loop.

In use, particularly if the person is unconscious, another short piece of rope should be used to link the three loops together at the back to prevent them from moving.

Without the Ends  9

Some knots intended to be normally tied with the use of one end of the rope may also be tied in the bight or body of the rope, without using the ends which may already be secured or out of reach. There are other knots which are more easily tied without using the ends. The majority of these are loops and some have already been described. Particular examples are the *Spanish bowline* (Fig. 6-9) and the *middleman's knot* (Fig. 6-13). Besides those knots that form single, double or multiple loops, there is another group used for shortening or taking up slack without undoing end knots.

The shortening knots are part of a *sheepshank* family. All of these are used to secure the surplus rope gathered up into a long S-shape. This points to a further use: strengthening a weak place in a rope. If the rope has had local chafing or wear, that part can be put at the center of a long S-loop and the two sound parts of rope on each side of it will relieve it of strain and take the load. This can cope with damage even as far as a complete break in the rope, as can be seen in the following story which is told to illustrate the point.

Three fishermen after Saturday night drinking decided that the ropes on the three bells in the local church would be of more use on their fishing boats than in the church tower. They decided to visit the church around midnight to get the ropes. The first fisherman climbed one rope and cut it above his head. He fell down and was killed. The second fisherman was not going to be as silly. He climbed the second rope and cut it below his feet. Eventually, he tired and fell. He was also killed. The third man would not be content with two ropes—he wanted the third. He climbed that rope, hung with one hand and gathered up the rope into a sheepshank with the other hand. He cut the center part and climbed down carefully, then shook the rope to release it. The first time I heard that story I was a young Boy Scout. We tied a rope to the branch of a tree and tried repeating that third fisherman's action. It worked.

SHEEPSHANK

If maximum tension is not needed, a sheepshank is made by gathering up the long S-shape (Fig. 9-1A), then half hitches are turned in the standing parts (Fig. 9-1B) and slipped over the ends of the loops (Fig. 9-1C). In large stiff rope, this is often the only possible way in any case.

If the rope is sufficiently flexible and the rope has to be taut after shortening, the S-shaped loops are made to use up as much rope as possible, then a half hitch is put over one end (Fig. 9-1D). Use the loop at the other end to force a half hitch into the standing part and get even more tension. Put the end of the loop over the standing part and turn it over (Fig. 9-1E) and up to force itself straight with a half hitch in place (Fig. 9-1F).

This standard sheepshank will hold as long as there is a steady tension on the rope. If the rope is in a situation where it is alternately tensioned and slackened, there is a risk of the half hitches coming off the end. In those circumstances, one of the variations is advisable. The formation of the sheepshank shows how having the loops formed around a weak part will share the load (Fig. 9-1G).

SECURED SHEEPSHANK

If a sheepshank has to endure varying tensions without coming undone it can be seized at each end. The seizing may go around the loop (Fig. 9-2A), but it should be stronger if only taken around one side of each loop (Fig. 9-2B) with frapping turns around the seizings.

Another method of securing is with a toggle. This is a spike or piece of wood put across each loop so as to trap the standing part (Fig. 9-2C). For anything more than temporary use, the toggle should be lashed in place with a few turns of light line (Fig. 9-2D).

DOGSHANK

Early knotting writers also called a sheepshank a *dogshank* or a *catshank*. Here the name is used for a sheepshank with *marline*

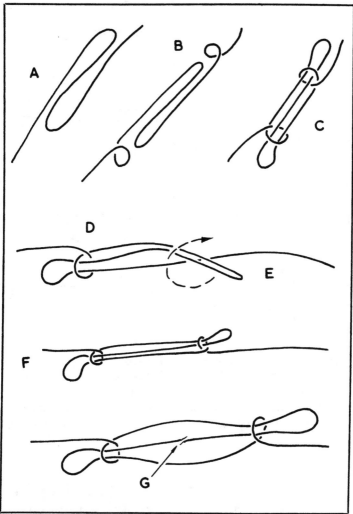

Fig. 9-1. The sheepshank is used to shorten or strengthen a rope: (A) s-shape; (B) half hitches are turned in the standing parts; (C) half hitches are slipped over ends of the loops; (D) half hitch is put over one end; (E) put end of loop over standing part; (F) it will force itself straight; and (G) loops share the load.

spike hitches at the ends. This form should be secure without seizings or toggle, even when there is considerable tightening and slackening of the rope.

Slack is gathered up as for an ordinary sheepshank, then the standing part twisted as if tying an overhand knot, but instead of passing the standing part through, the end of the loop is passed

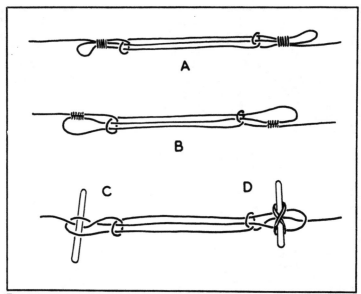

Fig. 9-2. A sheepshank can be secured with seizings or toggles: (A) seizing goes around the loop; (B) seizing around one side of each loop; (C) toggle; and (D) lashed toggle.

across in the way that a marline spike would be (Fig. 2-11E). Be careful to make the marline spike hitch so its twist is towards the center of the dogshank (Fig. 9-3A). It is possible to form it the other way so the twisted part is outward. That would pull out of shape. Adjust the length so the hitch is far enough from the end of each loop for there to be no fear of initial tensioning pulling the hitch off (Fig. 9-3B).

CLOVE-HITCHED SHEEPSHANK

Another way of locking the ends of the loops is to put on two half hitches close together to form clove hitches. Two hitches can be formed and put over together (Fig. 9-4A) if maximum tension is not required. For a tighter knot, put on one half hitch and add the second in the tightened line (Fig. 9-4B). It might also be possible to use the long end of a loop to force in the second half hitch (Figs. 9-1E and 9-1F).

Using clove hitches is preferable to single half hitches if a considerable amount of rope has to be brought together. In this case there can be many turns of rope instead of the long S-loops, and their ends are drawn together with clove hitches (Fig. 9-4C). Besides shortening under load this arrangement could be used to

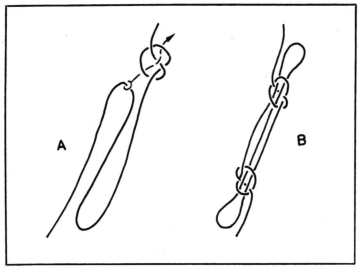

Fig. 9-3. Marline spike hitches make the knot into a dogshank: (A) twist should be toward the center of the dogshank and (B) adjusting the length.

gather up surplus rope temporarily so it hangs tidily and can be easily opened for use.

KNOTTED SHEEPSHANKS

Some knots used to form double loops can be altered to make variations of the sheepshank. Two are the *Tom Fool's knot* and the

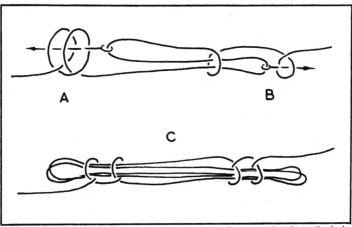

Fig. 9-4. Clove hitches may be used over the ends of a sheepshank, particularly if several turns have to be held: (A) two hitches; (B) tighter knot; and (C) ends draw together with clove hitches.

119

handcuff knot. There is probably no real advantage in making a sheepshank with a knot at the center except it will hold the loops together while the amount of slack to be accommodated is drawn through. The extra twists may provide some additional resistance to slipping.

For the Tom Fool version, hold the rope crossed with the hands towards each other (Fig. 9-5A) and reach across to pull the opposing standing parts so an overhand knot is made with the bights (Fig. 9-5B). Draw through the amount of slack which is to be taken up and put half hitches on the ends, as for a normal sheepshank (Fig. 9-5C). There could also be marline spike hitches on the ends, as in the dogshank.

For the handcuff knot version, two bights are knotted together (Fig. 9-5D) so the crossing standing parts lock against each other instead of going through the knot, as in first example. After adjusting the loops, half hitches are put on the ends (Fig. 9-5E). This is exactly the same formation as a handcuff knot for putting on wrists, except the half hitches are not run close to the central knot.

SHEEPSHANKS FROM HITCHES

There are several ways of making a sheepshank or variations of it from a series of hitches. In most of these examples there is little or no practical advantage in using the method, but it can be regarded as a trick to impress an audience. With practice it is possible to make the formation appear to be all one action with a knot resulting almost instantaneously.

For an ordinary sheepshank, form three half hitches as for a clove hitch, but with a third similar turn (Fig. 9-6A). Let the two outer half hitches overlap the sides of the central one. Grasp the sides of the central hitch through the side hitches (Fig. 9-6B) and pull through (Fig. 9-6C). The size of the resulting sheepshank depends on the size of the central half hitch. For a reasonable length start with a large central loop. The outer ones should not be much bigger than they will have to be finally.

Carry on to a fourth half hitch and it is possible to make a handcuff knot sheepshank. Make four identical half hitches over each other (Fig. 9-6D). Let the sides of the loops overlap each other slightly. Take the sides of the two overlapping at the center and pull them through the gaps between the others (Fig. 9-6E). The result is a handcuff knot (Fig. 9-5E). As with the previous example, it is the sizes of the middle two half hitches that control the final size of the knot, so it is better to make these larger than the end ones for the best effect.

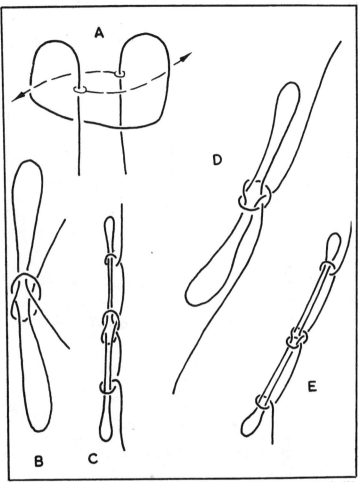

Fig. 9-5. Slack may be gathered with a knot before making a sheepshank: (A) crossed ropes; (B) overhand knot with bights; (C) half hitches on ends; (D) two knotted bights; and (E) half hitches on ends.

If the four hitches are pulled through in a different way, another form of crossing is made at each. To the love-sick sailor these crossings represented hearts and the whole thing was described as *two hearts that beat as one*. Apart from expressing feelings, the knot does not seem to have any use.

Have the four half hitches laid out and overlapping (Fig. 9-6D). Pull the overlapping sides of the center two loops through the other crossings in an over-and-under manner (Fig. 9-6F) to get the special end effect (Fig. 9-6G).

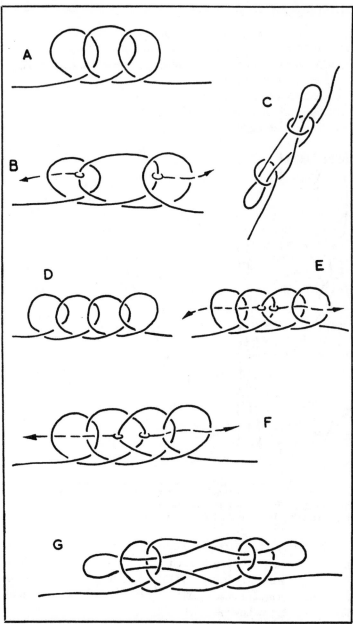

Fig. 9-6. Sheepshanks in various forms can be made from hitches in several ways: (A) third turn; (B) sides of central hitch; (C) pull through side hitches; (D) four half hitches; (E) handcuff knot; (F) over-and-under manner; and (G) special end effect.

SINGLE-ENDED SHORTENINGS

If a rope is hanging and the surplus part has to be gathered up temporarily it is possible to use a top part only of any of the sheepshank variations. The simplest is the *bell ringer's knot*. When the bell rope is out of use, it is gathered up as if to make a sheepshank, but only the top half hitch is used (Fig. 9-7A). There could be several turns gathered up as a coil, then it would be better to use two half hitches (Fig. 9-7B).

ROPE TACKLE

Although not especially a shortening, nor made without use of the end of the rope, this is an adaption of the bell ringer's knot that can be used to gain a purchase. Theoretically there is an advantage of two-to-one, but because of friction it is really less. This is used for tightening ropes over truck loads and anywhere that more tension is needed than can be provided by a direct pull.

The bell ringer's knot is made in the standing part of the rope, possibly coming from the other side of a truck and over the load (Fig. 9-7C) with enough free end hanging to complete the tackle. The end of the loop could be seized or toggled, but against a load the unsecured end is safe.

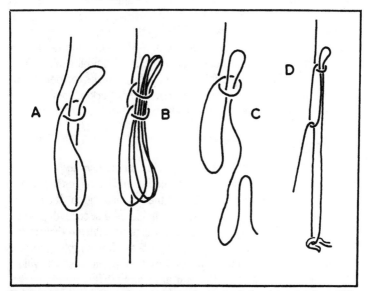

Fig. 9-7. Slack may be gathered using only one end of a sheepshank and this form can be converted to a rope tackle: (A) top half hitch; (B) two half hitches; (C) hanging free end; and (D) hanging loop.

The rope end goes to the hook or other anchorage point and back to pass through the end of the hanging loop (Fig. 9-7D). Pulling the end applies a similar two-to-one purchase to what there would be with a single block in place of the loop, but the friction of rope over rope lessens the actual gain.

LINEMAN'S LOOP

The middleman's knot (with its many alternative names) is one way of putting a loop in the body of a rope. Although it will take a strain satisfactorily in one direction, if the pull along the rope is the other way the sliding overhand knots may separate and the loop becomes a noose. The lineman's loop is a knot made in a comparable way but with the overhand knots interlocked so they cannot pull apart, whichever way the load comes along the rope. This is the knot to choose when the loops are needed along a rope for helpers to get their shoulders into for pulling a load either way.

Start by putting a complete twist in the rope (Fig. 9-8A). Use enough rope to form the size of loop required. Take the bottom of the loop over the standing parts (Fig. 9-8B). The form then is like that stage of a middleman's knot, but with a twist instead of an overlap. Draw the middle of the loop through the gap in the twist (Fig. 9-8C) and pull the knot into shape (Fig. 9-8D).

That is the usual way of making the knot, but there is an alternative. Make a complete loop (Fig. 9-8E). Turn another loop in its side, using the underneath part (Fig. 9-8F) and lift this to rest over the crossing of the first loop (Fig. 9-8G). Pull its top behind and down through both loops (Fig. 9-8H). When worked to shape the final knot is the same as that produced by the first method.

MAN-HARNESS KNOT

The man-harness knot is also called an *artillery loop* from its use in putting loops in the ropes attached to gun carriages for help in dragging. Its purpose is the same as the lineman's loop. If adjusted to its proper form when tightened it should be a secure loop when the pull comes in either direction, but it is possible to distort the knot so it slips and becomes a running noose. It is simpler to make than a lineman's loop and may suffice for temporary use. It will be seen to be an adaption of the marline spike hitch.

Make a loop using the amount of rope needed in the final loop (Fig. 9-9A). Lift the under part over the adjoining standing part (Fig. 9-9B), then take the side of the loop under and over (Fig. 9-9C) so it

124

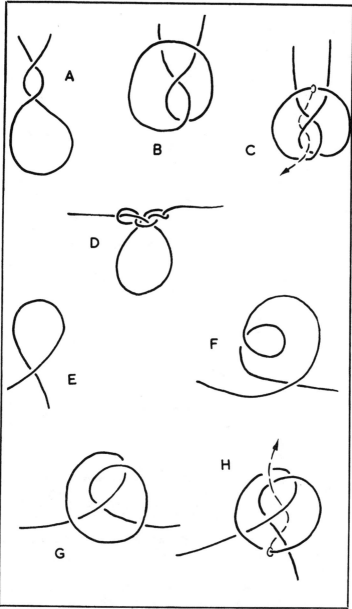

Fig. 9-8. There are two ways of making a lineman's loop to form a non-slip ring at the side of the rope: (A) complete twist in the rope; (B) bottom of loop over standing parts; (C) draw middle of loop through gap in the twists: (D) pull the knot into shape; (E) complete loop; (F) underneath parts; (G) crossing of first loop; and (H) pull through both loops.

125

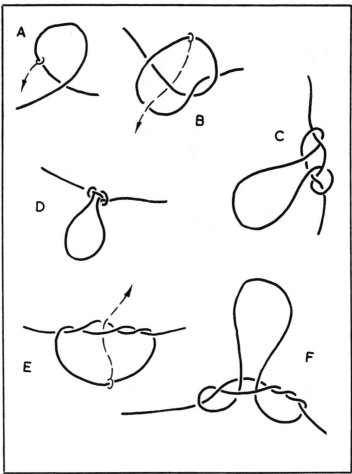

Fig. 9-9. The man-harness knot is used to put a loop in the body of a rope and it can be doubled for extra strength: (A) loop: (B) lift under past over adjoining standing part; (C) side of loop under and over; (D) finished loop; (E) overhand knot with second twists and (F) pass loop through middle of twisted part.

can be pulled through to make the finished loop (Fig. 9-9D). It is at this stage that care is needed to get the knot into its proper shape for safety.

A double man-harness knot is more secure, but as one end of the rope has to be used, it cannot be made if both ends are unavailable. Start with an overhand knot with a second twist (Fig. 9-9E). Pass the loop through the middle of the twisted part (Fig. 9-9F). the result will be similar to the single knot, but with an extra twist that should prevent the knot from pulling out of shape.

126

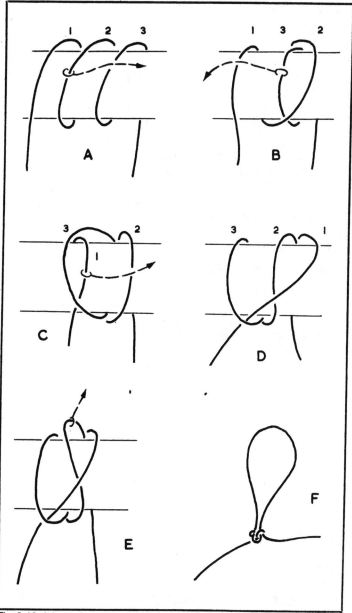

Fig. 9-10. A farmer's loop is another way of making a loop in the body of a rope and can be formed from loops around the hand: (A) two round turns; (B) lift middle turn; (C) take middle turn over its first part on left; (D) now take it over to the right; (E) middle turn loop has tube pulled out; and (F) ball-shaped knot at top of loop.

FARMER'S LOOP

One method of making this knot from a figure-eight slip knot was shown in Fig. 7-8. The knot produces a more secure and symmetrical loop than the man-harness knot, but it should be carefully worked to shape when tightening. An alternative method uses a number of loops made around the hand or a piece of wood.

Put two round turns on (Fig. 9-10A), keeping them loose enough to be moved over each other. Lift the middle turn over the one on its right (Fig. 9-10B), then take that over its first part on its left (Fig. 9-10C). That, in turn, goes over to the right (Fig. 9-10D). The middle turn will be the loop and it has to be pulled out (Fig. 9-10E). The hand or rod can be withdrawn so the end loops close and the middle loop can be drawn to size, then the whole thing closes to a neat ball-shaped knot around the top of the loop (Fig. 9-10F).

DOUBLE MIDDLEMAN'S KNOT

This knot is a rather complicated way of getting a result similar to a Spanish bowline or it may be regarded as a way of doubling the middleman's knot and altering it so it cannot slip in either direction.

Make an ordinary middleman's knot (Fig. 9-11A) and draw the two overhand knots close together, but keep them slack enough for the further movements. The loop should be large enough to make both parts of the final double loop. Lift this loop over the knotted part and pull the upper parts of both overhand knots together through it (Fig. 9-11B). Some slack will have to be pulled through these overhand knots to allow this. With these parts hanging down, pull both lower parts downward (Fig. 9-11C) through each other to gain the slack for the upper part of the first loop into the two final loops. The knot will then close to a non-slip double loop (Fig. 9-11D).

DOUBLE FIGURE-EIGHT LOOP

The ordinary figure-eight loop on a bight (Fig. 9-12A) will make a single loop. It can be made into a doubled loop with a form that might be mistaken for a bowline on a bight.

The final tucking of the end of the bight is not taken (Fig. 9-12B). Instead the loop is lifted behind the rest of the knot which will have to be held in shape (Fig. 9-12C). Its two sides are put down through the eye where the end of the bight would have gone in a single knot (Fig. 9-12D). It is these two parts that make the final

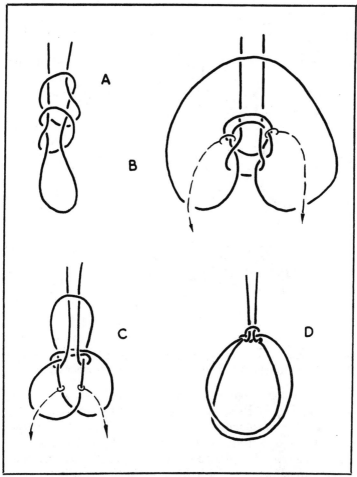

Fig. 9-11. A middleman's knot can be converted to a non-slip double loop: (A) ordinary middleman's knot; (B) lift this loop; (C) pull both lower parts downward; and (D) non-slip double loop.

loops, so the first part of the bight must be kept long enough to allow for this.

CATSPAW

The single catspaw (Fig. 8-6F) is used in the end of a rope that has to be attached to a hook. The name *catspaw* used alone means a knot for attaching a bight of rope to a hook, particularly when it is being used as a sling. There must be a load on both ends, as there would be when spreading the rope ends to lift a crate or broad load.

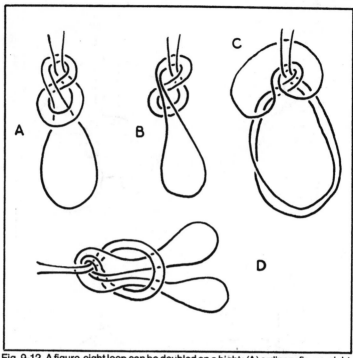

Fig. 9-12. A figure-eight loop can be doubled on a bight: (A) ordinary figure-eight loop: (B) final tucking; (C) loop is held in shape; and (D) end of bight.

Take a loop of rope and let the loop fall back over the standing parts (Fig. 9-13A). Hold the tops of the standing parts, one in each hand and twist them outward (Fig. 9-13B). It is common to make three twists, then the parts being held are put over the hook (Fig. 9-13C). The twists will draw up under strain, but the load cannot tilt as the two parts will not slide over the hook.

FORKED LOOPS

This knot is finished with two loops forking from the knot and the standing parts projecting from above it. It has possibilities as a sling for something like a horizontal ladder where the loops are each put over one side. A loop is allowed to drop between the hanging standing parts (Fig. 9-14A). The sides of the hanging loop are extended so each can be taken across and tucked through the top near each opposing standing part (Fig. 9-14B), then they are drawn tight to close the knot (Fig. 9-14C).

There are several developments of the forked loops that bring in complications that are not necessarily improvements for the

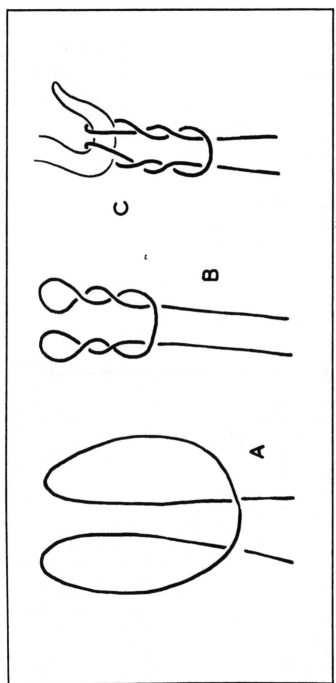

Fig. 9-13. A catspaw is made by doubling back and twisting a bight to hang a sling on a hook: (A) loop; (B) twist tops of standing parts; and (C) three twists.

practical applications of the knots, but some of them provide bases for decorative ropework that will be described later.

Some other knots not primarily intended to make double loops in the bight can be used for ladder or other slings in a similar way to the forked loop. If a sheepshank has its half hitches brought to the center it can be treated as a forked loop (Fig. 9-14D), although with uneven loading one loop can pull rope through from the other. This risk can be avoided by using the Tom Fool or handcuff version of the sheepshank, with the half hitches close to the center part of the knot (Fig. 9-14E).

JURY MASTHEAD KNOT

The jury masthead knot is tied without using the ends. It is particularly devised to fit around the top of a temporary mast with three or four loops projecting to which stays or supporting ropes can be attached. The greater the load on the loops, the tighter will be the grip on the mast. It is also possible to draw the knot close and use the projecting loops as handles around anything that has to be lifted, particularly anything round.

In the usual formation, three overlapping hitches are made (Fig. 9-15A). The inner parts of the two outer hitches are drawn in an over-and-under manner through to each side and at the same time the center of the middle hitch is pulled upwards (Fig. 9-15B). This will produce three projecting loops and the ends projecting in the fourth position. The center of the knot goes over the mast or spar (Fig. 9-15C). The two ends have to be secured, either by using them as mast stays or by knotting them together to serve as a fourth loop.

If only three loops are required, the two ends should be knotted close to the mast. As they come out on each side of the crossing ropes it is not easy to make a neat close knot there, and a slightly different way of forming the jury masthead knot is preferred.

Instead of three identical hitches, start with one hitch and put a round turn on top of it, followed by a hitch similar to the first. Notice that this puts the crossing of the parts of the center loop opposite to the other two (Fig. 9-15D). From this point pull the three loops in just the same way as in the first method, but because of the different crossing of the middle loop, the two standing parts come out together (Fig. 9-15E). They can be joined against the spar with a reef knot and the three loops arranged as needed to take the stays.

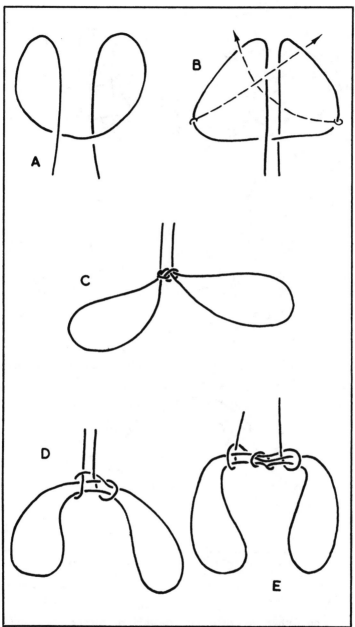

Fig. 9-14. A forked loop can be made in several ways and used to sling a load:
(A) loop drops between hanging standing parts; (B) extended sides; (C) sides
are drawn tight; (D) sheepshank treated as a forked loop; and (E) half hitches
close to center part of knot.

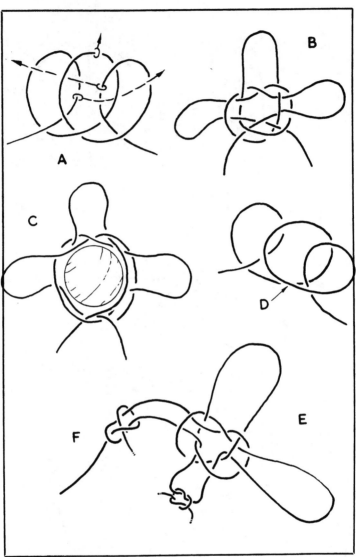

Fig. 9-15. The jury masthead knot forms three or four loops around a spar for attaching guy ropes: (A) three overlapping hitches: (B) center of middle hitch is pulled upwards: (C) mast or spar; (D) opposite crossing; (E) two standing parts; and (F) sheet bend.

Some other knots of similar formation are primarily ornamental and not as effective for practical applications. If a jury masthead knot is used to support a mast or upright spar, it is advisable to do something to stop it from slipping down. This may be accomplished by nailing on or by grooving around the spar so the knot pulls into the hollow. Stays attached to the loops to extend outward as supports can be attached in a similar way to reeving a sheet bend, either single or double (Fig. 9-15F). When used in this way it is called a *becket hitch*.

BOTTLE KNOT

There are several other names and more than one version of this knot. Some other names are *bag knot, beggarman's knot, jug sling,* and *hackamore.* The last name indicates a use as a temporary bridle, but otherwise the knot is a means of tying a rope handle to the neck of something solid, like a bottle, or as a way of pulling the top of a bag closed. In both cases there are opposing loops that serve as handles.

A *single bottle knot* is made from a continuous rope loop. This could be made by splicing or knotting the ends together. A bight is twisted in one side of the loop (Fig. 9-16A). This bight is treated as a half hitch and slipped over the side of the loop (Fig. 9-16B). The middle of the knot is put over the neck of the bottle (Fig. 9-16C) so the extending parts can be turned upward and used as a handle. There has to be a rim or flange on the bottle, then the sling is

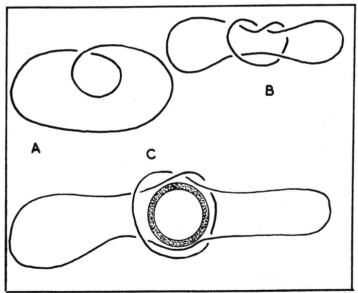

Fig. 9-16. A single loop can be made into a bottle knot to grip under the rim of a bottle neck: (A) twisted bight; (B) bight slipped over side of the loop; and (C) middle of knot is put over the neck of the bottle.

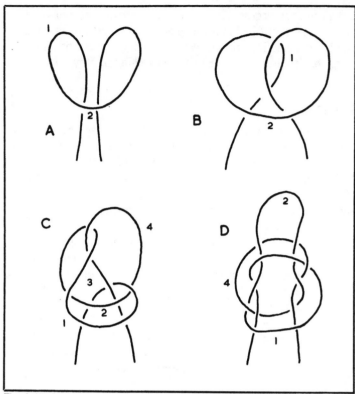

Fig. 9-17. Another bottle knot has more turns to grip the bottle neck: (A) turn back a bight over standing parts; (B) overlap the standing parts; (C) turn part over part 2; (D) resulting formation.

satisfactory, but it is not as tight as the following versions and is not advised for drawing the top of a bag together.

For the standard type of bottle knot, turn back a bight over the standing parts (Fig. 9-17A), then overlap the standing parts (Fig. 9-17B). Note parts 1 and 2. Take part 1 and turn it over 2 (Fig. 9-17C). Reach through space 3 under the nearest standing part, grasp part 2 and pull it through to get the formation shown (Fig. 9-17D). The bottle or bag goes in the central space and the ends are tied to form the second loop handle.

Another way of getting the same result starts with an overhand slip knot (Fig. 9-18A). The slip loop is twisted into an eye (Fig. 9-18B) which is opened large enough to rest over the overhand knot (Fig. 9-18C). Take the end of the first bight over the eye and back up through the first knot (Fig. 9-18D). When pulled into shape the result is the same as by the first method.

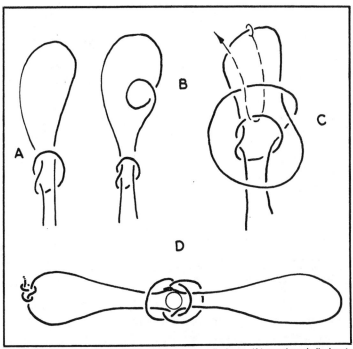

Fig. 9-18. A very similar bottle knot starts as a slip knot: (A) overhand slip knot; (B) slip loop is twisted into an eye; (C) opened eye rests over overhand knot; and (D) end of first bight goes up through first knot.

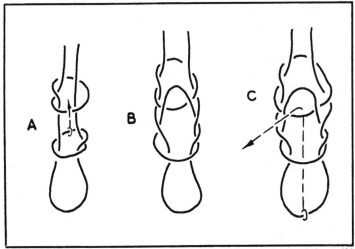

Fig. 9-19. A similar result can be obtained by converting a fisherman's knot: (A) make the knot; (B) pull overhand knot through; and (C) pull end of bight up through the space.

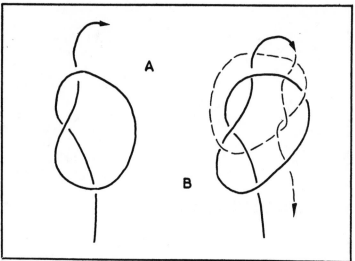

Fig. 9-20. Another way of making the knot uses interlocking overhand knots: (A) working end and (B) standing part.

A variation converts a fisherman's loop or middleman's knot into the later stages of the previous method. Make that knot (Fig. 9-19A) and keep its parts loose. Pull through enough of the overhand knot nearer the bight to overlap the other (Fig. 9-19B). Reach down through this overlap and pull the end of the bight up through the space (Fig. 9-19C). When pulled into shape the result should be the same as that achieved by the other two methods.

Despite its apparent complication the knot is really very like two interlocking overhand knots, as can be seen if one knot is tied and another worked through it. Allow enough for the working end (Fig. 9-20A), take it back into the knot alongside its own part, then work around to make an opposing knot and come out alongside the standing part (Fig. 9-20B).

Hitches to Spars  10

In the days of large square-rigged sailing ships there were a great many situations where ropes had to be knotted to spars. The different loadings and directions of strain necessitated different ways of knotting. As with other knotting applications the seamen on particular ships or in different parts of the world sometimes evolved different knots for the same purpose. Records of many of these knots have survived and they may have applications today in circumstances very different from the original ones.

A knot to a spar is correctly termed a *hitch*. Although there are exceptions in naming, the exceptions to the rule are not as many as they are in some other branches of ropework. The basic hitches are the clove hitch (Fig. 3-8) and the round turn and two half hitches (Fig. 3-9). These serve in many situations where a line has to be attached to a spar, either within the body of the rope or at its end. A knowledge of the making of these two hitches will help in the making and understanding of most of the others.

Although the hitches in this chapter are primarily for attaching ropes to spars, most are also suitable for attachments to rings and hooks or other solid objects, but there are some special hitches noted later. Many of the hitches can also be used for joining one rope to another where a light line has to be attached temporarily to a much thicker rope that is under tension, so as to make an attachment such as to a tackle to add extra purchase to a pull. The thicker rope is then in a similar position to a spar and is not itself worked to shape to form the knot.

Most rope-to-spar knots include one or more half hitches. This is merely a complete encircling of the spar with the end on the side of the standing part that will trap it in position. The locking arrangement can be seen in the clove hitch. It is formed with two half hitches opposed to each other so both ends are inside and locked against each other (Fig. 10-1A). The clove hitch needs to have a load on both ends, otherwise it is liable to slip. It is normally used when both parts extending from the knot go on to be attached elsewhere. Except for temporary use, it is not the hitch to use for the end of a rope, unless it is locked in some way and then it may not be as satisfactory as some of the other hitches.

One way of locking a clove hitch in the end of a rope is to seize the end to the standing part (Fig. 10-1B). This may be called a *post hitch* and it would be a fairly permanent attachment. For a less permanent arrangement there could be a half hitch around the standing part (Fig. 10-1C). It would be safer with two half hitches, but in those circumstances it might just as well be a round turn and two half hitches.

With three- or four-strand rope the end could be tucked through the standing part (Fig. 10-1D). Sometimes the end is taken back on the spar to tuck through turns of the clove hitch, but this is less satisfactory than one of the snug hitches intended to be secured in that way.

It is possible to lock a single half hitch by tucking the end under the turn (Fig. 10-1E). This should be done further around the spar from where the standing part will take the strain and may be called a *half hitch with a nip*. What must be avoided is having the nip close to the pull, as this would slip under load (Fig. 10-1F). The nip can be made with a bight (Fig. 10-1G). As well as making it possible to slip the hitch easily, this gives an increased bearing area with greater security. Using just a single nip may not seem very secure, but providing there is a steady load on the hitch it is stronger than it seems. Such a hitch is used in displays by acrobats and it might be used by a climber to get down a rope and then shake it free. Obviously, discretion is advisable and one of the hitches with more turns is preferable.

TIMBER HITCH

The name comes from its use in attaching a rope to a log, but it is a slip knot that tightens on a spar and can be taken apart very easily when no longer required. It may also be called a *lumberman's knot*. The formation is a half hitch with a nip given more turns.

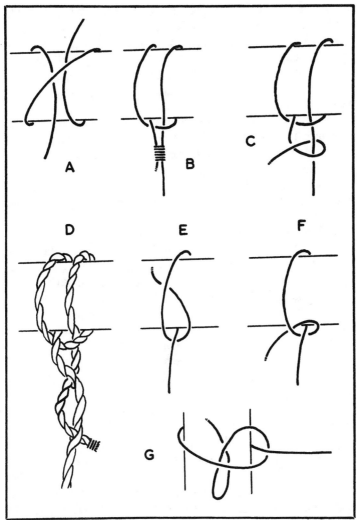

Fig. 10-1. Simple hitches to spars can be locked in various ways: (A) two half hitches; (B) locking a clove hitch; (C) half hitch around standing part; (D) end tucked through standing part; (E) tucking end under the turn; (F) avoid nip close to the pull; and (G) nip made with a bight.

Three times around itself will usually be enough (Fig. 10-2A), except if the tree trunk is very large in relation to the rope. Then a greater number of twists is advisable.

If three-stranded rope is used, the turns are best made in the same direction as the lay as this make the parts fit together better without any risk of kinking.

For a direct pull away from the spar or tree, this is all that is needed. If there has to be an endwise pull, as when dragging a log or towing a spar through the water, the timber hitch is put some way from the end and a half hitch put on near the end (Fig. 10-2B). For extra security, particularly if the spar is slender in relation to the rope, there could be a second half hitch, like widely-spaced parts of a clove hitch (Fig. 10-2C).

There is a further use for a timber hitch with a half hitch beside it—attaching a rope to a rock for use as a temporary anchor. The combination may be called a *killick hitch*. Killick is a sailor's name for an anchor. The timber hitch goes around the rock and the half hitch is brought close to it (Fig. 10-2D). The rope will be secure under load, yet it will not be difficult to cast off, despite the rope being tight and wet.

There are a few variations, but if the load is very great, the timber hitch as just described, should be used. A timber hitch with just one turn may be called a *figure-eight hitch* (Fig. 10-2E). This would be stronger than a half hitch with a nip and could be chosen for hanging something light from a spar. If a bight is used for the final tuck, the hitch is easily cast off (Fig. 10-2F). A *timber hitch with a round turn* is made in the usual way, except the line goes completely around the standing part before being taken back around itself (Fig. 10-2G). The round turn gives increased bearing around the standing part and may be preferable if the rope is weak or chafe is anticipated there.

COW HITCH

Like the clove hitch, this is really a hitch that should be loaded on both ends, yet the name comes from its alleged use in tethering a cow to a post driven in the ground, so the animal can walk around at the end of its rope. It is claimed that this hitch is less likely to snarl up around the post than any other. It is made like a clove hitch, but the direction of the second half hitch is reversed (Fig. 10-3A). It may be called a *lark's head*.

With a load on both ends this is an alternative to the *catspaw* for attaching a rope to a hook for slinging a load. It could then be made like a catspaw by throwing back a bight, without putting in any twists. It might then be called a *bale sling hitch*.

If used in the end of a rope, the end part should be attached to the standing part. One way would be to make a bowline in the rope before making the hitch, then turn back two loops in the bight (Fig. 10-3B) to slip over the end of the spar. A similar arrangement can be

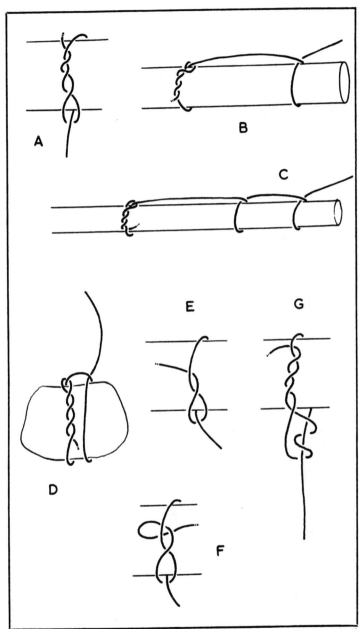

Fig. 10-2. The timber hitch is a slip knot that can be supplemented with half hitches: (A) three turns around itself; (B) half hitch near the end; (C) second half hitch; (D) timber hitch; (E) figure-eight hitch; (F) hitch is cast off; and (G) timber hitch with a round turn.

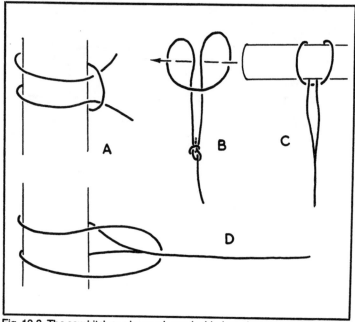

Fig. 10-3. The cow hitch can be used as a doubled running noose: (A) reversed hitch direction; (B) turn back two loops; (C) end of an eye splice; and (D) standing part is pushed through the end of the eye.

used in the end of an eye splice (Fig. 10-3C). This may be called a *running eye*, whether a splice or a bowline. Even if the end of the spar is unavailable for passing the hitch over, a long eye in the end of the rope can be passed around it or through a ring and the standing part of the rope pushed through the end of the eye (Fig. 10-3D).

SNUG HITCHES

These are a step further than a half hitch with a nip and they provide more tucks and therefore more security. Simplest is a round turn with the end over the standing part (Fig. 10-4A), then it is passed under the turn of the standing part (Fig. 10-4B).

In a better arrangement the end starts around in the same way, but it then goes around the standing part before crossing to tuck under its own turn (Fig. 10-4C). Besides being more secure it is easier to cast off. In any rope to spar knots, a turn around the standing part before tucking allows the strain to be relieved at that point first when undoing the knot.

There are several variations that have been named according to the job they did in attaching ropes to spars as part of the rigging in

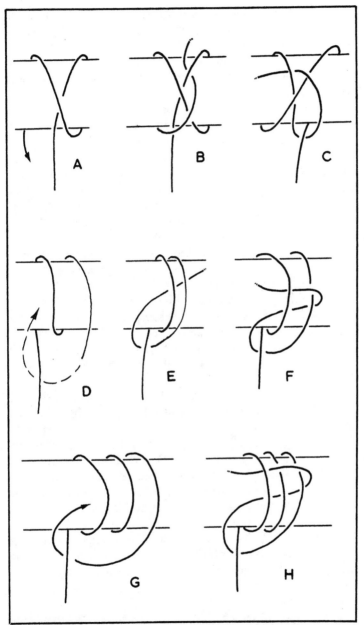

Fig. 10-4. Snug hitches use extra turns to limit slipping on a spar: (A) round turn; (B) passed under standing part turn; (C) crossing to tuck; (D) gaff topsail halliard bend; (E) passes under both turns; (F) studding soil halliard bend; (G) three turns around the spar; and (H) turns go under first turn.

large sailing ships. They could still be used for the direct attachment of halliards and other ropes to spars in smaller sailing craft, so metal fittings are not required.

The *gaff topsail halliard bend* differs from the previous hitch by bringing the end around the standing part (Fig. 10-4D) and passing it under both turns on the spar (Fig. 10-4E).

The *studding sail halliard bend* takes the tucking a stage further. After completion of the gaff topsail halliard bend, the end goes around one turn and under the other (Fig. 10-4F).

Even more complicated is the *topsail halliard bend*. If it has any advantages it is in the non-sliding qualities due to extra turns with their increased grip on a smooth surface. There are three turns around the spar and the end goes around and under them (Fig. 10-4G), as in a gaff topsail halliard bend, then over them and under the first turn (Fig. 10-4H).

These knots depart from the accepted method of naming by being called bends instead of hitches. All of them have the common quality of securing the standing part of the rope so it pulls directly from the spar without the risk of turning around it, and with the minimum part of the knot on the standing part. In the original applications there was an advantage in drawing the spar as close as possible to the block through which the halliard passed. They could still be worthwhile knots anywhere that the spar has to be drawn up close.

There are snug hitches that work the rope around the spar as if plaiting or making a three-part sinnet. They should be secure and the appearance may be attractive, but they are probably no stronger than earlier examples. The end goes under the first round turn and around the standing part (Fig. 10-5A) to be tucked under the next turn (Fig. 10-5B). That may be sufficient, particularly if the rope is fairly thick in relation to the spar, but when there is a greater difference, the three-part sinnet formation can be carried further (Fig. 10-5C).

Something like it is a snug hitch with the end taken around (Fig. 10-5D) and passed under both turns (Fig. 10-5E). Make sure the ends stay in the correct position as the knot is drawn tight.

ANCHOR BENDS

If a rope is used as an anchor cable the knot has to be one that can be trusted as it will be out of sight in use and there must be no fear that it will come undone, losing the anchor and allowing the boat to drift. Anchor bends can also be used on spars when their non-slip

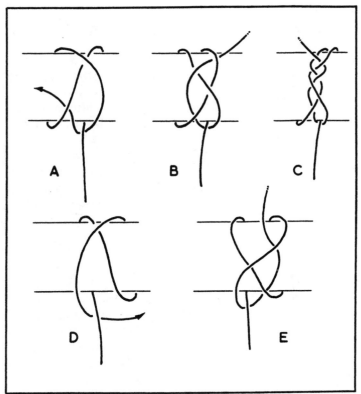

Fig. 10-5. The turns of a snug hitch can be worked together as if making a sinnet: (A) end goes under first round turn; (B) tucked under next turn; (C) three-part sinnet formation; (D) snug hitch; and (E) passed under both turns.

qualities would be an advantage. One anchor or fisherman's bend looks like a round turn and two half hitches, but the first half hitch takes up the middle of the round turn. Start with the round turn and commence the first half hitch, but take its end through the turn (Fig. 10-6A). Go on to make the second round turn in the usual way (Fig. 10-6B). That completes the knot, but it is common to seize the end to the standing part after the knot has been drawn tight (Fig. 10-6C).

When two half hitches are put on in a reverse direction they form a *buntline hitch* and they can be used in another version of the anchor bend. A half hitch around the standing part picks up the middle of the round turn (Fig. 10-6D), then instead of making another half hitch, what is in effect a complete clove hitch goes around the standing part towards the anchor ring (Fig. 10-6E). This arrangement need not be finished with a seizing. The ordinary

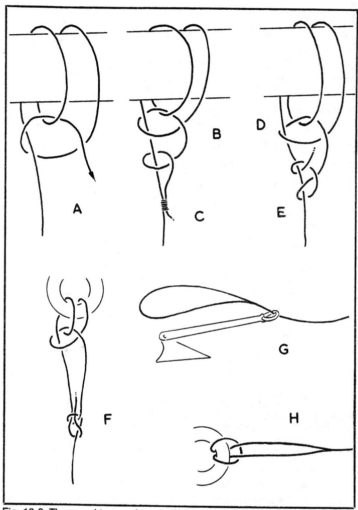

Fig. 10-6. The round turn and two half hitches converts to an anchor bend. A loop can used to pass over the anchor: (A) round turns; (B) second round turn; (C) knot drawn tight; (D) picking up middle of round turn: (E) complete clove hitch; (F) bowline; (G) anchor; and (H) running eye.

anchor bend can have its end tucked through the standing part as an alternative to seizing it.

An alternative strong way of finishing an anchor bend is to join the end into the standing part with a bowline (Fig. 10-6F). Make sure both parts share the strain.

If a rope may sometimes have to serve as an anchor cable or warp, but at other times it is to be used for mooring, it is possible to use a long bowline in the end of the rope with no other knotting. The bowline must be long enough to pass the length of the anchor through. The loop goes through the ring and is passed over the rest of the anchor (Fig. 10-6G) so it can be brought back to be a *cow hitch* or *running eye* at the ring (Fig. 10-6H).

FISHERMAN'S HITCHES

In some fishing gear light lines have to be attached to thicker ropes in a way similar to the ropes' attachment to some of the spars of sailing ships. Some of the same knots would seem to be suitable, but there are other ones favored by fishermen.

On some fishing nets the net itself is surrounded by a headrope and this has to be linked to a backing rope by short lines at frequent intervals. The backing rope is thicker than the headrope and two

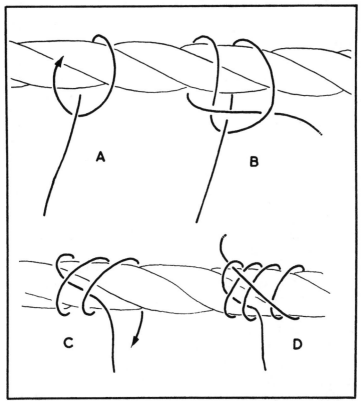

Fig. 10-7. Fishermen have their own special hitches for attaching nets to ropes: (A) headrope; (B) end turns; (C) two round turns; and (D) end goes under turn of the standing part.

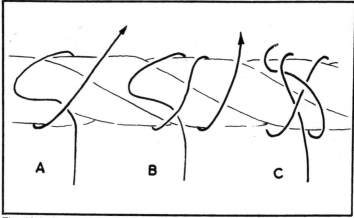

Fig. 10-8. A ground line hitch is used by cod fishermen: (A) loose loop; (B) another turn; and (C) standing part is pulled to tighten.

variations of a *net-line hitch* or *ossel hitch* are used to join on the lines.

The simpler hitch is used at the headrope. The end goes around the headrope, then behind the standing part (Fig. 10-7A), around the headrope again and across to the first turn (Fig. 10-7B). It is a compact snug hitch that could have other applications.

The hitch to the backing rope has more turns to give a better resistance to sliding on the thicker rope. Two round turns go over the standing part (Fig. 10-7C), then the end continues the same way and crosses to go under the turn of the standing part (Fig. 10-7D). It is then pulled to tighten the hitch. To distinguish this hitch from the other it may be called an *ossel knot*.

Another fisherman's knot with a resemblance to some snug hitches is the *ground line hitch* used by cod fishermen. A round turn goes over the standing part. It is allowed to remain as a loose loop (Fig. 10-8A). The end goes around to make another turn (Fig. 10-8B), then it crosses through the loose loop and the standing part is pulled to tighten on it (Fig. 10-8C).

MAGNUS HITCH

This is a name that goes back into knotting history. The name has not always been applied to the same knot and there has been confusion with the rolling hitch. Early writers gave that name and treated the two knots as interchangeable. By present definition a magnus hitch is really a clove hitch with an extra turn that is used when additional friction is needed to prevent slipping on a smooth

150

spar. The magnus hitch is intended for use where the load pulls across the spar approximately at right angles. The rolling hitch is used when the pull is in line with the spar or at a fairly close angle.

To make a magnus hitch, go around the spar or rope twice (Fig. 10-9A), then take the end over what has been done and put on the final half hitch (Fig. 10-11B). As with a clove hitch, the magnus hitch is really only satisfactory when there is a load on both ends. It is not intended for use at the end of a rope.

If the end of a rope has to be prevented from sliding on a smooth spar it is better to use *two round turns and two half hitches* (Fig. 10-9C). This has also been called a magnus hitch and a rolling hitch by early writers.

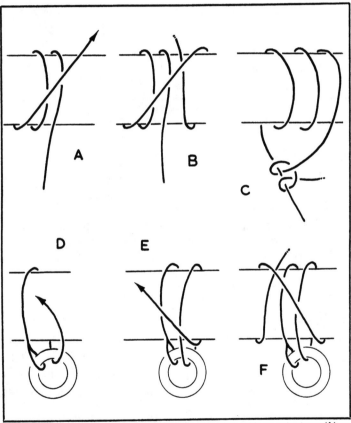

Fig. 10-9. The magnus hitch is made like a clove hitch with an extra turn: (A) go around rope twice; (B) final half hitch; (C) turn round turns two half hitches; (D) end goes through eyelet; (E) crosses the turns; (F) half hitch alongside other turns.

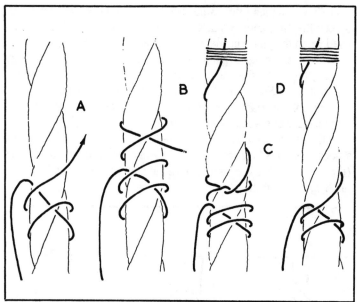

Fig. 10-10. A rolling hitch is intended to resist a slipping load along a large rope or spar: (A) working end; (B) half hitch; (C) seized end above the knot; and (D) wrapped tail.

ROBAND HITCH

The roband hitch is really an application of the magnus hitch. A roband was a rope spliced to an eyelet or grommet in the corner of a sail and used to lash the sail close up to a yard.

The end goes around the spar and back through the eyelet (Fig. 10-9D). It crosses the turns, without going through again (Fig. 10-9E) and makes a half hitch alongside the other turns (Fig. 10-9F). The sail is brought up close to the spar and the roband drawn tight with the last half hitch.

ROLLING HITCH

The confusion between this and the magnus hitch in the past has probably been due to the magnus hitch also having possibilities for resisting pulling along the spar or thick rope it is attached to. To distinguish the knots, the magnus hitch has one crossing turn, while the rolling hitch has two.

Take the working end twice over the standing part (Fig. 10-10A). Continue around the same way to put on a half hitch (Fig. 10-10B). The load is taken on the part covered by two turns. Be careful not to form it in reverse.

Although that is the complete knot, if it is to get a considerable load along the spar it is usual to seize the end above the knot (Fig. 10-10C). Sometimes it is not even completed. If the rope tail of tackle, sometimes called a *handy billy,* has to be attached to a cable to provide extra purchase temporarily, the first two turns are put on, then the tail wrapped around the cable with the lay and seized (Fig. 10-10D). For a brief pull, it might be sufficient for the end to be held by hand, while someone else pulls on the tackle.

SINGLE-TURN HITCHES

Usually if the end of a rope has to be attached to a spar it is better to completely encircle the spar with a round turn. The friction

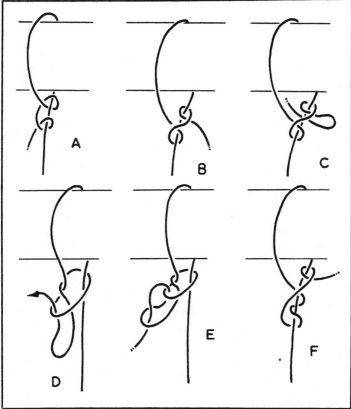

Fig. 10-11. Single turns can be secured in various ways with turns around the standing part: (A) two half hitches; (B) buntline hitch; (C) tucked-back bight; (D) slip noose hitch; (E) end is dipped through the bight; and (F) turns made towards the spar.

153

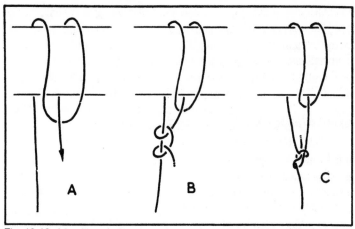

Fig. 10-12. A backhanded hitch can be used where it would be difficult to pass rope several times around an object: (A) end of rope is taken through end of bight; (B) two half hitches; and (C) bowline.

this causes may contribute as much to the strength of the fastening as any subsequent hitches. However, there are occasions when the rope need only be looped around.

Two half hitches can be used with a single turn instead of a round turn (Fig. 10-11A). However, if strength is required and the round turn is not to be used, it is better to make the two half hitches the other way and this is the basic *buntline hitch* (Fig. 10-11B). At sea it was a simple knot for attaching a rope to a yard. It can be made quick-release if the last turn is made with a tucked-back bight (Fig. 10-11C). A version of the buntline hitch uses a cow hitch instead of a clove hitch towards the spar. This is a *lobster buoy hitch*. It may hold as well as a buntline hitch, but the buntline is usually preferred.

A *slip noose hitch* is a simple overhand slip knot (Fig. 10-11D). The end is dipped through the bight (Fig. 10-11E) to prevent it from slipping back. One use of this knot is for hitching horses to rails.

Any sort of slip knot will pull close to the spar it is around, but if a knot is needed that will pull tight, but not too readily loosen when the load is relaxed, there can be an extra turn in the sliding part. In a *jam hitch* this is really a magnus hitch made around the standing part in place of the two half hitches of the buntline hitch. Note that the turns are made towards the spar (Fig. 10-11F).

BACKHANDED HITCH

In some circumstances it is difficult to get several turns around a spar or mooring place due to obstructions or narrow gaps. In that

154

case it is convenient to get a bight of the rope around and you not need to pass any more of it that way. The end of the bight is brought to the front and the end of the rope taken through it (Fig. 10-12A). Two half hitches may be put around the standing part (Fig. 10-12B) or the end can be joined into the standing part with a bowline (Fig. 10-12C).

HIGHWAYMAN'S HITCH

This hitch is a variation of a backhanded hitch that also allows a quick getaway. From its name, it is alleged to be a knot employed by a highwayman who used it to tie his horse to a tree while he waylaid a coach. After the robbery he jumped into the saddle, pulled the end of the rope and was away rapidly.

A bight of the rope goes around the spar, through a ring or anything else solid. The end is usually longer than the standing part. A small bight of the standing part is lifted through the end of the long bight (Fig. 10-13A) which is pulled to tighten it (Fig. 10-13B). Then a bight in the end piece is pushed through the small bight and the standing part is pulled to tighten on it (Fig. 10-13C). This completes

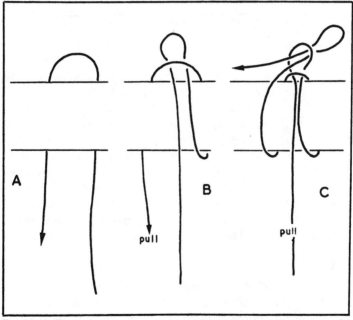

Fig. 10-13. The highwayman's hitch is a quick-release attachment to a solid object: (A) small bight is lifted through end of long bight; (B) pulled to tighten; and (C) standing part pulled to tighten.

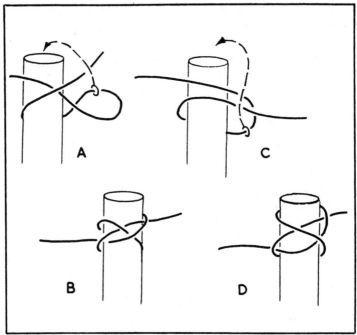

Fig. 10-14. A spar hitch uses a bight of rope passed over the top of a post: (A) loop lifted over top of post; (B) twist lifted over top of post; and (C) loop is lifted; (D) over the post.

and locks the knot. Any amount of pulling on the standing part will not upset the knot, but a pull on the end will release it.

This can be used in any quick-release situation. One modern example would be the single-handed use of an outboard motor on a small boat in a fast-flowing stream. The boat could be moored by a bow rope with a highwayman's hitch having a tail long enough to reach the user while he starts the motor at the stern. He can start his motor and get everything ready before pulling the end and gathering in the rope as the knot releases, so he gets away without the difficulty that might occur if he had to deal with a conventional mooring knot as well as handle his motor.

CROSSING KNOTS

Many of the hitches already described are suitable for situations where there will be a load on both sides, but there are some others that are mostly of use when the line goes across upright posts, as in making a temporary fence. The clove hitch is still a good choice in this situation, but there are some others.

Some of the simpler knots, such as the *marline spike hitch,* tend to slip down, particularly if it is an iron stake and not a stouter piece of wood that forms the upright. It is better to use a knot with several turns so there is more friction. It is also an advantage to use a knot that does not necessitate pulling an end through, particularly if there is a long piece of rope involved.

There are several *spar hitches* where a bight of rope goes over turns around the post. In one version a loop is lifted over the top of the post and the loop from the part under the other is twisted (Fig. 10-14A). This twist is then lifted over the top of the post (Fig. 10-14B). It pulls tight with a good resistance to slipping.

In another version the loop is lifted (Fig. 10-14C) over the crossing and over the post (Fig. 10-14D). The effect is to form a constrictor knot. As the twisted parts tighten under strain, the crossing part presses over them and further tightens them. It becomes very difficult to undo, so should only be used in rope in a permanent situation.

A *towing hitch* is used to attach a rope to the post in the bow of a boat taking a tow. It takes the strain and does not seize so it becomes difficult to cast off. A bight of rope is pulled around the post (Fig. 10-15A), then lifted over the turns and around the top of the post (Fig. 10-15B). In this form it can be used for making a temporary fence.

A post hitch that has a good bearing on the post and finishes with a regular appearance starts by twisting a bight (Fig. 10-16A). The crossing towards the standing parts is lifted through the end of the bight (Fig. 10-16B) so there are two overlapping loops ready to

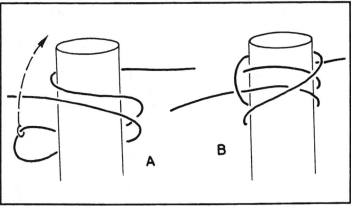

Fig. 10-15. A towing hitch has a bight passed over the post when securing a tow rope: (A) bight of the rope and (B) lifted over the turns.

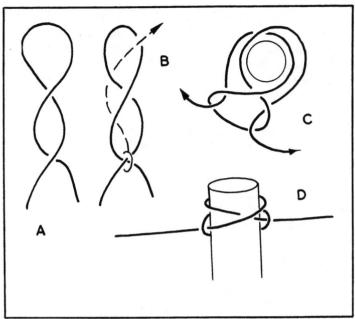

Fig. 10-16. A post hitch with the parts on the same side starts with a twisted bight: (A) twisting a bight; (B) crossing; (C) two overlapping loops: and (D) tighten the knot.

put over the post (Fig. 10-16C). Pull both standing parts in opposite directions to tighten the knot (Fig. 10-16D).

POSTS WITH HOLES

If ropes are to pass through holes in posts they should be knotted at each post, otherwise pressure on the rope at one place may slacken it excessively there and tighten at another place. Actual knots in the rope on each side of each hole can be avoided by looping the rope over the posts.

In the simplest arrangement a loop is turned back on itself to make a half hitch (Fig. 10-17A) to drop over the top of the post (Fig. 10-17B). For a stronger attachment and to reduce the risk of someone releasing the knot, the half hitch is twisted in the same way (Fig. 10-17C), but passed under the opposing standing part before putting over the top of the post (Fig. 10-17D).

The need to reeve the rope through the holes in the post can be avoided if the hole is large enough to take the doubled rope. A loop is taken through (Fig. 10-17E) and turned back on to the tops of the post without a twist (Fig. 10-17F).

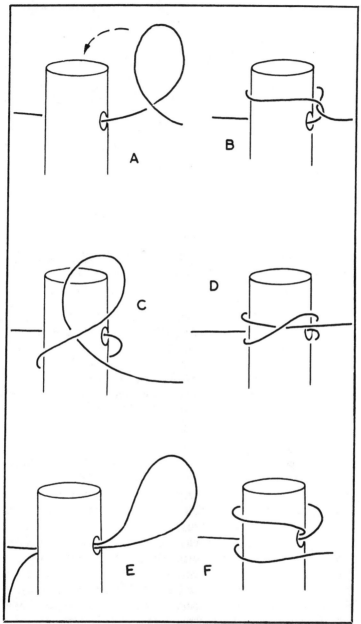

Fig. 10-17. If there is a hole through a post the rope may be passed through and secured with turns over the end: (A) half hitch; (B) drops over top of posts; (C) twisted half hitch; (D) passed under opposing standing part; (E) loop; and (F) loop or top of post without a twist.

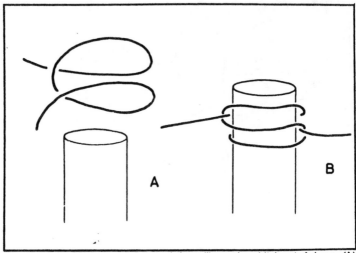

Fig. 10-18. An Oklahoma hitch is made by pulling a clove hitch out of shape: (A) two loops slip over top of post and (B) distorted crossing part.

OKLAHOMA HITCH

The Oklahoma hitch is a way of using a clove hitch on a fence post that increases the amount of bearing surface on the post and therefore reduces the risk of slipping. An ordinary clove hitch is made by forming two loops to slip over the top of the post (Fig. 10-18A), then instead of tightening under the crossing part, the ends are pulled around the post so they go the opposite ways and distort the crossing part (Fig. 10-18B).

SCAFFOLD HITCH

A similar distortion of a clove hitch can be taken even further. The center part is allowed to pull around until the two ends are pointing the same way (Fig. 10-19A). This is one way of slinging a spar or plank on edge, either for lifting it or using it as a hanging seat. It is also suggested as a way of making a sling for an injured arm.

However, for slinging a plank for use as a seat there is a better scaffold hitch. The plank is held flat without the risk of it turning, as there is with the simpler hitch. The rope is wrapped over the plank so there are three parts on top (Fig. 10-19B). Lift the inner part to the center (Fig. 10-19C). Draw up some slack on the part that is now the inner one and take that over the end of the plank without disturbing the other turns (Fig. 10-19D). Draw the whole thing tight and carry the end up to join it into the standing part with a bowline (Fig. 10-19E).

160

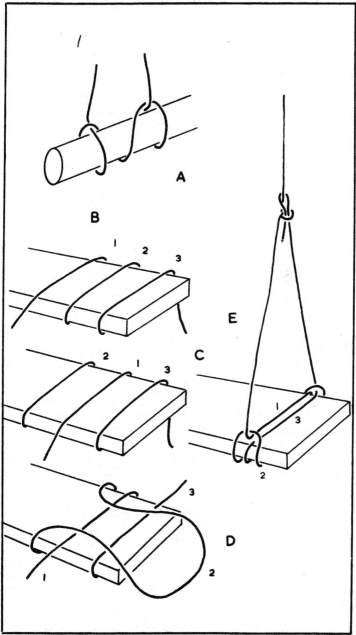

Fig. 10-19. A spar can be slung with a similar hitch, but a better scaffold hitch slings a board level: (A) center part pulls; (B) rope wraps over plank; (C) lift inner part; (D) draw some slack; and (E) draw tight.

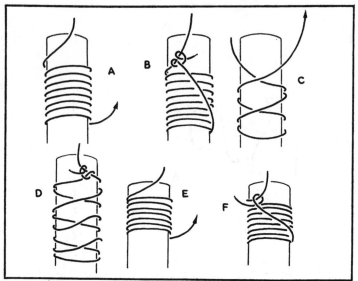

Fig. 10-20. When a spar has to be lifted endwise there have to be many turns to provide enough friction to grip the surface: (A) large number of turns; (B) two half hitches; (C) bight taken spirally around; (D) end joined to standing parts; (E) end brought back over turns; and (F) half hitched around standing part.

LIFTING HITCH

The alternative name—*well-pipe hitch*—indicates the main use of the lifting hitch. If a spar or pipe has to be lifted endwise, there has to be plenty of friction in the knot used so the rope will not pull along the surface. The knot is also used on the main poles of a circus or other large tent to secure the end of the rope after it has been used for hoisting.

A large number of turns are taken around the spar of pipe, then the end brought back to the top over the turns (Fig. 10-20A) and knotted to the standing part. Two half hitches are suitable (Fig. 10-20B), but other fastenings are possible.

Another knot for the same purpose is the *telegraph hitch*. This does not give as much friction, but it would be enough to grip the rougher wooden surface of a telegraph pole. A bight of rope is put across the pole and that and the standing part are taken spirally around, crossing back and front (Fig. 10-20C). The end is then joined to the standing part with two half hitches (Fig. 10-20D).

A similar knot is a *fire hose hitch* used for hoisting a hose vertically. Many turns are put on, then the end is brought back over them (Fig. 10-20E) and half hitches around the standing part (Fig. 10-20F).

Special Hitches to Spars and Posts

11

The many hitches described in Chapter 10 should cover the majority of needs when rope has to be attached to a spar with the load across or along it, but there are other hitches for special purposes and some of them are associated with particular activities. Many can be adapted to other needs. When specialist knot formations have been developed over many generations of users, the result can usually be assumed to be as near perfection as can be achieved and the knots would obviously be good choices in comparable circumstances.

CIRCUS KNOTS

Circus staff need to attach ropes to spars and be certain that the knots they use will not slip, despite the exceptional loads that may have to be taken in a large circus tent. Although cleats might seem the best form of attachment because they are afloat when halliards have to be secured under similar circumstances, they are avoided in circus tents where the poles have to be stacked for transport and they are better with no projections.

In most circus rope-to-spar knots, the first load is taken with a half hitch. As the rope is hauled taut, the quickly-applied half hitch takes some of the strain while the rest of the knot is made.

One side-wall pole hitch for temporarily taking a light strain is a *wrap hitch*. The line out of the first half hitch is turned back and a bight goes under the standing part (Fig. 11-1A). A stronger and more permanent hitch in the same place is a *one-length hitch*. The

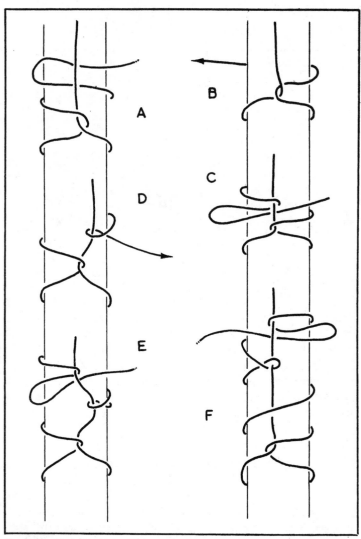

Fig. 11-1. Ropes are attached to circus tent poles in many ways that provide friction to prevent sliding: (A) bight under standing parts; (B) spar; (C) bight is tucked the other way; (D) quarter-pole hitch; (E) reversed tucked bights; and (F) another variation.

first half hitch is taken, then the end goes back and around the spar (Fig. 11-1B). A bight is turned over the standing part to tuck in the other way (Fig. 11-1C).

The circus quarter poles are larger and the load on the rope is greater, so the hitches are given more turns and locks. One *quarter-pole hitch* takes the end around after the half hitch and it twists around the standing part (Fig. 11-1D) before going back for a reversed tucked bight (Fig. 11-1E). A variation which should be stronger, wraps over the standing part on the way (Fig. 11-1F).

In yet another variation, called a *jumper hitch,* the turns on the standing part are arranged as half hitches (Fig. 11-2A) with the working end zig-zagging around the pole. How many half hitches are put on before finishing with a reversed tucked bight (Fig. 11-2B) depends on the size and smoothness of the pole and the load.

The knots used for lifting poles (Fig. 10-20) may also be used for securing the end of a rope used for lifting.

Besides the rolling hitch and magnus hitch there are other knots, basically similar, that get a resistance to slipping by putting many turns.

TREE SURGEON'S KNOT

The tree surgeon's knot is for attaching a rope to a tree branch, or if it is made around its own standing part to form a noose, it can be adjusted by sliding the knot. It is unlikely to slide unintentionally

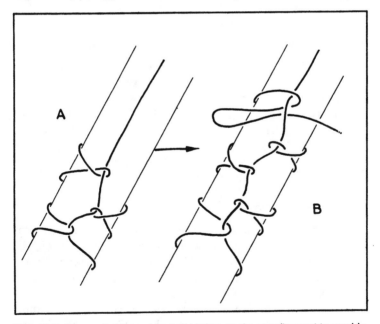

Fig. 11-2. Other pole hitches use half hitches on the standing part to provide friction and tension: (A) turns as half hitches and (B) finish with a reversed tucked bight.

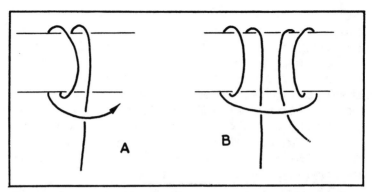

Fig. 11-3. A tree surgeon's knot attaches a rope to a branch: (A) working part crosses two turns of the standing part and (B) reverse the direction.

because of the number of turns providing friction.

Start as if making a magnus hitch, with the working part crossing two turns of the standing part (Fig. 11-3A). Instead of following around the same way, reverse the direction around the branch and put on two turns towards the center (Fig. 11-3B). The effect is something like a cow hitch with an extra turn under the crossing part at each side.

SWING HITCH

This hitch is intended to attach a rope to a tree branch so the standing part hangs from the center of the knot and can be used as one support for a swing.

Bring the rope up behind the branch and around and over itself at one side (Fig. 11-4A). Cross to the other side and do it again (Fig. 11-4B), then dip the end behind the standing part and tuck it under the turns of the first hitch (Fig. 11-4C). Push all the parts close together before drawing taut.

STEEPLEJACK'S KNOT

When a steeple or other tall building has to be climbed a rope is hung down and the steeplejack wears a safety belt attached to it with a knot that can be moved along. When under load it does not slip, but when the load is relaxed the knot can be moved to a new position with one hand.

The knot is a magnus hitch with an extra turn. Put on three turns and take the working end over them (Fig. 11-5A) to make a half hitch above (Fig. 11-5B). The loaded part must be the one included in the treble turns.

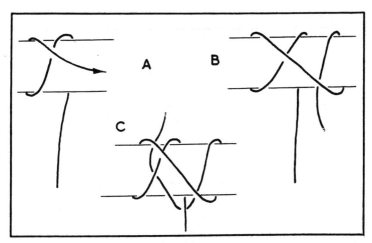

Fig. 11-4. The swing hitch attaches a rope to a spar so the standing part leads from the center of the knot: (A) bring rope up behind the branch; (B) cross to other side; and (C) dip the end and tuck it.

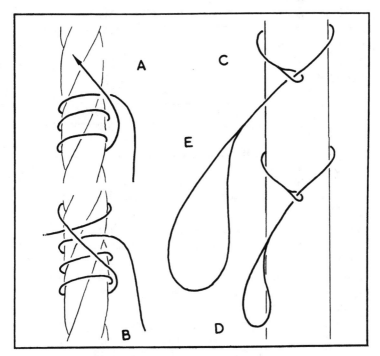

Fig. 11-5. A steeplejack uses a magnus hitch with an extra turn as a knot that can be slid to a new position. Two slings are aids to climbing a pole: (A) three turns; (B) half hitch; (C) noose around the pole; and (D) stirrup.

167

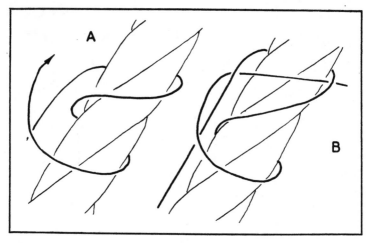

Fig. 11-6. The slack line hitch puts a grip around a rope that is not under a steady tension: (A) make the turn and (B) pull under the first part of the knot.

For a similar purpose, when climbing a flag pole or when working down it while painting it from the top, two slings are made up. Each has a noose around the pole (Fig. 11-5C). One is given another loop to serve as a stirrup for one foot (Fig. 11-5D). The other may have a large loop to sit in (Fig. 11-5E) or there may be a wooden seat. Either noose will take a man's weight, but to move up or down he puts all his weight on one sling while moving the other to its new position. He transfers his weight to that if he wants to move the other further.

SLACK LINE HITCH

Most hitches are intended to be used on a rigid spar or on a large rope that is under tension and is just as rigid as the spar for practical purposes. Many of these hitches would be unsatisfactory if the main rope was slack or no bigger than the one being attached. If a temporary line has to be attached to such a rope, as when needed to give assistance in pulling or to make fast while adjustments are made elsewhere, there is a hitch that is quickly applied and should not slip once it has been pulled tight.

Take the end around the rope and make a turn towards the direction the pull will come (Fig. 11-6A). Go around the standing part and under the first part of the knot (Fig. 11-6B). This hitch could be used on a spar, but some of the other hitches would then be more appropriate.

TAIL BLOCKS

Some tackle is made up with blocks. Rope is reeved through them with a hook or ring on one block and a long rope tail spliced to the other block. Such an assembly may be called a *handy billy*. Its

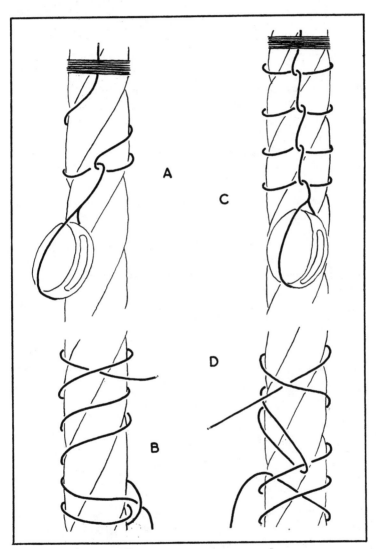

Fig. 11-7. A tail block can be attached to a rope in several ways, depending on how much friction is needed to prevent slipping: (A) half hitch; (B) seizing; (C) series of half hitches with seizing on the end; and (D) double back turn.

purpose is to provide the means of applying extra purchase anywhere it is needed by using the tail to secure one end of the tackle to whatever is to be pulled, while the hook is attached to a secure point to take the strain.

The rope tail can be used to make a *rolling hitch* around a larger taut rope. The *slack line hitch* may be more appropriate if the larger rope is not already tensioned.

There are several other ways that have been used. Some rely on a number of turns to finish with a seizing. The simplest is a half hitch and a few turns with the lay (Fig. 11-7A). It would be better to make the two turns of a rolling hitch at the start.

Another way is to put on one or two turns with the tail, then go back around the larger rope in the direction of the lay and finish with a seizing or a half hitch (Fig. 11-7B).

There could be a series of half hitches along the rope and a seizing at the end (Fig. 11-7C).

A complication is to start as for a rolling hitch, then double back a turn before finishing with a half hitch (Fig. 11-7D). This could be done more than once, depending on the length of the tail.

STROPS

A strop is an endless band. It may also be called a *strap*. It may even be a length of rope with the ends spliced together, or even knotted for temporary use. It might be a *selvagee strop* or it could be a *grommet,* but the last, made by twisting together a loop with a single strand, is more appropriate to smaller things than the means of attaching something to a spar or larger rope.

A long strop can be used to attach a hook to a spar or stout rope, either for arranging lifting tackle on a vertical spar or for getting increased temporary purchase on a large rope when the tackle has hooks instead of a tail at one end.

A selvagee strop is a made-up continuous rope. It is flexible and easy to work, so it beds down tightly. Being made of a large number of small lines laid around the circle, the strength is greater than the equivalent amount of yarns twisted in the normal laid rope pattern.

Traditionally, with natural materials, a selvagee strop was made of marline or spunyarn, but in modern synthetic materials any light line can be used, but it should be quite small stuff in relation to the spar or rope it is to be used on.

To make the strop, drive two nails into a piece of wood at the distance that will give a strop of the required size when line is wound around them.

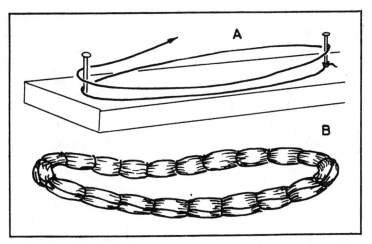

Fig. 11-8. A selvagee strop is made up of many turns with marline hitches holding them together: (A) strop of sufficient thickness and (B) close marline hitches.

Attach one end of the line temporarily to a nail with a clove hitch, then put on enough turns to make a strop of sufficient thickness (Fig. 11-8A). How much to put on will have to be found by experience. When sufficient turns have been made, go all around with fairly close marline hitches (Fig. 11-8B). Take the strop off the nails and tie the two ends of the line together.

The simplest way to use such a strop is to pass one end through the other and hang the block from that (Fig. 11-9A). If this does not have enough friction on the spar, put the middle of the strop behind the rope or spar and wrap it around (Fig. 11-9B) several times, then the hook engages with the final loops (Fig. 11-9C).

Another way with a very long strop, possibly spliced rope, is to wrap around until only enough is left for one loop to be passed through the other (Fig. 11-9D), then the hook or other load goes into the hanging loop.

Sometimes a load has to be taken nearer right angles to the spar, as when using an assembly of spars above a load that has to be lifted with the load-bearing spar horizontal. Similar conditions occur when a spar has to be hoisted horizontally with a tackle.

In both cases the strop is laid across the spar and wound around, with one part going through the other (Fig. 11-10A). Sufficient turns are taken to use up the strop, then one loop is passed through the other to take the hook (Fig. 11-10B) or the lengths can be arranged so the hook engages with both parts (Fig. 11-10C).

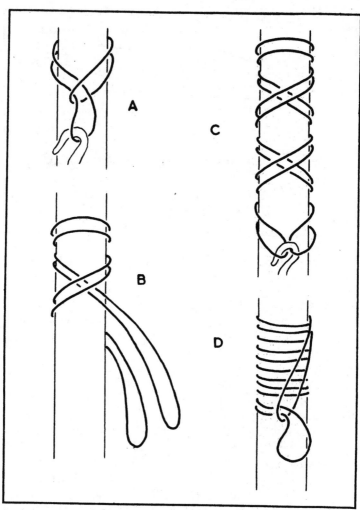

Fig. 11-9. A strop may be passed around a pole many times to support the hook of a block: (A) hang the block; (B) put middle of strop behind the rope; (C) hook engages with final loops; and (D) hanging loop.

MOORING HITCH

When a vessel comes alongside its way may have to be checked with a mooring rope around a bollard or post, then the mooring line secured. Way is stopped by having a turn around the post with the end part under the loaded one (Fig. 11-11A). Resistance on the end and friction around the post stops the vessel's movement, then a loop is lifted over the top of the post (Fig.

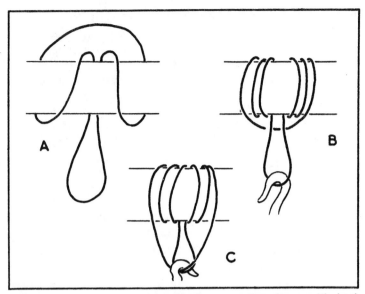

Fig. 11-10. A strop on a horizontal spar is given several turns to support the hook of a block: (A) one part of strop goes through the other part; (B) loop takes the hook; (C) and hook engages with both parts.

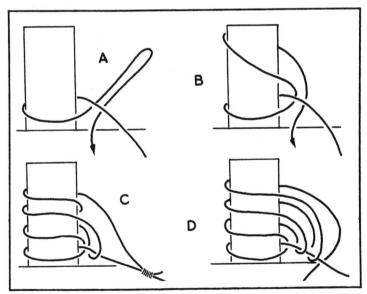

Fig.11-11. A mooring line to a post is secured by several turns taken over the top of the post which are easily cast off: (A) end part is under loaded one; (B) loop is lifted over top of post; (C) end is half hitched or seized and (D) lift alternate bights.

173

11-11B). More of the rope may be twisted around the post and the end half hitched around the standing part or seized there (Fig. 11-11C), but it is stronger to lift alternate bights from under the standing part over the top of the post (Fig. 11-11D). This will withstand the pull on the mooring rope, yet eventually the knot is easily cast off.

When a vessel is already stationary, moorings can be made with any of the end of rope knots, but it is convenient to have an eye spliced or a bowline tied in the end of the rope to drop over the post or bollard.

GUY LINE HITCHES

Ropes to support a tent have to be tied to stakes or posts. Although synthetic cordage does not expand and contract with difference in moisture as much as natural fiber ropes did, many tents are still made of natural fabrics. They expand and contract and it is necessary for the supporting ropes to be adjustable. There are several sorts of runners that slide on the lines to provide adjustment, but if rope has to be used without them, it is better to use an adjustable knot along the line than to tie at the end and have to untie and adjust frequently.

One suitable knot is a magnus hitch used as a noose (Fig. 11-12A). The knot is arranged far enough from the stake and the load arranged to come at the end of the knot with double turns (Fig. 11-12B). This should not slip inadvertently, but it can be moved by hand to adjust the tension of the tent.

Another adjustable hitch has two overhand knots tied in the main part of the line and the end taken down through them (Fig. 11-12C). A variation has the end taken down through one overhand knot, then the second knot is tied in itself (Fig. 11-12D) to make a version of a fisherman's knot.

If adjustment is not required, the rope could be joined to the stake with a round turn and two half hitches, but if it is a heavy load, as there would be with a circus tent, it is necessary to be able to hold on to the load while completing the knot. A round turn might be difficult to hold while the half hitches are made. There is a *backhand hitch* which puts a nip on the standing part (Fig. 11-10E) so it is easier to hold a strain, while the end is made into the two half hitches (Fig. 11-12F).

A circus man has a hitch for the same purpose, which he calls a *wet weather hitch*. It is easily released and re-adjusted if there are changes in the weather. The line goes around the stake and nips the standing part (Fig. 11-12G). One hitch is put on with a bight (Fig. 11-12H).

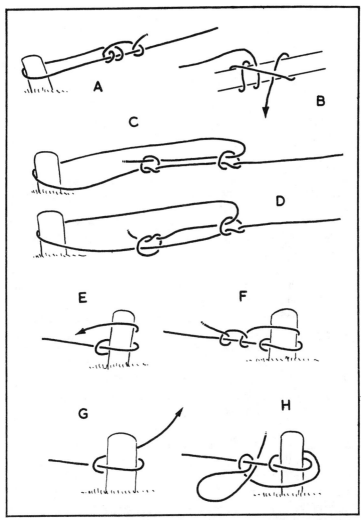

Fig. 11-12. Guylines can be made adjustable through knots or secured to stakes that are easily cast off: (A) magnus hitch used as a noose; (B) knot with double turns; (C) adjustable hitch; (D) second knot is tied in itself; (E) backhand hitch; (F) two half hitches; (G) line nips standing part; and (H) one hitch is put on with a bight.

SLIPPERY HITCHES

The *highwayman's hitch* (Fig. 10-13) is probably the most useful quick-release hitch, but there are others.

One slippery hitch is particularly appropriate when taking a tow in a small boat. Any hull has on optimum speed through the water. If

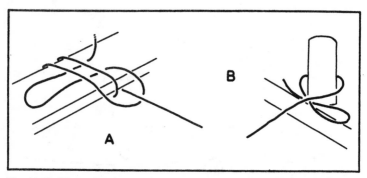

Fig. 11-13. Slippery hitches can be arranged with turns over a bight in the end of the rope: (A) bight tucked under standing part and (B) end hanging within reach.

a small boat is towed by a power boat at much higher speed than its optimum, the bow will be pulled under and the boat will capsize. Consequently, it is always wise to lead the tow rope through an eye or fairlead at the bow and make it fast with a slippery hitch to a thwart or seat within reach in the boat. It can then be cast off and the line will run out to let the small boat stop in an emergency.

A turn is taken around the thwart and a bight tucked under the standing part (Fig. 11-13A). The end is kept within reach so a jerk on it will let the whole knot go. A simpler version of this could be used for a mooring if the mooring rope comes from the bollard over the edge of the dock. A bight is tucked under the standing part with its end hanging within reach (Fig. 11-13B). This is obviously only a temporary expedient and unsuitable to be left unattended.

Several of the knots for attaching a rope to a spar can be tucked with a bight so a pull on the end releases the knot. Any of the knots made like a clove hitch will come away if the second half hitch is made with a bight that can be pulled. One special *high post hitch* uses the principle for a mooring rope that may be out of reach at some states of the tide. It is something like a buntline hitch. A single turn goes around the post and this continues to a single turn around the standing part (Fig. 11-14A). The end goes around both parts of the loop around the post (Fig. 11-14B) and between the crossing and the standing part with a bight (Fig. 11-14C).

These special slippery hitches involve letting go of the end after the knot has been upset. It has to run out around the post. If there is a considerable length of rope involved this could be a nuisance or even a danger, as when quick recovery of the rope might not be possible and its end could become tangled with a boat propeller. It would be better to have the quick-release hitch made

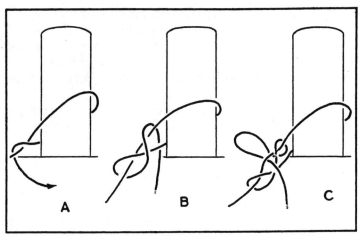

Fig. 11-14. A high post hitch is a slippery hitch for a mooring that may become out of reach on a falling tide: (A) single turn; (B) end goes around both parts of loop; and (C) crossing and standing part.

on a bight. Pulling the end should also pull in the surplus rope without the need to let go at any stage. The *highwayman's hitch* is made in this way and satisfies the conditions. Another knot with similar properties is a *high post hitch on a bight*.

A bight is taken around the post or through the mooring ring and its end turned back over the standing part and the hanging end (Fig. 11-15A). A small bight in the hanging part is used to tuck under the turns around the post and lock the end of the main bight (Fig.

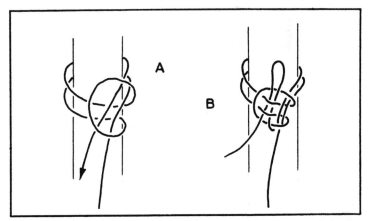

Fig. 11-15. A high post hitch on a bight uses a bight for a slippery hitch to a post: (A) bight is taken over hanging end and (B) locks the end of the main bight.

11-15B). Pulling the hanging end should free the knot and let the bight run away around the post. The only possible difficulty comes if there has been considerable load and the knot is very tight around the post so the friction on the small bight is very great and resists pulling free. This trouble does not occur in the highwayman's hitch as the locking bight is not against the solid object.

Some other slippery hitches are described in Chapter 12. Although primarily intended for securing to rings, most of them could also be used around a post.

Hitches to Rings and Hooks

12

Many of the hitches for attaching ropes to spars or stretched ropes may also be used on rings, hooks and other solid objects, but the curved shape of the ring or hook may limit the number of turns that can conveniently be passed through without the risk of them riding over each other. If the rope is small in relation to the size of the curve there may be several turns, but normally a hitch to a ring does not have many turns passing through. The limit is reached when the rope is almost as big as the hook, which it sometimes is for a sling.

Some of the common knots, such as the *round turn and two half hitches* and the *anchor bend* variation are as much ring knots as spar knots. Similarly, the *catspaw* may get more use on a hook than for attaching to other solid objects. Any of the hitches with few turns around the spar and described in chapters 10 and 11 may be used on most solid objects, including rings and hooks.

HALF HITCHES

For light loads and temporary situations, such as when hanging things on rings for storage, or to keep them out of reach or off the ground, there is no need for the strong and sometimes complicated hitches that are needed for hoisting loads. Variations on the half hitch may suffice.

A simple half hitch can be taken around the standing part and tucked so the end is nipped against the ring (Fig. 12-1A). It is probably better to tuck with a bight (Fig. 12-1B). Not only does this

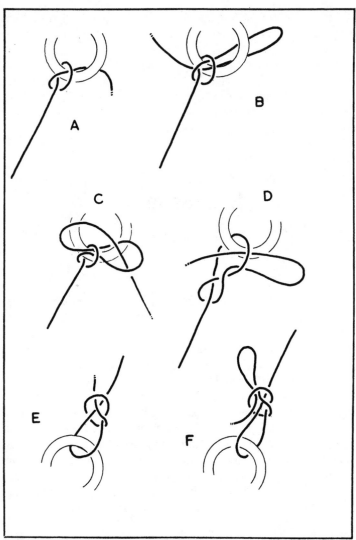

Fig. 12-1. Lines may be secured with half hitches to rings: (A) end is nipped against the ring; (B) tuck with a bight; (C) drop the end through the bights: (D) bight used for final tuck; (E) overhand knot; and (F) tucking a bight.

allow the attachment to be slipped by pulling the end, but it gives extra bearing and a more secure grip. A further step to prevent inadvertent releasing is to drop the end through the bight (Fig. 12-1C) without pulling the bight tight around it.

If a slightly stronger knot is wanted there can be a figure-eight knot instead of the half hitch. If a bight is used for the final tuck (Fig.

12-1D), the knot can be slipped by pulling the end. The end can be dropped through the bight in the same way as with the half hitch.

A noose is often used through a ring or over a hook. There is really little reason for having a slipknot tightening on the metal and one of the other knots might be preferable, but for a quick attachment an overhand knot can be made around the standing part (Fig. 12-1E). Note that the twist of the knot should be done in the way· that brings the end out alongside the standing part. Twisting in the other direction brings the end across the standing part and the knot does not close as tightly or neatly. The knot can be made quick-release by tucking a bight (Fig. 12-1F) and the end can be dropped through the bight to prevent accidental release, as described for other hitches. This last is the *halter hitch*.

LOOM HITCHES

At the lower end of the scale regarding size are knots for use in thread and yarn. One *loom harness knot* is more suitable for a hook

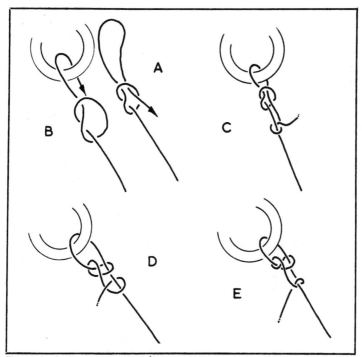

Fig. 12-2. Variations on the hitch are used for looms and hammocks: (A) tie an overhand knot; (B) over the hook; (C) knot is drawntight;(D) an extra tuck goes through the ring directly; and (E) or with a twist.

than a ring, as it is most easily made when it can be passed over a point. Tie an overhand knot near the end, but only push through a bight (Fig. 12-2A). It goes over the hook or the end is passed through a ring and threaded back (Fig. 12-2B), then the knot is drawn tight and is locked with a half hitch (Fig. 12-2C).

Hammock hitches are slip knots with two half hitches around the standing part, but with an extra tuck through the part that goes through the ring, either directly (Fig. 12-2D) or with a twist (Fig. 12-2E). There does not seem to be any great advantage in this for ropework, but the additional grip may be an advantage for very small stuff.

ANCHOR HITCHES

Besides the *anchor bend* developed from the round turn and two half hitches, there have been many others devised for the same purpose—a secure attachment to a ring that can be trusted out of sight and under water.

Many of the bowlines have been used. In particular, a long bowline loop that is doubled back in a cow hitch on the ring (Fig. 12-3A) is a good way of joining a rope to a ring for other purposes besides anchoring. It is also a good way of joining a spliced eye in the end of a rope to a ring. With a long eye it may be possible to pass an anchor through to avoid pulling through the standing part, but where this is impossible, as with a ring attached to a wall, the length of the eye permits a coil of rope to pass through instead of having to pull its length through a small eye.

Instead of the cow hitch there can be a clove hitch on the ring and a bowline further up the standing part (Fig. 12-3B). This cannot be made with an existing loop on a ring, although the clove can be formed on a loop and slipped over a hook. If the attachment is to a ring, the clove hitch must be made in the free line, then the bowline formed afterwards. Less satisfactory is the use of two half hitches on the standing part instead of the bowline.

A *Portugese anchor hitch* is based on the Portugese bowline, which could be used in its normal form, but in this hitch it is started by passing a bight through the ring. Quite often it is less trouble to do this than to reeve an end through more than once. Turn back a sufficient length of bight through the ring (Fig. 12-3C). Leave the standing part behind the bight, but bring the end through. Make an eye for a bowline in the standing part within the length of the hanging bight (Fig. 12-3D) and take the end around the standing part to complete the normal bowline pattern, but taking in the end of the

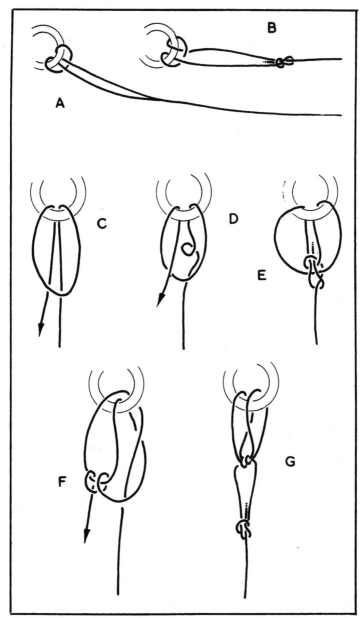

Fig. 12-3. A line can be attached to a ring with a loop. Anchor hitches may be based on the Portugese bowline or an ordinary bowline with a round turn: (A) long bowline loop; (B) clove hitch on the ring; (C) turn back the bight; (D) eye for bowline; (E) take in the end of the bight; (F) pull bight through; and (G) complete the knot.

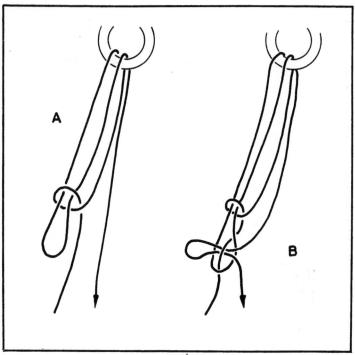

Fig. 12-4. A sheepshank hitch can be used for a quick-release, with the knot formed some way from the ring: (A) sheepshank and (B) bight locks the standing part.

bight (Fig. 12-3E). The knot then stands away from the ring and can be made any length desired. This might be an advantage if the ring is not easily reached, then when the bight is pulled through the knotting can be done in a more convenient position. The strength of the knot is unaffected by the length of the loops.

A *bowline and round turn* is another anchor bend with a bight through the ring and the knot away from it, suitable for similar circumstances to the previous knot. Pull a bight through and take the end through it and around the standing part (Fig. 12-3F) twice before going further along the standing part to work a bowline (Fig. 12-3G) to complete the knot.

SHEEPSHANK HITCH

This hitch is a slippery hitch with similar advantages to the knots just described in having the knotted part some way from the ring after a bight has been passed through it. The particular advantage is seen when mooring a boat to a ring in a place where there is a considerable rise and fall of tide. Once the bight has been passed, the knot can be made in the boat and released later in the same position.

The bight is brought through as far as required, then a half hitch of the standing part goes over it, as in one end of a sheepshank (Fig. 12-4A). A bight of the end locks the standing part under the end of the first bight (Fig. 12-4B). A pull on the end releases the knot and strain on the standing part upsets the half hitch so the long bight can pull through the ring.

SLIP BOWLINE

A bowline through a ring can be arranged to slip by pulling the end. It may be any length, so it can be close to the ring if there is no reason for making it elsewhere. It can also be of considerable length if more convenient, but when casting off the rope has to be allowed to run free through the ring, therefore a great length might delay a quick get away.

Start with the usual bowline formation, but with a bight through the rope eye (Fig. 12-5A). Twist this bight over the knot (Fig. 12-5B) so part of the twist is over the standing part. Form the rest of the end part into another bight and push it across to lock the

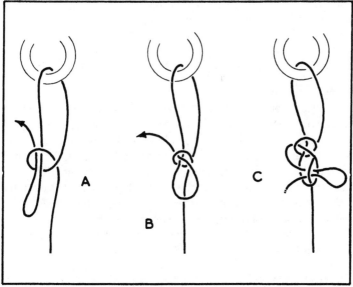

Fig. 12-5. A bowline can be arranged to slip by using a bight against the standing part: (A) bight through the rope eye; (B) twist the bight over the knot; and (C) form end part into another bight.

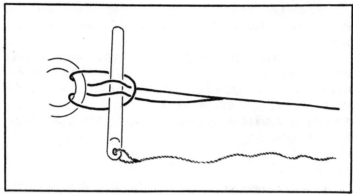

Fig. 12-6. A loop in the end of a rope can be made quick-release by using a toggle.

twisted bight to the standing part (Fig. 12-5C). A pull on the end allows the knot to upset.

TOGGLED LOOP

A certain quick release comes from using a wooden peg on a lanyard to lock a knot. Of course, the toggle or peg is separate from the rope and is an extra item that could be lost, but if it is on a long line with its other end secured to the boat or other item being tied, it should always be there when required.

Use a bight or the end of a long loop. Pass it through the ring as if to make a cow hitch, but instead of passing the rope through, use the toggle across to trap the end of the bight on its sides (Fig. 12-6).

SAMPAN HITCH

This hitch is the mooring hitch commonly used by oriental river boatmen. The knot starts by taking the end through the ring and making an overhand knot with a bight (Fig. 12-7A). It is turned back over the standing part and another bight of the end part tucked to lock it (Fig. 12-7B). The knot could be left at that stage, but for greater security the end of the second bight is turned over the standing part and locked with yet another bight (Fig. 12-7C). The effect is a chain of locked bights with the hanging end in the boat. When the end is pulled, the series of bights will come apart and the knot releases.

HOOK HITCHES

For many purposes there need be no distinction between knots used on rings and hooks, but there are a few hitches that are

186

particularly intended for hooks and some of them would be unsuitable for rings or spars. These include some which were traditionally used as temporary attachments when setting up the complicated rigging of a square-rigged ship. Those uses have gone and the particular hitches have few uses today. In any case, they should be used with discretion, although some of the apparently over-simple hitches have stronger grips than might appear at first glance. In their original applications the hitches were of a very temporary nature, being used to quickly join a tackle to some part of the rigging that needed one pull. Then they were released and ready for the next job.

BLACKWELL HITCH

Blackwall is part of the London dock area. This hitch is only suitable when the size of rope almost fills the throat of the hook. The end is laid in the throat (Fig. 12-8A) and the standing part taken around the neck of the hook and crossed over it (Fig. 12-8B). The part behind the hook should be high enough to fit into the hollowing of the neck of the hook and not lower on the thicker back of it.

In a *double Blackwall hitch* there is a second turn around the neck of the hook (Fig. 12-8C). Older books describe this as a way of strengthening the Blackwall hitch, but as the second turn lifts the standing part so it does not press as tightly on the end, it is probably weaker.

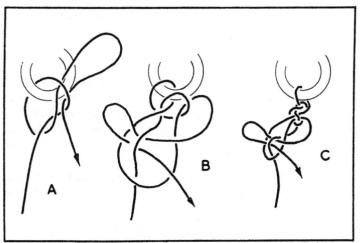

Fig. 12-7. The sampan hitch is an oriental quick-release mooring knot: (A) overhand knot with a bight; (B) bight of end part tucked; and (C) locked with another bight.

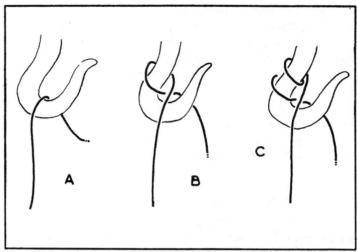

Fig. 12-8. The Blackwall hitch is a simple attachment to a hook: (A) end is laid in the throat; (B) standing part crosses over; and (C) double Blackwell hitch.

STUNNER HITCH

The stunner hitch may also be called a *double Blackwall hitch.* It differs from the other version by having the extra turn taken above the hook, going above the shackle or eye there. Put the end in the hook (Fig. 12-9A), then loop around above the hook and down to cross the end in the hook (Fig. 12-9B). Like the other hitches it is the pressure of the standing part over the end in the throat of the hook that provides the grip, so extra turns may have little effect and may actually weaken the grip.

MIDSHIPMAN'S HITCH

This name is given to several other knots, but here it is an alternative to the *Blackwall hitch.* It may also be called a *bill hitch.* Its formation is the same as a *sheet bend* or *becket hitch* with the hook in the position of the turned-back bight or loop in those knots. As with the earlier hook hitches, this is only secure if the rope almost fills the throat of the hook.

It is possible to pass the end around as if making a sheet bend, but a better way is to first put in the end (Fig. 12-10A), take the standing part around the neck of the hook and over it as for a Blackwall hitch (Fig. 12-10B), then lift the rear part of the end loop over the bill of the hook (Fig. 12-10C). This completes the hitch, but see that the rope fits into the hollows of the neck and the bill as the standing part is tightened (Fig. 12-10D).

188

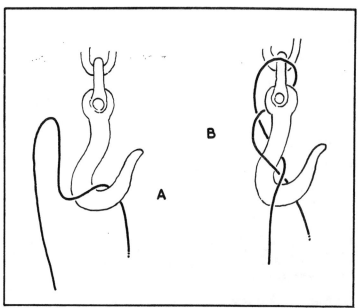

Fig. 12-9. The stunner hitch or double Blackwall hitch takes a turn above the hook: (A) end in the hook and (B) cross the end in the hook.

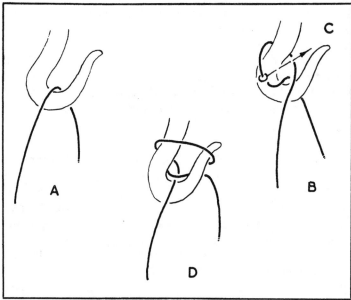

Fig. 12-10. A midshipman's hitch is formed from a Blackwall hitch: (A) put in the end; (B) Blackwall hitch; (C) lift rear part over bill of the hook; and (D) standing part is tightened.

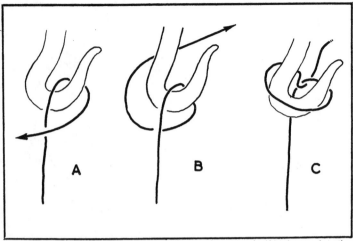

Fig. 12-11. The marline spike hitch can be used on a hook: (A) tale rope into the throat and around the bill; (B) around itself and the back of the hook; and (C) tuck it under the standing part in the throat.

MARLINE SPIKE HITCH

This simple hitch has already been described for levering and pulling, but here it is used as a means of attaching a rope to a hook and would seem to have a better grip than those just described, particularly if the rope is not large enough to be a fairly close fit in the throat of the hook.

Take the rope into the throat and around the bill (Fig. 12-11A), back around itself and the back of the hook (Fig. 12-11B). It is to be tucked under the standing part in the throat (Fig. 12-11C). See that the crossing stays within the hook as the knot tightens.

RACKING HITCH

If the relationship between the size of the rope and the throat of the hook is such that there is room for two turns of rope alongside each other in the space, none of the simple hitches are suitable. Instead, it would be better to use a round turn and two half hitches, or the single type of *catspaw* at the end of the rope, or the normal double-twist catspaw in a sling or the bight of a rope.

The common use of the catspaw is shown by its other name of *hook hitch*, but it is sometimes wrongly called a *racking hitch*. That is made in a very similar way by throwing back a bight (Fig. 12-12A). In the catspaw the two parts are twisted in the opposite way (Fig. 12-12B) before being put over the hook. In a racking hitch they are twisted the same way (Fig. 12-12C). The lower part of the bight then passes between the standing parts instead of across them and there is a tendency for the two parts to twist on each other as the sling hangs from the hook. There is probably little to choose between the two hitches for strength, but the catspaw keeps a better shape under load.

ENDLESS SLINGS

For many loads a continuous rope ring is spliced or knotted. This can be looped around the load and one part passed through the other as a *bale hitch* (Fig. 12-13A). The other part may go directly over the hook with some types of load, but otherwise there may be a *cow hitch* on the hook to stop the rope from slipping through and tilting the load (Fig. 12-13B). For a heavy load it would be better to use a catspaw.

With the same sling being used for different sizes of loads there may be too great a length in some circumstances. Making a long catspaw will use up some surplus rope, but there are other ways of shortening.

The surplus part of the sling can be divided into two parts. They are knotted together (Fig. 12-13C) and the two parts are put over the hook (Fig. 12-13D).

Another way that gives some adjustment has the surplus loop turned down and crossed between the standing parts (Fig. 12-13E).

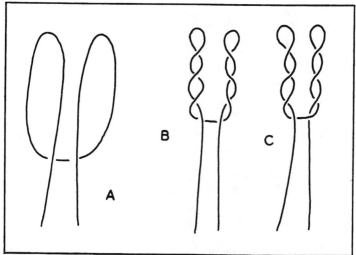

Fig. 12-12. A racking hitch is like a catspaw, but the turns are made the same way: (A) throw back a bight; (B) two parts twisted in the opposite way; and (C) in racking hitch, they are twisted in the same way.

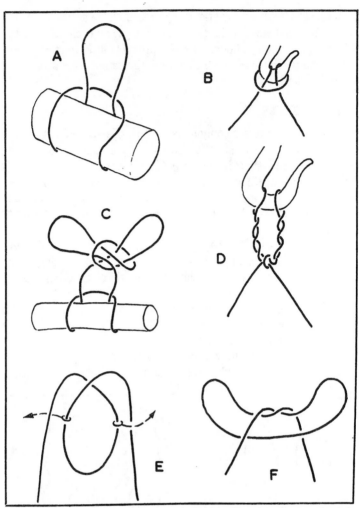

Fig. 12-13. A bale sling may loop around a load, but if too long there are knots to shorten it: (A) bale hitch; (B) cow hitch; (C) two parts knotted together; (D) two parts put over the hook; (E) surplus loop; and (F) lower part is left straight.

If the crossed parts are pulled outward they will knot the upper part and leave the lower part straight (Fig. 12-13F). When the crossed part is kept low as the end loops are put over the hook the total sling will be shorter than if the crossing is adjusted to come nearer the hook.

With both methods of shortening, the rope may go directly over the hook or be treated as a catspaw when it can be used to produce further shortening.

Constricting Knots  13

Besides knots that go around solid objects, go through rings and make attachments involving encircling something that is unaffected by the ropework, there is another group of knots whose main purpose is to squeeze whatever they are put around. This occurs when the neck of a bag has to be drawn tight or a bundle of loose things have to be pulled together and held. Some of these binding knots may also be suitable for attaching a rope to a solid object where the tightening action will be of value in preventing the knot from moving once it has been tightened. However, many of the binding knots are difficult or impossible to cast off and the line has to be cut to release them. They serve more uses for cord and string for a once-only knot that will be discarded rather than undone to be made again.

Many of the knots already described might have constricting applications. For instance, the reef knot joining the ends of a rope around something is constricting, particularly in its original use of joining the ends of reef points around the gathered slack of a sail being reefed. Several slip knots that can be pulled tight and then locked serve as good constricting knots. Other uses of some have been described already, while further varieties are described in this chapter.

Some binding knots have developed into ornamental knots. They may still bind, but their main purpose is decorative. The

Turk's head is one of these with a great many ramifications and it is described with other decorative ropework, but it might be considered for an application where there is a need to constrict and a pleasing appearance would be welcomed.

Whippings and seizings might be regarded as constricting knots, although the large number of turns involved and the fact that they are made in light line, puts them into a different group. The *West country whipping* idea of alternately knotting on opposite sides could be used for just a few turns in larger cordage as a binding, but some of the other knots would usually be more suitable. Similarly, there are constricting knots that would make temporary whippings or seizings. Where strands have to be held to prevent them from unlaying while working on a splice, a binder knot may be easier to put on than a whipping and it would be just as effective. For more permanently preventing the end of a rope from fraying a proper whipping is better than a constricting knot.

There are two main groups of binder knots. In one type the line goes around and the ends are knotted together, either with a slip knot to tighten and then lock, as with the packer's knot (Fig. 3-10). In the other type the action of going around the object is the knot and there is no further joining of the ends as they get their security by tucking in the turns that encircle the bag or other item being squeezed.

Not all of the uses are direct squeezes. Lacing through eyelets of shoes or canvas covers may be pulled up and tied with a knot in this group. There are occasions when a constricting knot may be used to pull things together and then they are held in some other way. In some cases the knot may take in something else, as in the *roband hitch* (Fig. 10-9), which pulls a sail to a spar with a binding action.

REEF KNOT VARIATIONS

When a line goes around something solid or semi-solid, like the gathered sail or the neck of a bag, the knot for joining the ends is the reef knot. There is no need to consider any other if all that is required of the knot is to join. This is where the reef knot comes into its own. Be careful not to tie a *granny knot* by making both twists the same way. The ends must come out alongside their standing parts—right over left, left over right if you need to think about it.

If the reef knot has to be untied there is a way of pulling one end to capsize the knot. Much depends on the original tightness and the

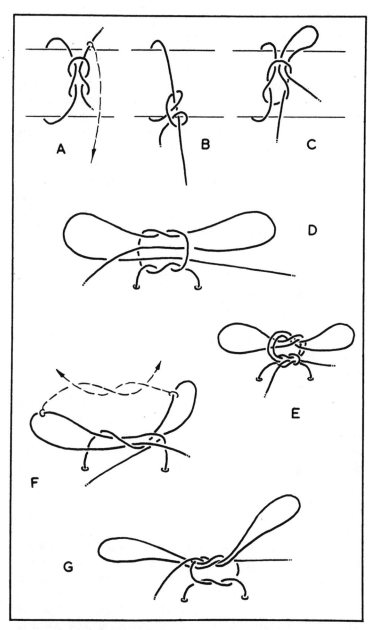

Fig. 13-1. The reef is a binding knot that can be made with bights for appearance or quick release: (A) straight standing part; (B) cow hitch; (C) slip reef knot: (D) reef bow knot; (E) tied bights on top of reef knot; and (G) second twist made with bights.

type of cord used, but it is worth trying. Take one end and pull it so it and its standing part come straight (Fig. 13-1A). When it is straight, the other part will be left as a *cow hitch* around it, ready to slide off (Fig. 13-1B). If a granny knot is capsized in this way, there will be a *clove hitch* instead of a cow hitch.

As that method of untying cannot always be relied on, it is better to make a *slip reef knot* by forming one of the final tucks with a bight (Fig. 13-1C). That is all that is needed for a quick release, but there is often a bight both ways to make a *reef bow knot* (Fig. 13-1D). This is the knot that should be tied in shoe laces, and often is not. A reef bow across the top eyelets of a shoe will finish with the two bights across the foot. If the bights are in line with the foot it is a granny bow. This may hold well enough under the circumstances, but anyone who claims to understand knots would always tie the reef version of a bow.

With very slippery shoe laces—as some synthetic ones are—the bights of the bow could be tied again on top of the reef knot (Fig. 13-1E). The knot is no longer quick release, but this may be the only way of avoiding laces coming undone in use.

Another way of dealing with slippery laces, if they are long enough, is to tie the whole knot with bights to make a *bight reef knot* (Fig. 13-1F). It cannot be released by pulling an end, but it can be upset by straightening one part and sliding the other off, like a doubled cow hitch.

Another way of getting increased friction to provide grip on slippery laces is to make the first part of the reef knot normally, then make the whole of the second twist with bights (Fig. 13-1G). The result is less bulky than the previous knot and probably secure enough in most circumstances. Unless drawn exceptionally tight, it can be released by pulling one or both ends.

If a *surgeon's knot* is used, the double twist of the first part holds on to any strain better while the second part is made, either as in a normal reef knot or in any of the bow variations.

Those who regularly tie string around packages have their own versions of reef knots. In one type of *parcel knot* a slip reef knot is made and the one bight pushed through, then its own end is used to put a half hitch over it (Fig. 13-2A) and it is pulled close to the center of the knot. Another version has the other end doubled back and put through the bight (Fig. 13-2B). It is drawn tight on it by pulling its own end. A third way is very similar, but a double bow is made and one bight put through the other (Fig. 13-2C), which is tightened on it.

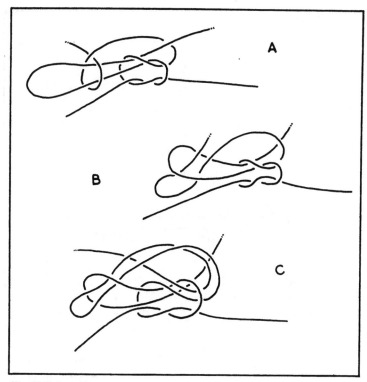

Fig. 13-2. A reef bow can be locked by interweaving the bights: (A) parcel knot; (B) end doubled back and put through the bight; and (C) double bow and one bight.

HITCHED LOOPS

The *packer's knot* uses a figure-eight slip knot and locking is by a half hitch on the end. This serves well in string for a parcel, but if something similar is needed in rope it does not hold well enough to be trusted. Instead, it is better to make a loop, which may be an eye splice or a bowline. Use the end through it to tighten around the spar or bag (Fig. 13-3A).

Hold on to the tautness gained while passing the end around the loop to make a half hitch (Fig. 13-3B). This part of the knot is then the same as a *becket hitch*. Some users prefer to turn the end back around its own standing part and make the half hitch there (Fig. 13-3C). If the loop is long enough, the first method is preferable.

A simple and effective way of getting an equally tight bind has the two parts first twisted like the first part of a reef knot (Fig. 13-3D) and one end is hooked around the other (Fig. 13-3E). There

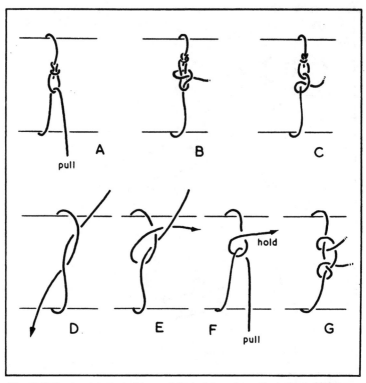

Fig. 13-3. Packages may be drawn tight and then the string locked: (A) tighten around the spar or bag: (B) hold tautness; (C) turn the end; (D) twisted parts; (E) one end hooked around other end; (F) end is pulled back; and (G) tautness held for half hitch.

can be two stages of pulling taut—when the first twist is made and after hooking the end around the other. The hooked piece is held against the object being enclosed with one hand, while the other end is pulled back in the same way as when tightening a packer's knot (Fig. 13-3F). Now all the tautness gained has to be held while a half hitch is made with the end that was pulled (Fig. 13-3G).

JAM KNOTS

Sometimes a binder knot is needed that has enough friction in it to hold, yet it can be slid loose without untying anything. This may happen when a roll of paper or cloth has to be kept reasonably tight, but the roll has to be opened occasionally. The strain involved on the constricting knot is never very great. What is required then is a slip knot with enough turns involved to provide the friction needed.

198

A *buntline hitch* can be used. A clove hitch is made with the end around the standing part, working towards the object enclosed (Fig. 13-4A). This slides tight and holds by bearing against the roll. If that does not grip, it can have an extra turn included so the sliding part is a *magnus hitch* (Fig. 13-4B). Several other ways of providing enough turns to produce friction are possible, but those two should serve all purposes up to the stage where a locking half hitch is needed to resist the pull.

CONSTRICTOR KNOT

Rather surprisingly this knot does not appear in the older manuals. This may be because those books were directed at seamen and they had little need for a knot to draw up the neck of a bag or sack. There was also the problem at sea of conserving materials. Most constricting knots intended for sacks are once-only and the string used is discarded. At sea there might have been no opportunity to replenish supplies for a long time and any waste was discouraged. Millers and others who had to tie sacks would have been using constrictor knots at least as far back in history as the heyday of sailing ships, when contemporary writers were describing knots, but as the writers were usually seamen, they never got around to describing knots used ashore.

There are several knots for constricting where the parts are tucked within the turns. They are distinct from the end-knotted types so far described in this chapter. The one that gets the name of

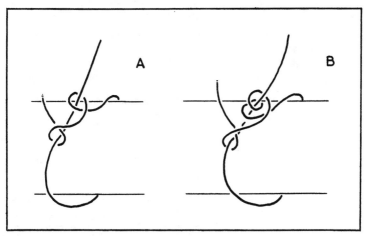

Fig. 13-4. A buntline hitch has enough friction to hold the amount pulled through while it is locked: (A) clove hitch and (B) magnus hitch.

constrictor knot has been used for mail bags and grain sacks for a long time. Of this group, it is probably the best version.

Basically the knot is an overhand knot with an extra turn going over it (Fig. 13-5A). The effect of the covering turn is to provide a lock as it presses on the twisted part. As the ends are pulled to tighten the twists, the top turn is also tightened and the whole effect is to bind or constrict the item encircled. This and other similar knots are shown as if around a spar for the sake of clarity, but in practice, this is a knot to go around cloth or canvas when tightening a bag neck or a roll.

Put a round turn on (Fig. 13-5B), then go around with the part that is on top and twist it into the under part as it meets it (Fig. 13-5C), taking care to twist in the opposite way to the angle of the covering piece and to keep the twisted part under the covering turn as the ends are pulled to tighten the knot.

If the end of the object is accessible, it is possible to make the knot without using the ends of the string. Put on a round turn (Fig. 13-5D), then take the loop of the under part and lift it over the end of the object (Fig. 13-5E). The parts will then fall back together as a complete knot.

Although it is usually expected that the knot will be cut to release it, there is a slip version where the final tuck is made with a bight (Fig. 13-5F).

For extra security, as when using a constrictor knot around a bag neck which is very large in relation to the size of line used, or when using the knot as a whipping, there can be an extra turn outside (Fig. 13-5G). The knot is made by going around twice before twisting the parts together under the crossing turns. With even more turns it may be called a *strangle knot*.

MILLER'S KNOTS

Millers and farmers who have to tie up sacks of grain and flour could use the constrictor knot, but there are some other versions that have been used traditionally.

A *bag knot* finishes like a constrictor knot having part of the overhand knot outside the covering turn. Go around as if starting a clove hitch (Fig. 13-6A), but instead of tucking the end under the crossing part, go over it and under the first part (Fig. 13-6B). That tuck could be made with a bight to allow easy release (Fig. 13-6C).

The knot usually described as a *miller's knot* is like the bag knot, but the working end goes over the crossing part and under the first part the other way (Fig. 13-6D).

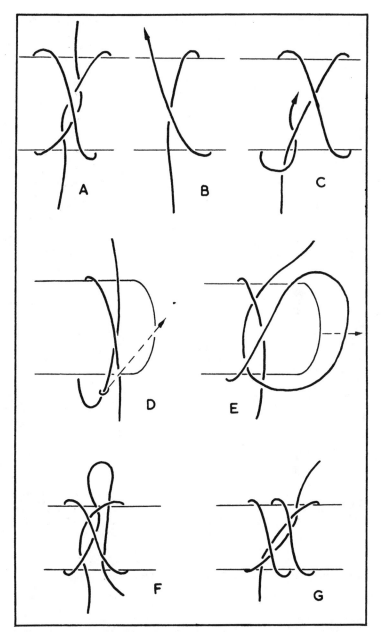

Fig. 13-5. Constrictor knots draw tight and lock as they are tightened: (A) overhand knot with an extra turn; (B) round turn; (C) twist top part into under part; (D) round turns; (E) lift loop over end of objects: (F) final tuck; and (G) extra outside turn.

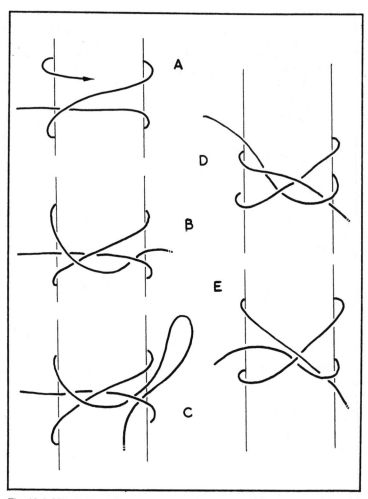

Fig. 13-6. Miller's knots are used to draw the necks of sacks tight: (A) start as for a clove hitch; (B) go over end and under first part; (C) tuck made with bight; (D) Millers' knot; and (E) ground line hitch.

Both knots are made by some users without the working end going over the starting part. The second type is then the same as a *ground line hitch* (Fig. 13-6E).

NET LINE HITCH

This hitch is a version of a constrictor knot particularly intended to pull together two ropes of opposite lay at the head of a large sea fishing net. There are local versions, but in general there

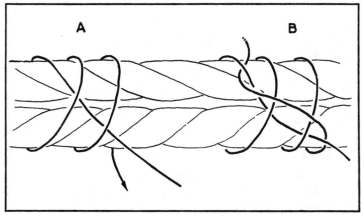

Fig. 13-7. A net line hitch is a version of a constructor knot for pulling ropes together: (A) two to three turns and (B) the end is tucked under the turn of the first part.

are two, and sometimes three, turns over the first part (Fig. 13-7A). The parts are drawn tight, then the end is tucked under the turn of the first part (Fig. 13-7B).

STRAW BINDER KNOT

When corn or straw had to be dried in the field it was stacked in *stooks* formed by several bundles gathered into armsful and tied

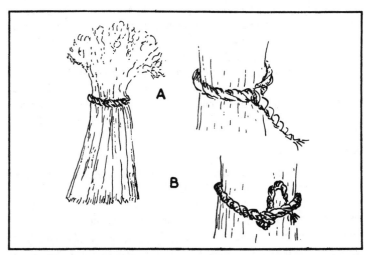

Fig. 13-8. A straw binder knot uses rope made from straw and twisted in the field: (A) ends twisted together and (B) tucked under the turn.

around. Originally the rope for tying was twisted on the spot from straw picked up to make a crude rope long enough to go around the bundle. The ends were twisted together (Fig. 13-8A) and tucked under the turn (Fig. 13-8B). The same knot could be used with a hankerchief or cloth tied around as a temporary bandage. It might also be used with a rolled-down stocking where the rolled edge is pulled out and twisted to tighten around the leg. The twisted part is then tucked inside.

WINDLASS CONSTRICTOR

The name *Spanish windlass* is applied to several ways of getting leverage or applying pressure. Here a similar idea is used to draw things together. It is a particularly appropriate method for larger work where other constricting and binding knots would be unsuitable for use with rope, as when gathering logs together for roping around before loading on a wagon. The windlass does the pulling, but another rope is used for securing.

You need an endless rope, such as would be used for a sling (Fig. 13-9A). It must be long enough to go around the load with a little to spare when doubled. Pass a piece of wood through the loops and start twisting (Fig. 13-9B). This is rather hard on the rope as the friction in the twists is considerable and the piece of wood should be stout enough and long enough to withstand the strain. Although the assembly is often arranged with the wood extending by equal amounts, it is better to have one long end. When the load has been drawn together the end of the wooden lever may be temporarily tied to prevent it from unwinding, either to its own rope (Fig. 13-9C) or to another one (Fig. 13-9D).

This technique has been described as a tourniquet. It was to be put around a limb to stop bleeding, but modern thought on first aid discourages its use and it would be unwise to consider that application.

DEADMAN'S GRIP

The deadman's grip is not strictly knotting, but it is a mechanical arrangement for getting a bundle of saplings pulled together after they have been cut in the forest. The saplings are put together by hand, then two poles linked by a cord are put over them and levered downward to tighten the bundle (Fig. 13-10A). As an alternative to pushing with both hands or feet, one pole may be hooked under a forked post driven into the ground (Fig. 13-10B). This allows one

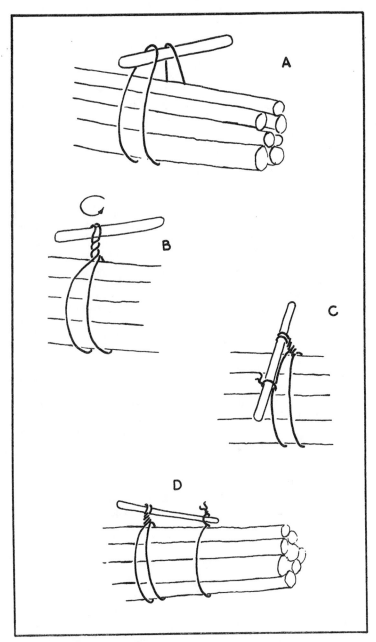

Fig. 13-9. A windless constrictor uses rope twisted with a pole to draw a loose bundle together: (A) endless rope; (B) with wood through loops. start twisting; (C) temporarily tie end of wooden lever; and (D) tied to another rope.

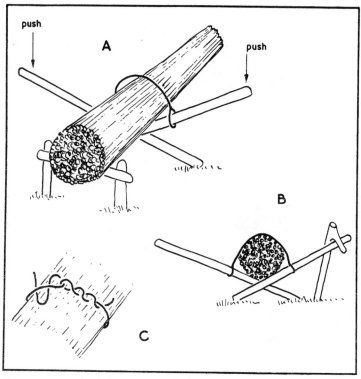

Fig. 13-10. A deadman's grip is an aid to single-handedly drawing bundles of saplings together: (A) tighten the bundle; (B) one pole may be hooked under a forked post; and (C) pulled end looped under its own part.

hand to be used to keep on the pressure while the other one ties the bundle.

Traditionally tying was done with a piece of split sapling, twisted back on itself to make a timber hitch, then the end that had been pulled was looped under its own part (Fig. 13-10C).

Fisherman's Knots  14

The sea fisherman who gathers fish in commercial quantities by netting them uses knots for his ropes which are comparable with those used for other purposes. Some are adapted to his needs and there are local preferences, but in general knots are made that can be cast off later and the rope used again. The ropes used are too valuable for permanent splices and immovable knots to be employed. Most of these knots have been described in earlier chapters alongside variations and similar knots used for other activities.

The line fisherman, whether he is fishing at sea or on a river or lake, uses material which is very much finer and his knotting needs are very different. The line used may be described as gut and the traditional fishing lines were quite thin and smooth. A series of special knots gradually developed to suit these lines, but in recent years synthetic fishing lines have been developed, alongside the development of man-made fibers for ropes and cloth. These are even stronger and finer than the older materials. They are smoother and this, coupled with thinner lines for the same strength as older thicker lines, has caused rethinking about knots for use with them.

If the line is more slippery, knots have to be given a greater number of turns to provide a grip. This leads to complications and some fishermen tie the older knots and put in a few extra turns and hope the whole thing will pull up and lock securely. Fortunately, such a knot will usually seize solidly and be safe enough, but it may finish rather bulky and this could be a nuisance. Knots that have been designed for the material close with a better form and less bulk. The majority of knots described in this chapter are suitable for modern fishing lines, although some of them are of traditional types.

Much historic information on fishing and the knots used goes back to the book *The Compleat Angler,* written in England early in the seventeenth century by Izaak Walton. The development of fishing knots is recorded by a great many writers since then. As with other branches of knotting, names are not always the same. Those used here are believed to be those generally accepted today.

Knots in fishing line are not meant to be undone. They are expected to tighten to a state where they will not slip, then if they are no longer required, the line is cut. If necessary, the cut is on each side of an unwanted knot. Then the parts are knotted again rather than attempting to open a knot and use the ends again. This allows knot formations that would be unacceptable for use in rope. The majority of knots for line fishermen are suitable for their materials, but are not adaptable to larger cords and ropes.

Fishermen's knots are mostly for joining one piece of line to another, sometimes with a branch line leading from the knot, and for forming loops, which are then joined to something else, particularly to hooks.

KNOTS TO LOOPS

A reel line may have its end already made into a loop, then more line has to be joined into it. A sheet bend or becket hitch may be used, either single (Fig. 14-1A) or double or made with a bight (Fig. 14-1B) for increased friction and to allow slipping if the line has to be changed. As it may be better for the free end to point back along the line there is a variation tucked the other way (Fig. 14-1C).

Another way uses a figure-eight knot around the loop (Fig. 14-1D). Many fishermen tend to go for a blood knot (see later) on every possible occasion and the adaption of it here puts several turns around the standing part and tucks the end against the eye (Fig. 14-1E).

A more secure joint is made by using two interlocking loops. The end of the new line is taken through the existing loop and a new loop made around its standing part (Fig. 14-1F). The two loops then pull up so their parts interlock in a form that looks like a reef knot (Fig. 14-1G).

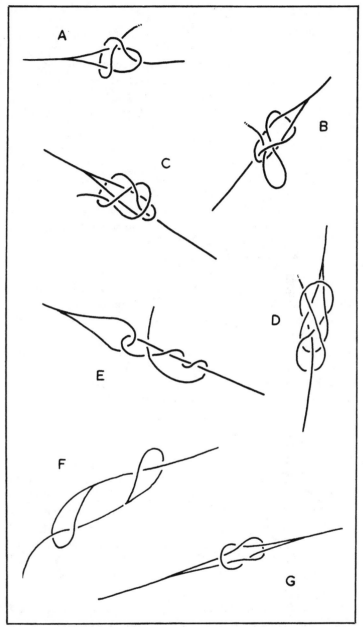

Fig. 14-1. Fishing line knots to loops need many turns to prevent slipping. Two loops can be interlocked: (A) single as double becket hitch: (B) with a bight; (C) tucked free end variation: (I) figure-eight knot around the loop: (E) end tucked against the eye; (F) new loop around standing part; and (G) reef knot likeness.

LOOP KNOTS

The simplest loop in the end of a line is made with an overhand knot in a bight (Fig. 14-2A). With modern materials this may not have enough friction to prevent slipping. A figure-eight knot could be used (Fig. 14-2B). A better formation is a *double overhand loop*, which is made as an overhand knot in the bight, but with an extra turn before pulling tight (Fig. 14-2C). This may also be called a *blood bight knot*.

All of these knots are *leader loops,* but the knot that gets that name is a locked overhand slip knot. An overhand knot is made with the bight pushed through to form the loop (Fig. 14-2D), then the end goes across the knot under the sides of the bight (Fig. 14-2E). This is not very different from a *bowline*. A bowline is an acceptable knot for a loop in fishing line, as it is for larger cordage, but some of the other knots with more turns may be better.

The knot called a *fishermen's knot* by others has its uses for making a loop in the end of a line (Fig. 14-2F). It is made by pushing the bight through an overhand knot and making another overhand knot with the end around the standing part, taking care to form the second knot in the direction that puts its end alongside the standing part and not across it.

Another way of dealing with this avoids the second overhand knot. After pushing through the bight, the end is twisted twice towards the loop (Fig. 14-2G). The overhand knot must be drawn closer before the other part of the knot is pulled to it.

JOINING KNOTS

The *fishermen's knot* is a long established method of joining pieces of fishing line, but in modern, thinner and slippier materials it is advisable to put on a half hitch in each direction after pulling the two overhand knots together (Fig. 14-3A). They should be tucked so the ends conform to the way the overhand knots slope.

Another way of strengthening a fisherman's knot is to use figure-eight knots instead of overhand knots, tucked so the ends come alongside the standing parts (Fig. 14-3B). The slight bulk is not very apparent.

There is a *double fisherman's knot,* also called a *grapevine knot.* It is made by having enough end after tying each overhand knot to go around and knot again (Fig. 14-3C). It can be pulled up so the turns fit against each other and the thickness is no more than with the other knots.

210

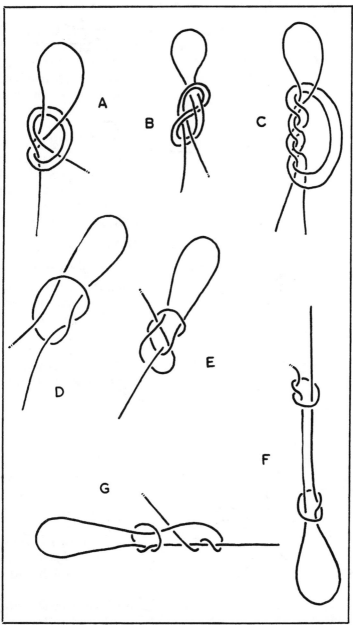

Fig. 14-2. Loops in fishing line can be made with a bight and locked with knots using many turns: (A) overhand knot in a bight; (B) figure-eight knot; (C) put extra turn in before pulling tight; (D) overhand knot; (E) end goes across knot under sides of the bight; (F) fisherman's knot; and (G) end is twisted.

211

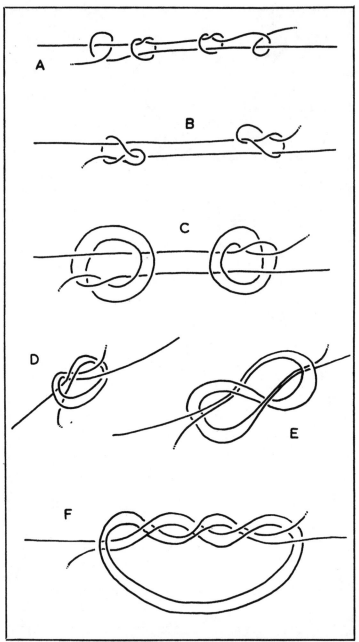

Fig. 14-3. Knots to join fishing line need many turns for security: (A) two overhand knots together; (B) tuck the ends; (C) double fisherman's knot; (D) new end; (E) figure-eight knot; and (F) double overhand knot.

Simple and commonly-used joining knots are made by forming a knot in the end of one line and following it back with the other end. The simplest one is the overhand knot. The new end goes in where the old end comes out and follows around until it comes out alongside the first standing part (Fig. 14-3D). In modern materials this probably does not have enough friction to be trusted. An alternative is a figure-eight knot (Fig. 14-3E). Both may be called *water knots*. A stronger knot for synthetic line is a *double overhand knot*. There is an extra twist in the overhand knot before the second end is followed round (Fig. 14-3F).

BARREL KNOT

This uses two knots sliding on the opposing part in the same way as the fisherman's knot, but the overhand knot around the opposing piece is given an extra turn around it before tucking the end through (Fig. 14-4A). This is repeated with the other end (Fig. 14-4B). With both knots closed and pulled together the effect is a neat parallel cylinder with the minimum bulk and the ends along the line.

BLOOD KNOT

There are many variations of this knot, depending on the numbers of twists and their direction. In all of them the opposing parts are twisted around each other and the ends are brought back to the center where they cross between the two parts. The *barrel knot* is sometimes confused with a simple blood knot when that is

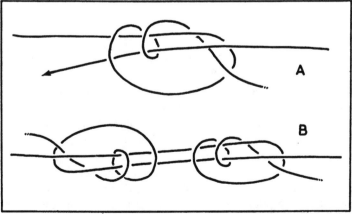

Fig. 14-4. The barrel knot in fishing line uses opposing sliding knots: (A) tuck the end and (B) repeat with the other end.

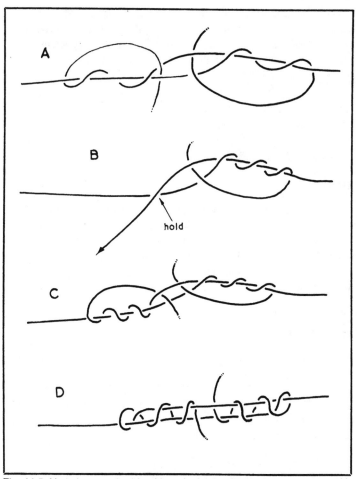

Fig. 14-5. Variations on the blood knot for joining fishing lines use turns with ends crossing at the center: (A) blood knot; (B) hold the crossing; (C) turn the whole thing around; and (D) twists are started away from the center.

made with two turns each way (Fig. 14-5A), but the twists can be seen to be in the other direction. The ends of a blood knot finish at the center and the ends of a barrel knot are along the standing parts.

The more common blood knot has each part twisted around the other, usually three times. Hold the crossing and twist one end around the other and bring the end back to be held through the center (Fig. 14-5B). Turn the whole thing around and do the same the other way (Fig. 14-5C). Each half of this knot and the other versions of it should be the same—both sides of the center. It would be wrong to twist one half one way and one the other, which could happen if the knot is made without turning it to repeat the action the second way. Note how the two ends cross at the center. Pull up slack and tension the knot equally both ways, then cut off the surplus line.

In another version, the twists are started away from the center and made back towards it (Fig. 14-5D), but this knot is not as good. Other variations have the turns in the first version made the other way and varied in number.

DROPPER KNOTS

If there has to be a branch piece off the line so the knot has a T-shape, with one part hanging from the other two parts which are in line, there are adaptions of joining knots and others specially devised.

A blood knot can be used with one of the projecting ends long enough to form the dropper. This is a good way of satisfying the requirements with no fear that the dropper line could come away from the others as it is part of one of them.

Any of the joining knots that use opposing knots sliding on the other part can be opened to allow a dropper to be added. The parts are moved enough to make a gap, then the dropper line has its end knotted so it will not pull through (Fig. 14-6A). The joining knots are then closed on it.

Another way of bringing in the dropper is to put a loop in it and have a knot tied in the line. The loop then goes over the line and the end of the dropper is passed through it in the cow hitch formation (Fig. 14-6B). An advantage of this method is that it helps to keep the dropper and its fly standing out well from the cast.

The makers of synthetic fishing line suggest a variation of the blood knot. In this *blood loop dropper knot* enough of the line is made into a loop and the ends twisted around each other a total of 10 times (Fig. 14-6C). The center gap in the twists is opened with a spike or the point of a pencil and the other side of the loop is pushed through (Fig. 14-6D). The pencil is then put through this projecting loop to hold it in shape while the whole knot is pulled tight to finish with close turns on each side of this part. The dropper is attached by any of the knots for joining to a loop (Fig. 14-6E).

A common way of attaching a dropper is to tie its end around the casting line. It has a knot in it to prevent the dropper from sliding along. Any knot is made in the cast and an overhand knot is made with the end of the dropper around the line above it (Fig. 14-7A) in the direction that brings the parts along the line. A half hitch is put

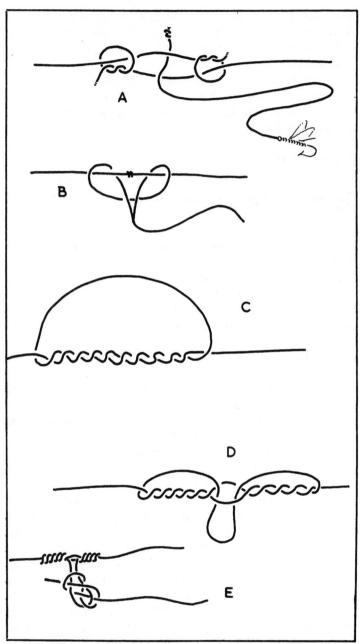

Fig. 14-6. Dropper knots allow branch pieces off the main fishing line: (A) knotted dropper line; (B) loop goes over the line; (C) blood loop dropper knot; (D) loop is pushed through; and (E) dropper is attached.

around the cast beside it (Fig. 14-7B) and pulled tight against the knot. It could be made with the half hitch first to avoid having to pass through the fly on the end of the dropper.

It is possible to take the end of the dropper through an overhand knot in the cast and finish it as a fisherman's knot around the cast (Fig. 14-7C). A variation on this takes the end through and uses a bulkier knot on its end (Fig. 14-7D) to provide increased resistance to the slippery parts of the line releasing.

One way of attaching a dropper or snell avoids having to use the end of the cast to pass through and tie a knot in it. Make a large eye in the cast and take the dropper through it (Fig. 14-8A), then around the standing part of the cast, so the actual formation within the knot is a sheet bend (Fig. 14-8B), which will be seen when it is drawn tight.

Another dropper knot uses an overhand knot in the cast, then the end of the dropper goes through the twisted part of it (Fig.

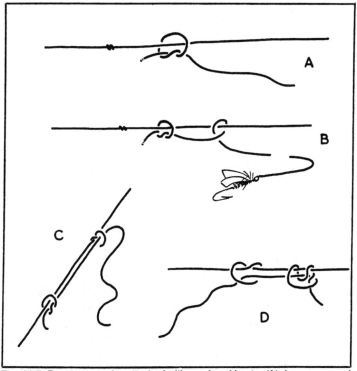

Fig. 14-7. Droppers can be attached with overhand knots: (A) dropper around the line; (B) half hitch pulled tight; (C) fisherman's knot around the cast; and (D) bulkier knot on the end.

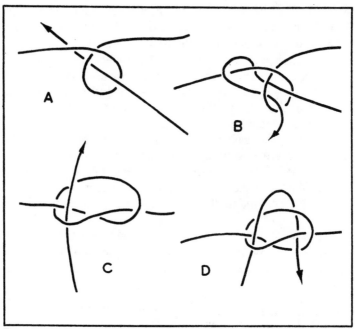

Fig. 14-8. A dropper can be attached to a fishing line by a sheet bend or by looping through an overhand knot: (A) large eye in the cast; (B) sheet bend; (C) dropper knot using overhand knot; and (D) end of dropper goes down through twisted part.

14-8C), over its loop and down through the other side of the twisted part (Fig. 14-8D).

Several of the loop knots that could be made without using the ends of rope that were described earlier can be used in fishing line. They provide a loop projecting from the side of the cast, to which the dropper can be separately knotted. They also have the advantage of avoiding having to pull through what could be considerable length of line to form the knot.

The loop which older books describe for the purpose is known to others as the *man-harness knot*. Start to twist the line as if to make an overhand knot, but at the point where an end would have to be pulled through, grasp the other side of the knot and pull it through the gap (Fig. 14-9A) so the knot closes with a loop projecting from the side (Fig. 14-9B). The size of the loop is governed by the amount first turned to form the knot.

The *middleman's knot* is another way of making a loop without using the ends, but it is better when the two projecting parts lead away close to each other than when they extend in opposite direc-

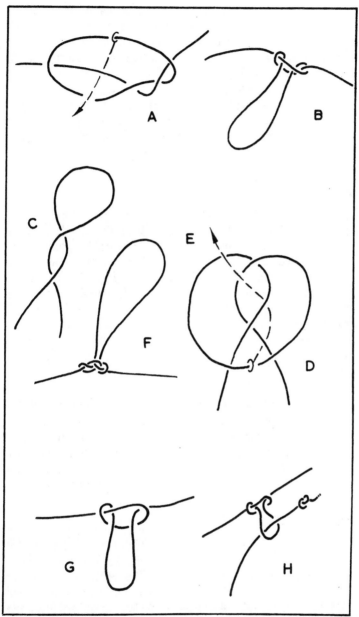

Fig. 14-9. Droppers can be attached to loops made in the same way as some intended for larger lines: (A) pull side of knot through gap; (B) knot should close with loop projecting from the side; (C) lineman's loop; (D) loop of line is turned back; (E) bottom of bight pulled up through the crossing; (F) knot is tightened; (G) overhead slip knot; and (H) pass knotted end of the dropper.

tions, as they have to in a cast. The rather similar *lineman's loop* is better. A loop of the line is twisted (Fig. 14-9C) and turned back (Fig. 14-9D). The bottom of the bight is pulled up through the crossing (Fig. 14-9E) and the knot is tightened with its ends in opposite directions (Fig. 14-9F).

One of the simplest ways of adding a dropper to a loop is to make an overhand slip knot in the cast (Fig. 14-9G) and pass the knotted end of the dropper through it (Fig. 14-9H). There is a slight risk of the slip knot pulling open in one direction, but in fishing line pulled taut, the parts should lock securely enough.

SWIVEL HITCHES

When a swivel is to be included in a line, the knots to the metal eyes at each of the swivel could be any of these described for making loops. It may be sufficient to use the first knot of a fisherman's knot and put a half hitch above it (Fig. 14-10A). A long loop in the line can be passed through in the cow hitch manner (Fig. 14-10B) and this allows the swivel to be taken out without cutting the line. A bight can go through the ring and be half-knotted, so pulling the end will release the knot (Fig. 14-10C).

A more complicated swivel hitch has a round turn through the eye, with the middle of the round turn held out so the end may go through it, as it does in an anchor bend (Fig. 14-10D) with two turns towards the ring (Fig. 14-10E).

Another knot claimed to give maximum strength in synthetic material is a *four-turn half blood knot*. As its name indicates, this is made like one half of a joining blood knot. After going through the metal eye, the end is wound four times around the standing part (Fig. 14-10F), then it is taken down and through the turn near the ring (Fig. 14-10G). It pulls tight neatly (Fig. 14-10H).

KNOTS TO HOOKS

Fish hooks are in many forms and many sizes. All have barbed ends and need careful handling. Because of this, many knots for attaching line to them are formed further back on the line and manipulated over the hook after the tucks have been made. This avoids having to work the line in close proximity to the dangerous point. Almost all hooks have eyes set at an angle so the standing part of the line goes through them parallel with the wire of the hook. A hook without an eye is a *tad hook* with a flattened and broadened end.

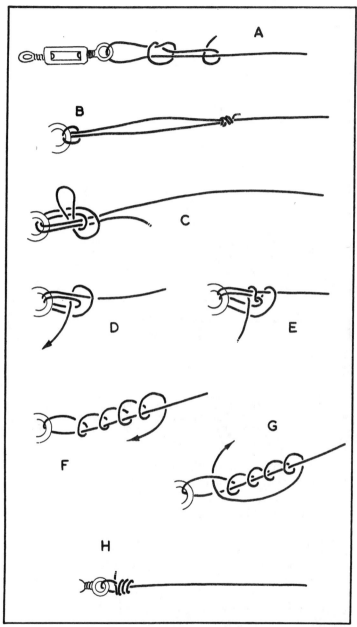

Fig. 14-10. Ring knots may be adapted for attaching fishing line to swivels: (A) half hitch above fisherman's knot; (B) cowhitch manner; (C) half knotted bight; (D) anchor bend; (E) turn; (F) four-turn half blood knot; (G) end is taken through turn near the ring and (H) pull tight neatly.

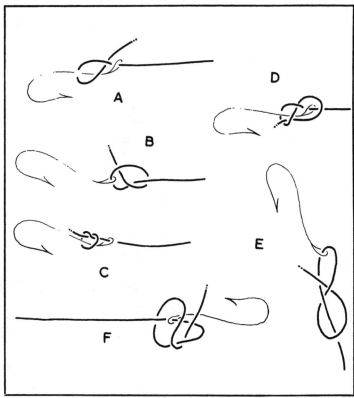

Fig. 14-11. Hook hitches have to provide ample turns to prevent the line from pulling out of the eye of a fishing hook: (A) half hitch; (B) overhand knot; (C) overhand knot pushed over the eye; (D) figure-eight knot on the hook; (E) tying a figure-eight knot; and (F) line pulled back through hook eye.

The simplest knot to a hook with an eye is a half hitch (Fig. 14-11A). If an overhand knot is made in the line above the eye (Fig. 14-11B) and then pushed over the eye (Fig. 14-11C), a jammed half hitch is formed. Other knots for attaching hooks are developments of this.

A half hitch (Fig. 14-11A) can have the end follow round and pass back alongside the hook to make a *figure-eight knot* on the hook (Fig. 14-11D). This can be made by tying a figure-eight knot in the line above the hook (Fig. 14-11E). The line is then pulled back through the hook eye at the same tim   as the knot is pushed over the hook (Fig. 14-11F).

The *Turle knot* is named after its inventor. The line goes through the eye and is allowed to project, where an overhand slip knot is made (Fig. 14-12A). The loop of this is passed over the hook

222

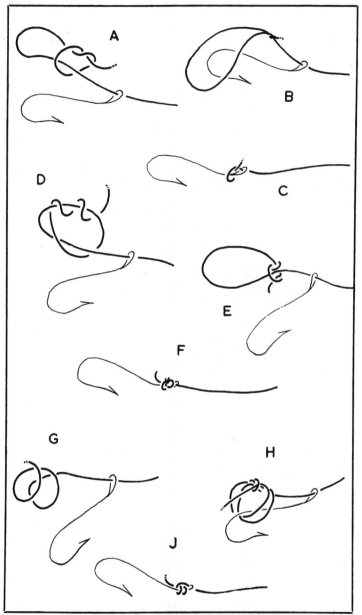

Fig. 14-12. If the parts of a hook hitch can be made away from the hook, there is more space to work and less risk from the hook: (A) overhand slip knot; (B) loop is passed over the hook; (C) knot drawn tight; (D) two-turn Turle knot; (E) loop is held open; (F) knot is tightened around neck; (G) two-circle Turle knot; (H) knot over loops with the end; (I) turns of the knot are below the eye.

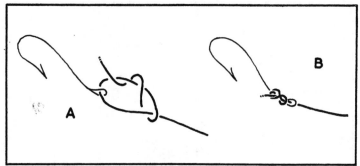

Fig. 14-13. An overhand knot converts to a simple hook hitch: (A) double overhand knot; and (B) close around the neck.

(Fig. 14-12B) and the knot is drawn tight around the neck of the hook (Fig. 14-12C). This differs from most of the other knots in having to pass the line over the hook. If there is a fly formed on the hook, this needs care to avoid damaging the fly.

For more slippery modern line there is a *two-turn Turle knot.* The line goes through the eye and is twisted twice back on its own loop (Fig. 14-12D). The twisted part is drawn close, but the loop is held open (Fig. 14-12E) so the hook and the free end of line alongside it can be pushed through and the knot tightened around the neck of the hook (Fig. 14-12F).

An alternative is the *two-circle Turle knot.* The line through the eye is turned into a pair of loops, one over the other (Fig. 14-12G). Knot over these loops with the end (Fig. 14-12H) and draw tight so the end finishes alongside the hook with the turns of the knot below the eye (Fig. 14-12J).

There are several versions of overhand knots with extra turns. A double *overhand knot* is given the extra twist around the standing part above the hook eye (Fig. 14-13A) and this is pushed over the eye to close around its neck (Fig. 14-13B).

A *Wood knot*, also named after its inventor, is something like a figure-eight. The end half hitches around the neck of the hook (Fig. 14-14A), then continues around the standing part to tuck alongside the hook (Fig. 14-14B). The whole knot is pushed to below the eye where it settles to neat turns as the line is drawn tight (Fig. 14-14C).

For larger hooks it is more common to use some sort of loop to the eye. In one method for salmon flies, the end of the line goes through the eye, around the neck of the hook and back through the eye (Fig. 14-15A) to form an overhand knot around the standing part (Fig. 14-15B). This should pull tight against the eye. If there

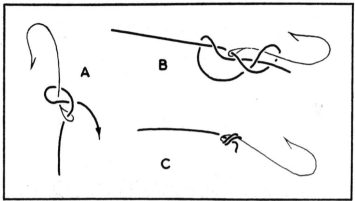

Fig. 14-14. A wood knot converts a figure-eight to a hook hitch: (A) end half hitches around the neck; (B) tucks alongside the hook; and (C) line is drawn tight.

seems a risk that it would pull through the eye, a figure-eight knot could be used instead of the overhand knot as it finishes with slightly more bulk.

Another way of attaching a long loop is to pass it through the eye and back over the end of the hook (Fig. 14-15C) to finish as a

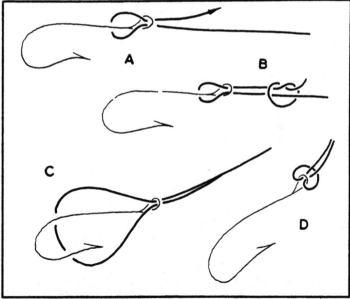

Fig. 14-15. Large hooks are more securely attached with an eye in the line: (A) method for salmon flies; (B) overhand knot around standing part; (C) attaching a long loop; and (D) cow hitch.

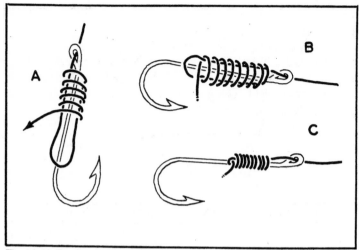

Fig. 14-16. The Domhof knot grips a large hook with a great many turns: (A) tight whipping of eight turns; (B) last tuck projects towards the turn of the hook; and (C) bring knot close to the eye.

cow hitch (Fig. 14-15D). More likely it is called a *lark's head knot* in this case.

The *Dumhof knot* gets its grip by a large number of turns around the hook. Although it is for attachment to a hook with an eye, its formation is not very different from variations on knots described by Izaak Walton for joining line to tad hooks. In this case, take the line through the eye and along the back of the hook far enough to double back and put on what is, in effect, a tight whipping of about eight turns (Fig. 14-16A). These turns go over the line and the hook, with the last tuck through the loop of the standing part projecting towards the turn of the hook (Fig. 14-16B). Pull the standing part back through the eye to draw up surplus line and bring the knot close to the eye (Fig. 14-16C). Exactly the same formation can be used on a hook without an eye, then the knot is tightened before it is slid up towards the broadened end of the wire.

If tad hooks are found still in use they are of the larger types and the line is fairly stout. Some traditional knots were suitable for the less-slippery older lines, but for modern material on hooks without eyes, it is advisable to choose knots with many turns to provide enough friction for a grip.

The simple attachment is a clove hitch with the end taken up to join into the standing part with a bowline (Fig. 14-17A). If the loop is already there, it can be taken around the hook and its end passed over the top of the hook (Fig. 14-17B). Another way has a lark's head knot over the top of the hook and a half hitch put below it (Fig. 14-17C) and drawn close up to it.

A single line can be attached with a clove hitch and a half hitch put below it (Fig. 14-17D). Like the other hitches so far described, the pull does not come directly at the top of the hook, so the hook may not hang upright. This probably does not matter as when a fish is caught the strain comes sufficiently in line to retain the catch. If

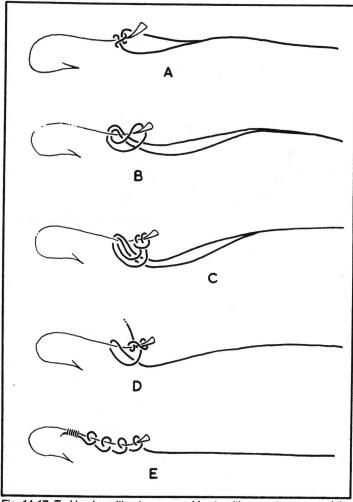

Fig. 14-17. Tad hooks, without eyes, need knots with many turns around the stem of the hook: (A) simple attachments; (B) loop is passed over the top of the hook; (C) lark's head knot; (D) single line attachment; and (E) several half hitches are put on towards the top.

Table 14-1. Percentage Strengths of Fishermen's Knots.

Percentage Strengths of Fishermen's Knots.	
Tucked sheet bend	65%
Two loops	85%
Blood bight knot	74%
Blood loop dropper knot	80%
Four-turn half blood knot	85%
Two-turn Turle knot	85%
Two-circle Turle knot	88%
Domhof knot	75%

the pull is to come from the end, the *Domhof knot* (Fig. 15-16) is one of the best to use. Another way has the line seized around the hook far enough down for several half hitches to be put on towards the top (Fig. 14-17E).

RELATIVE STRENGTHS OF FISHERMAN'S KNOTS

Knotted line is weaker than unknotted line. That is a fact and no knot has been devised that does not weaken the line. Tests on several knots devised for synthetic fishing line have been published. Some of these strengths quoted as percentages of the unknotted rope are found in Table 14-1.

Climber's Knots  15

A climber is more dependent on knots for his own safety than most other users of knots. Climbing should never be an individual activity. There should always be two or three in a party and they should be linked by ropes when tackling anything hazardous, whether it is a comparatively small rock climb or an assault on a mountain. This means that ropes and the knots used with them are of great importance to a climber and his concern with them may go much further than many other users of rope. Other users might make a mistake in the choice of a rope or knot and suffer inconvenience or discomfort, but there is not usually a risk to their life.

At one time climbing ropes were made of natural fibers, like all other ropes. They were the best in their class, but they were made of short fibers so they had a hairy surface that was far from smooth and this allowed a variety of knots to be used with certainty of holding. Most of the knots used by climbers were the same as those used by seamen and others. Much of the knotting information used by climbers with natural fiber ropes came from the lore of the sea. The science of knotting afloat was adapted to the needs of the climber, with little alteration.

The coming of synthetic fiber climbing ropes has caused a considerable amount of rethinking. Some earlier knots still have uses, but there are a few new knots which have been devised to particularly suit synthetic ropes. Of the many synthetics it is nylon which has proven particularly attractive to climbers. It is more elastic than the others. In other applications, such as a halliard for a sail, where a positive tension is needed, this elasticity is a disadvantage, but for climbing some springiness in the ropes serves to absorb shock.

The shock-absorbing quality due to the elasticity is particularly valued because tests have shown that a nylon rope will sustain five times the falling load of the best natural fiber rope of the same size. Other advantages in climbing are: it is lighter, both wet and dry; it does not suffer from rot or mildew; frost does not weaken it; its flexibility is better, both wet and dry. Although more costly, the useful life of nylon is much greater.

The only real snag with nylon rope is the possibility of it melting if it gets too hot. It begins to deteriorate at 400°F. The only time there is a risk of these temperatures being reached is when there is friction across the rope. Friction due to the rope slipping lengthwise over something could never raise the temperature enough to matter, but suppose one rope under load passed quickly through a loop of another rope. Rubbing on one spot of the loop could heat it to a dangerous level. The risk is slight, but climbing knots and arrangements of ropes have to be planned so there is no risk of excessive local friction. Where a rope has to run through something it is now common to have it slide through a metal snap link or *karibiner*. Instead of the moving rope passing through a rope loop, the karibiner is clipped on to the sling and the rope slides through that.

WAIST BAND

It is usual for a climber to coil a rope around his waist and despite the general change to nylon, some users still prefer this to be hemp or other natural fiber rope. In any case it would be thinner than the climbing rope—¼-inch diameter is suitable and the total length may be as much as 20 feet, taken around as many times as necessary. This is a useful spare rope and the multiple turns lessen the shock on the body in the event of a fall while linked to a rope with a karibiner.

It is common to join the ends of the rope around the waist with a reef knot, but the ends are tucked through the rope for security (Fig. 15-1). Like all other climbing ropes, this is three-stranded and the ends are well whipped as well as heat-sealed. The reef knot has no other use in climbing.

END LOOPS

Many of the knots for making loops described earlier in the book can be used at the end of a climbing rope. The *bowline* is as

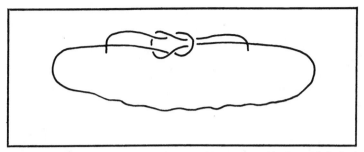

Fig. 15-1. A climber's waist band has its reef knot secured by the ends tucked through the rope.

suitable here as in ropework for many other purposes. Some climbers appear to be satisfied with an *overhand loop* tied on a bight (Fig. 15-2A), but tests have shown that this knot formation weakens more than some other knots and it tends to seize so it is difficult to undo. In nylon rope the reserve of strength should be more than enough for the weakening effect of this, or any other knot.

Kenneth Tarbuck is a climber who has carried out research into knots for climbers using nylon ropes and his recommended *Tarbuck knot* is very different from other loop knots, but it is claimed to weaken the rope less than any of them. It uses the friction of many turns around the standing part to provide a grip. It is made in a position where it still has space to slide and close onto the karibiner or other attachment point. The friction on a normal climbing rope is claimed to be enough to take the load of a man, but in an emergency the ability to slide acts as a shock absorber.

The arrangement of turns is important. The end is brought to the standing part and round turns are put on towards the loop (Fig. 15-2B). It is covered as it returns to the standing part above the first turns, to make a turn (Fig. 15-2C). This is followed by tucking the end towards the loop (Fig. 15-2D). Draw the parts together firmly so all the turns are close around the standing part (Fig. 15-2E). With any normal load on the loop the knot should stay put wherever it is made. The inventor suggests that for the normal connection to a karibiner the turns of the knot should be left about 1 foot up the standing part, where they would stay under normal loads, but would slide to act as a shock absorber in an emergency.

If the *Tarbuck knot* is used to form a loop around the waist, it has to be prevented from closing tightly and performing as a noose in a fall. A stop is arranged by passing the end through the standing part (Fig. 15-2F) at a point that would allow the loop to close only far enough for it to still be a comfortable fit.

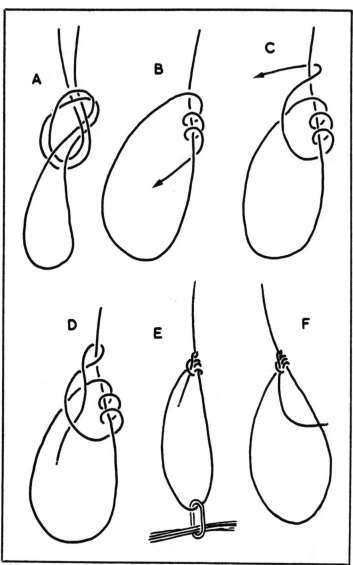

Fig. 15-2. An end loop may be a simple overhand knot or the Tarbuck knot, which can be adjusted: (A) overhand loop; (B) arrangement of turns; (C) turn; (D) tucking the end; (E) draw the parts together firmly; and (F) a stop.

MIDDLEMAN LOOPS

In the past the need to join in another man when the two ends were already knotted to other climbers was taken care of by some of the loops described in Chapter 9. The *middleman's knot* was the one with the name, but its tendency to close up when the load comes in one direction has always made it undesirable. The *man-harness knot* could also be upset and tighten with uneven loading. The *lineman's knot* is a better one.

There is an adaption of the manharness knot, called the *Alpine butterfly knot*. From its name this is another climber's way of putting in a loop for a middle man. The twist in the loop may reduce the risk of slip. The rope is taken as if to tie an overhand knot, up to the stage where one part would be pulled through (Fig. 15-3A). Instead, a twist is put in the opposite side of the loop (Fig. 15-3B) and this is passed through where the end would have gone (Fig. 15-3C). Keep the twisted part within the knot as it is tightened (Fig. 15-3D) or the knot will finish as an ordinary man-harness knot.

With nylon rope there is a preference for attaching a middle man with separate ropes. One rope goes between the first and second man and another goes between him and the third man—all

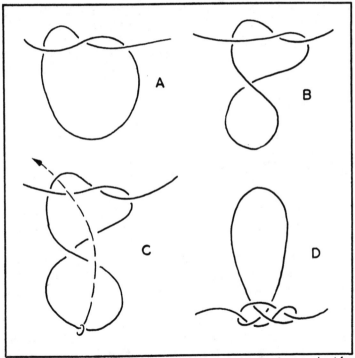

Fig. 15-3. The Alpine butterfly knot is an adaption of a man-harness knot for putting in a loop for a middle man in a climbing rope: (A) take rope as if for an overhand knot; (B) put twist in opposite side of loop; (C) pass it through where end would have gone; (D) keep twisted part within the knot.

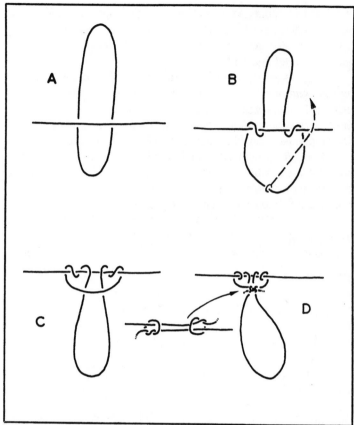

Fig. 15-4. A Prusik knot is used to join in a middle man with a separate loop: (A) loop is put across the man rope; (B) one part is wrapped; (C) pull up with the projecting loop; and (D) formed Prusik knot.

the attachments being by karibiners to waist bands. It would then be possible for climbers to change places merely by unclipping karibiners.

If another man has to tie into a continuous rope a knot in that rope can be avoided by joining in another rope in a way that uses the quality of friction due to many turns that can be employed with nylon rope.

The second rope should be in the form of an endless loop or sling, and preferably supple. It need not be very long, as it will be attached to a karibiner and not usually around the man's waist. A climber calls this a *Prusik knot*. In fact it is the same arrangement as has been described for using a strop to sling tackle from a horizontal spar.

234

The loop is put across the main rope (Fig. 15-4A) and one part wrapped around so as to pass through the other part (Fig. 15-4B) and to pull up with the projecting loop ready to connect with a karibiner (Fig. 15-4C).

Ideally the loop would be made up with a rope having its ends spliced together. If it has to be made by knotting the ends together, this can be done with a *fisherman's knot*. When this is pulled up and the Prusik knot formed, arrange the joint to come on the part of the loop over the extension to the karibiner (Fig. 15-4D).

Friction will hold the Prusik knot in place, but putting the hand over it allows it to be moved to a new position. In this way the amount of rope between the climbers can be varied. However, for a considerable move, it is better to slacken the knot first.

ANCHOR KNOT

If a climber needs to anchor himself to a rock he has to use the rope linking him to another man in most circumstances. To do this the rope from his own karibiner goes around the anchorage, then back in a bight to his waist rope. After tucking under, the end of the bight goes over the other parts (Fig. 15-5A) and is twisted in a figure-eight fashion back through the turn around the waist rope (Fig. 15-5B).

If a separate rope is used to an anchorage, it may be a sling made up with its ends joined with a fisherman's knot (Fig. 15-5C). Tarbuck also suggests his knot for making an adjustable sling. In this case the end to be knotted is brought around so it points towards the loop and not up the standing part, then the knot is made in the reverse direction (Fig. 15-5D). The knot will hold under strain at whatever position it is put to vary the size of the sling, but there should be a knot tied in the end of the rope as a stopper (Fig. 15-5E) to prevent the Tarbuck knot from sliding off in an emergency.

EMERGENCY KNOTS

If a mountaineer has to perform a rescue and a patient has to be brought down, he may have to do what he can with the facilities available. As he is likely to be in a situation where there is nothing of any use except what he has with him, he may have to use rope for purposes where other things would be better at normal levels.

For lowering a person any of the double loops has possibilities. If one loop is to go under the knees and the other under the armpits, the *bowline on a bight* or one of the other versions with the two loops

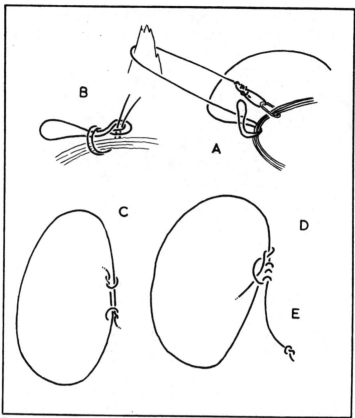

Fig. 15-5. A climber's anchor knot can be made in the main rope or a sling can be used: (A) end of bight goes over other parts; (B) twisted in figure-eight fashion; (C) ends joined with a fisherman's knot; (D) knot is made in reverse direction; and (E) knot in end serves as a stopper.

in the same direction is suitable. If it would be safer to have one loop around each thigh, the *Spanish bowline* is better as its loops project at opposite sides. In both cases, if the man is sensible he holds the standing part of the rope. If he is insensible, there could be a half hitch under his armpits above the loop knot or one of the middleman knots there would be less constricting. The three-loop knot that is most appropriate has been described (Fig. 8-8).

ALPINE BASKET

A major problem comes if the patient is a stretcher case, but there is no stretcher or anything that could make one, except rope. This is a way of using rope to immobilize a patient to reduce the risk of further injury. Padding should be used between the rope and the body, particularly where there is any injury. A considerable length of rope is used up in dealing with a normal adult. Allow about 120 feet.

Lay the rope on the ground in a series of S-bends that are about 20 inches near the feet and about 40 inches across at the upper part of the body (Fig. 15-6A). Leave some surplus rope at each end. The patient is laid over the rope and the projecting loops brought up around him. Working from the feet up, each loop passes through the opposite one. Slack is gathered and pulled through as these tucks are made, so the rope tightens as it goes (Fig. 15-6B).

When the body is enclosed from the ankles to the armpits, take the end through the loops and over the shoulders (Fig. 15-6C). Finish through the top loops, where it can be knotted. It may be needed for lowering. At the foot end use up the rope there to keep the ankles together, with loops around the feet as well (Fig. 15-6D).

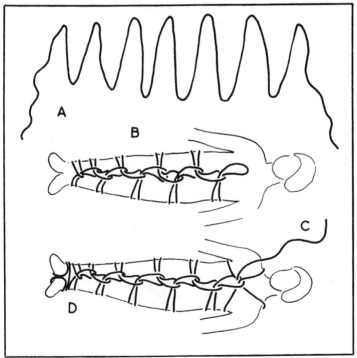

Fig. 15-6. An Alpine basket is a way to use rope to support an injured person who has to be transported: (A) series of S-bends; (B) rope tightens as it goes; (C) end goes through the loops and over the shoulders; and (D) loops around the feet.

If the patient has to be carried, slings can be passed under him. If he has to be lowered, the load should be taken from the ropes in front of his chest.

RELEASE HITCHES

If a climber has to come down a rope and then recover his rope, he has to make sure the rope is safe to climb down, yet it has to be released after he has gotten down. He may actually climb down the rope or he may abseil, using a sling sliding on the rope. If the rope is twice as long as the height to be dealt with, it is best to use the doubled rope, if the upper anchorage is something that will take the rope without the need for a knot there. The ends would then be tied together and may be held by someone at the lower level. Untying the ends and pulling one of them would bring down the rope.

If the upper end has to be knotted and the rope is long enough for a second end to reach the ground or lower level, one of the slippery hitches can be used, with a tucked bight locking the knot and a pull on the end freeing this to allow the knot to come away. The *highwayman's hitch* and others have already been described. There is a choice between knots with a bight around the anchorage and those where the rope has to be pulled around it after releasing. The second type gives a reserve of safety, particularly if someone at the lower level holds both ends. Failure of the knot still leaves the rope around the anchorage, instead of coming away, as it would with a bight. A simple knot with the rope around is a *slipped buntline hitch*. Turns are taken as if to half-hitch around the standing part (Fig. 15-7A) and a tuck taken with the bight above the turns (Fig. 15-7B). Close the knot tight and with the standing part already in the direction it has to be for the climb down. It is unwise to load any rope to a rock so it pulls around to take up the direction of the load because it may become frayed or cut.

If the rope is only long enough to reach the distance required in a single length there cannot be any knot that requires a second end to be pulled to release it. The attachment has to be released by shaking the single end of rope. Any knot that allows this will not be up to the usual standard of safety, so salvaging a rope in this way should be regarded as an emergency rather than a normal practice.

The *precipice knot* is made by putting a knot in the end of the rope and taking a turn over it (Fig. 15-7C). Under the steady load of a careful climber the knot should hold, but flicking the free rope from the bottom will release it.

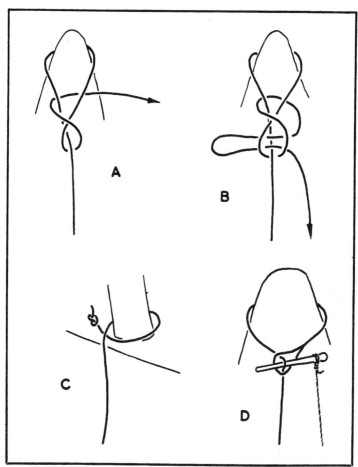

Fig. 15-7. If a rope has to be released after climbing down there has to be a hitch that can be pulled free: (A) turns are taken as if to half hitch; (B) tuck is taken with the bight above the turns; (C) precipice knot; and (D) piece of wood locks the rope.

If there is a piece of light line or even string or stout thread available the rope can be secured with a *toggled loop*. The end of the rope may have an eye spliced in it or a loop can be made with a bowline. A piece of wood goes across to lock the rope (Fig. 15-7D). To release the rope, the toggle is pulled out. So long as the second line is strong enough to do that, it does not have to withstand any other strains. The toggle can be any piece of wood, providing the section through the rope parts is smooth enough to slide out when pulled.

Belaying
and Making Fast

A seaman rarely uses the word *tie*. If he attaches a rope to anything, he *makes it fast*. What he is doing when he attaches the rope to something solid, he describes as *belaying*. It is a useful comprehensive word that includes tying to all sorts of things other than another rope. To be strictly correct, a rope is belayed when turns are taken around the object and they are made fast when something is done to prevent them from unwinding.

SECURITY

In many cases security is provided by half hitches. As with many knots, a number of turns provide the friction that is almost all that is needed to prevent slipping, but a final half hitch or other locking tuck holds them in place. In some cases the design of the solid object provides a lock in itself.

In recent years, with the development of racing sailing craft, there have been a large variety of cleats, bollards and similar things for securing ropes becoming available. In many cases these are refined versions of earlier types and in other cases they are ingenious ways of providing locking without the need for knotting, usually by including a taper that pinches the rope which can be released by pulling away from it. In these cases the only knotting is the provision of a stopper knot in the end of the rope to prevent it from running away. With the other type there is still a need for locking hitches similar to those on traditional attachment points.

240

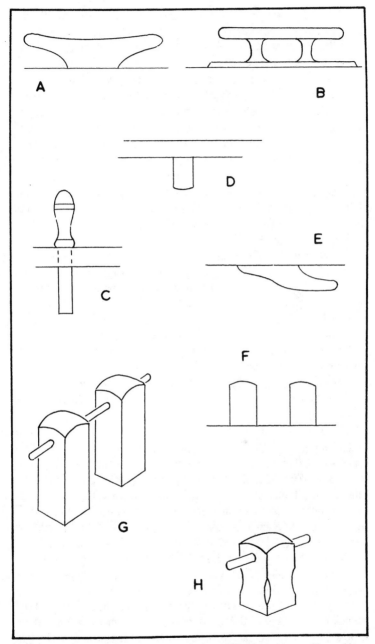

Fig. 16-1. Cleats, belaying pins, bitts and other solid objects are used for making ropes fast: (A) cleats; (B) bollard; (C) belaying pins; (D) projecting fixed peg; (E) thumb cleat; (F) bitts; (G) stag shorn; and (H) samson post.

Basically there are *cleats* with two horns (Fig. 16-1A). These come in a variety of shapes. Larger ones may be mooring *bollards*, but if there are two horns, the method of attaching the rope is the same. Sometimes a bollard may have a hole in it (Fig. 16-1B) and that allows some other methods of belaying. Less common today are *belaying pins*. Traditionally the pin had a turned top and a parallel or slightly tapered round lower part through a hole in a rail or thwart (Fig. 16-1C). In a sailing ship the belaying pins were not fixed in their holes, then they could be knocked out in an emergency to spill the rope attached to them, no matter how complicated the way it was made fast. In some modern arrangements the pin is plain and parallel, fixed in the rail so it projects an equal amount above and below. Sometimes there is only a fixed peg projecting below (Fig. 16-1D). There may also be a *thumb cleat,* which is like half of a normal cleat (Fig. 16-1E).

Cleats are usually screwed or bolted to a wooden surface, but they may be lashed in the rigging, possibly for a light flag halliard. At the other extreme are *bitts,* which are posts standing up, usually in pairs for rope to be worked around in a similar manner to a cleat (Fig. 16-1F). There may be an iron rod through the bitts, called a *stags horn* or *norman* (Fig. 16-1G) to give something extra for turns to be taken around. A single post with or without a bar through it may be called a *samson post* (Fig. 16-1H). Bitts and samson posts are used in the bows of a boat for attaching the anchor cable or a towing hawser, but they may be used ashore and elsewhere when a strong roping point is needed.

A single hitch is the simplest attachment under part of a belaying pin (Fig. 16-2A) or one horn of a cleat (Fig. 16-2B). This makes a safe hold under a steady strain. Even better is another turn around the other side of the cleat (Fig. 16-2C) or the pin. Making the hitch with a bight allows quick release (Fig. 16-2D).

Rope may be taken around a cleat or pin and then in a S or Z form, depending on whether it is a right-handed or left-handed person doing it. The direction does not matter. The horn opposite to the direction of pull is enclosed first (Fig. 16-2E). Other turns are put on in a figure-eight manner (Fig. 16-2F). The number of turns depend on the load, but the final turn should be made into a half hitch, preferably on the horn or end of the pin towards the pull of the standing part (Fig. 16-2G). A belaying pin normally has to be upright, but if a cleat can be angled in relation to the load, as it might be on a flag pole to take a halliard in a direction along the pole, it provides a better lead to the standing part as the first strain is taken

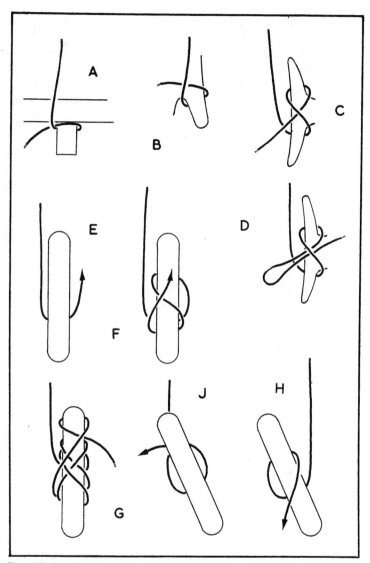

Fig. 16-2. Security when belaying is by hitching with or without several turns: (A) single hitch; (B) one horn of cleat; (C) turn on other side of cleat; (D) hitch with a bight; (E) horn is enclosed; (F) figure-eight turns; (G) final turn; (H) belaying pin; and (J) risk of jamming.

(Fig. 16-2H), but if the rope is started the wrong way, there is a risk of jamming when casting off (Fig. 16-2J).

A direct pull to the cleat or pin often has to be accepted, but if it is possible, a turn around or through something else, allows a better pull and tension to be given. This may be a *fairlead*. In its simplest form this is a piece of wood with a hole through it (Fig. 16-3A), although there are more elaborate arrangements. A wooden or metal thumb cleat may be used (Fig. 16-3B). The line then leads to this and from it to the cleat or pin (Fig. 16-3C). The turn through the cleat or fairlead provides friction to hold on to the strain while turns are put to the main attachment.

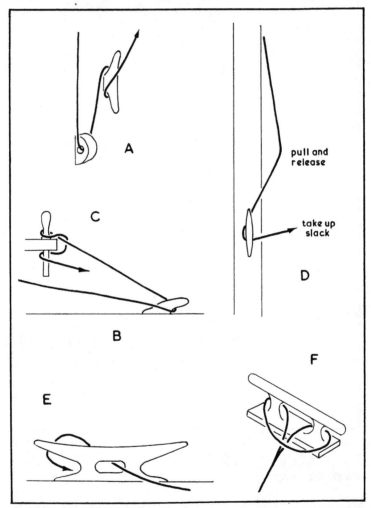

Fig. 16-3. The direction of pull may be altered with a fairlead. Extra tension can be obtained by swigging on the line: (A) fairlead; (B) metal thumb cleat; (C) line leads to cleat; (D) extra amount is pulled on the end; (E) line may go through the hole and (F) it is then turned back.

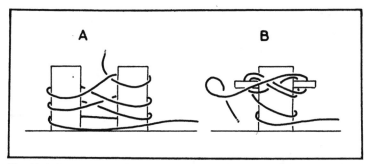

Fig. 16-4. Figure-eight turns around posts provide friction to prevent slipping: (A) figure-eight turns and a half hitch and (B) single samson post.

When a rope has to be set up with the maximum tension, the last bit of pull can be gained by *swigging* on it. A strong pull is put on the rope hooked under the cleat, then its standing part is pulled outwards with the other hand. As it is allowed back, the extra amount gained is pulled up on the end (Fig. 16-3D) and secured with turns around the cleat.

If the cleat is made with a hole through it, it is used as a boat mooring bollard. The line may come at it from different angles and could lift off with pulls in some directions. The line may go through the hole before being taken around (Fig. 16-3E). This is particularly suitable when there is a spliced or tied eye in the rope. It goes through and is turned back (Fig. 16-3F) for a safe simple attachment.

With double bitts, the first strain is taken around the one further from the direction of the pull, then figure-eight turns and a half hitch over one (Fig. 16-4A). Individual users have their own methods of putting on turns. Providing there are sufficient turns under the circumstances, the actual arrangement is not so important. With a single samson post, it is common to put on figure-eight turns across the bar after a turn below the post, finishing with a half hitch (Fig. 16-4B).

The surplus rope left hanging after a rope has been made fast to a cleat has to be disposed of. Unless it is very short, it should not be left loose. There may be a bin below the cleat for the coiled rope, but otherwise it will be necessary to gather up the rope and secure it safely. Although the coil must be kept out of the way, it should be possible to free it and cast off the rope from the cleat without knots to untie or any other complication. Sometimes the coiled rope is pushed between a halliard and a mast, but that is not considered seamanlike.

COILING

If there is a long enough horn or the top of a belaying pin projecting, the coil can be hung over it with its upper part between it and the rope (Fig. 16-5A). When the tail of a rope is coiled, it should

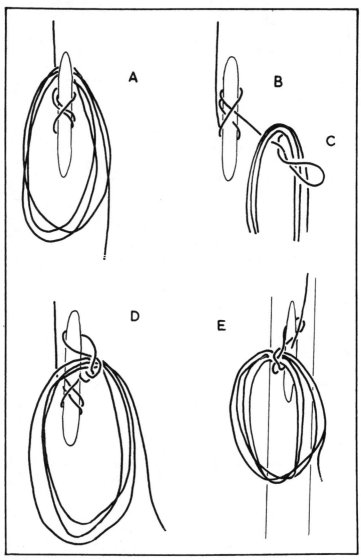

Fig. 16-5. Coils of rope may be held to a cleat with a twisted loop: (A) projecting belaying pin; (B) pull through the coil; (C) twist the loop; (D) put it over the horn of the cleats; and (E) pass twisted loop behind standing part.

be done from the cleat part and not from the end. If the rope is coiled back from the end it will kink or twist. If done from the cleat, the coil can be dropped on the deck and it should run smoothly after the standing part has been cast off the cleat.

Whether there is a long horn or not, it is better to do something to prevent the coiled turns from coming away. One way of doing this is to coil the rope from the cleat outwards, then hold the coil in one hand while reaching through it with the other to grasp where the rope comes from the cleat. Pull this through the coil (Fig. 16-5B) and twist this loop (Fig. 16-5C) before putting it over the horn of the cleat (Fig. 16-5D). The parts of the coil then go in front of the cleat and not over the horn or top of the belaying pin. How much to pull through has to be judged, but to a certain extent this can be adjusted by increasing the number of twists. Normally the twisted part goes over the horn in front of the standing part, but if the pull is along a mast there can be some extra security by passing the twisted loop behind the standing part before putting it over the cleat (Fig. 16-5E).

Allied to this is coiling rope for stowage. There are several ways of securing the turns so the coiled rope is kept tidy and ready for later use, whether it is hung or laid flat. A simple way of making up a coil is to work it into convenient loops and take the end part to hold the turns together. Hold the coils together with enough of the end projecting from the hand. Twist a half hitch into the end (Fig. 16-6A). Hold this behind the coils and pass the end through the coils and through it (Fig. 16-6B). The coil can then be carried or hung by the projecting end. If a bight is passed through instead of the end, that can be used for hanging.

A tighter way of coiling for storage has the sides of the coil brought together and several turns taken around (Fig. 16-6C) away from the end that will be hung. A bight of this end is pushed through the top of the coil (Fig. 16-6D) and turned over it. The effect is to put on a half hitch above the other turns, leaving the end projecting (Fig. 16-6E). In this and the previous method, the end should be left long enough to be knotted if it has to be attached to a hook in storage.

Other ways of coiling for storage finish with a loop upwards for hanging. In one method, a sufficient length of the working end is left to make a half hitch on the last coil, then it goes around the coils and back through the half hitch and the coils (Fig. 16-7A) as a bight. When pulled tight the end of the bight projects upward for hanging (Fig. 16-7B). In another method, the whole bight is extended to a

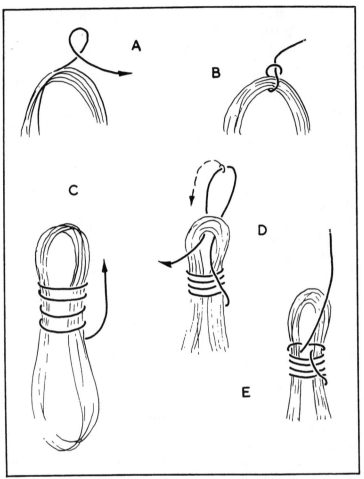

Fig. 16-6. Coiled rope can be held with turns of its end part: (A) twist a half hitch; (B) pass end through coils; (C) several turns around the coils; (D) bight; and (E) projecting end.

half hitch (Fig. 16-7C) and is taken around the coils and through itself and the coils (Fig. 16-7D) to get a similar result.

A *Portugese bowline* can be made with any number of turns in the coil, but that is a more complicated way of dealing with a coil for storage.

A coil can be flattened and two or more half hitches put along it, something like a *sheepshank* (Fig. 16-8A).

If the coiled rope is to remain round, possibly for storing flat, there can be turns of light line put around at intervals, but it will

248

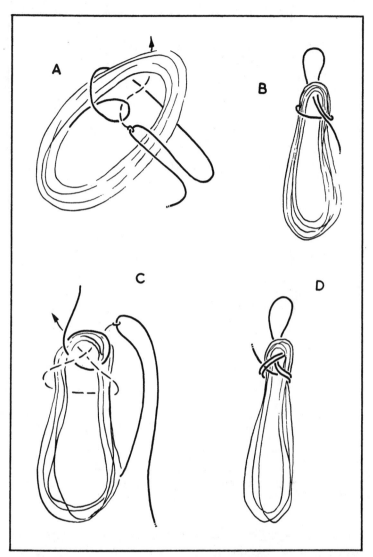

Fig. 16-7. Rope coiled for storage can be secured with a loop: (A) bight; (B) end of bight projects upwards; (C) whole bight is extended; and (D) half hitch around the coils.

usually be sufficient to use the rope itself to knot around. The coil can be marline hitched (Fig. 16-8B).

Clove hitches and similar knots around the coil have the disadvantage of leaving their parts projecting, so part of the coil is pulled across the center and the end projects. It is better to choose a

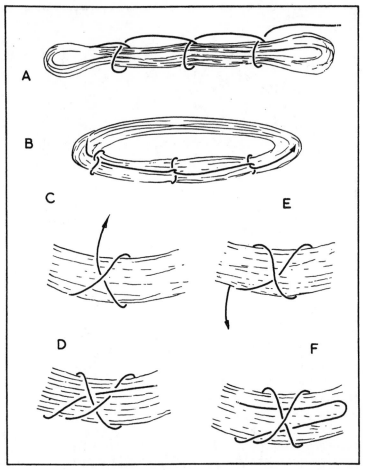

Fig. 16-8. A coil can have half hitches across it or light line can be used to make half hitches around it: (A) sheepshank; (B) marline-hitched coil; (C) ground line hitch; (D) half hitch; (E) strangle knot; and (F) push a bight under the turns.

method of knotting around the coils that leaves the standing part and end more in the direction of the circumference. One method uses a version of the *ground line hitch*. Take the end around the coil and under its own part (Fig. 16-8C). Continue around and make a half hitch (Fig. 16-8D).

Another version is based on the *strangle knot*. Take a turn with the end (Fig. 16-8F). Go around again and push a bight under the turns (Fig. 16-8F) so the knot can be slipped later. Knotting without finishing with a bight may cause the knot to become so tight that it is impossible to undo.

250

Basic Splicing

17

A splice is a form of knotting in which the strands of the rope are worked together to provide the joint. A splice is a more permanent thing than a knot. It is not intended that a splice should be taken apart and the rope laid up to be used again or joined in some other way. If, for instance, an eye is needed temporarily in the end of a rope, it would be correct to use a bowline or one of the other loop knots, but if it is expected that the eye will be needed permanently, it would be better to use an eye splice.

Besides the convenience of a neat splice that does not have the lumps and projections of a knot, a splice is stronger. There must be some weakening of the rope compared with a plain length of rope, but the weakening with a splice is less than with any knot for the same purpose, so when maximum strength is to be retained in a made-up rope assembly, it is always better to splice. A spliced eye is about 90 per cent and a bowline about 80 per cent of the strength of the rope.

Most splicing is done with stranded rope. In most cases this is three-strand rope laid up right-handedly. Traditional splices can be used with synthetic ropes made in this way, but because of the smoother strands, a greater number of tucks are used to prevent slipping. Although there have been braided ropes made of natural fibers, the development of synthetic filaments has made possible the production of ropes in braided forms different from anything done before. In some cases the construction does not permit satisfactory splicing, but for other new rope constructions there are new types of splices. However, most splicing is done in three-stranded rope and it is advisable to master the ordinary eye, back and short splices before moving on to the special splices.

As it is necessary to force strands apart in splicing, some sort of spike is needed. It may be a metal marline spike, either on the back of a clasp knife or one with a wooden handle for more comfortable pushing. There are special spikes with hollows or grooves to make space beside them for a tucking strand to pass. Others have been devised to lead a strand through, but for general splicing a round tapered spike is what most ropeworkers use.

In the small sizes the spike has to be steel for sufficient strength, but wood is less hard on the fibers than metal and a wooden *fid* is better for larger ropes. This is a spike made of a close-grained hardwood. For very large ropes the fid may be quite large and have its end bound with metal, so it can be driven with a mallet or hammer.

The end of the spike may be a round point, but some workers prefer to have the end ground like a small screwdriver with rounded corners. The narrow end can then be put between strands and turned to open them more. It is possible to use a screwdriver instead of a spike on small ropes, but any sharpness of the edges should be taken off so there is no risk of cutting fibers. The screwdriver goes in the flat way and is turned on edge to widen the gap, possibly for the insertion of a normal round spike. With very hard-laid ropes, this may be the only way to start a gap.

The only other essential tool is a sharp knife, probably in addition to a general-purpose one used for cutting rope. Fibers have to be scraped away and this is best done with a finely-sharpened knife, or even a razor blade. A pair of pliers may sometimes be needed to pull stubborn strands through. Other tools for special purposes are mentioned as the need arises.

The strands have to be separated for splicing. Some natural fiber rope will stay in the same state after opening, but synthetic rope has to be restrained or fibers will unlay from strands. They will also unlay themselves much further than intended if nothing is done to prevent it.

Strands have to be unlayed far enough for tucking, but with some extra length for convenience in handling. It is impossible to make a splice properly if only just enough is allowed for the tucks, and there is nothing left over. A little waste must be expected. How much to allow depends on several factors, but as a guide, about 8 inches should be allowed on rope up to ½-inch diameter.

Before unlaying, put in a temporary seizing at the selected distance from the end. This can be thread or any thin twine. A constrictor knot or a few turns of a West Country whipping will do. The seizing stays there until the splice is almost complete, then it is cut off.

The end of a synthetic rope will usually have been sealed by heat when it was cut. This bonds the ends of the strands together. It may be possible to cut through the fused end between the strands so each is still bonded within itself. It is more likely that the end will have to be cut and each strand separately melted with a flame. Try to keep the end no thicker than the rest of the strand. This is best done by using a flame to melt the end, then moisten your finger and thumb and roll the soft end as it sets.

Try to keep the fibers in each strand twisted in the way they were in the normal rope. Be careful that the strands below the seizing keep in shape. If synthetic rope goes out of shape, it is almost impossible to lay up most of these materials again so they are exactly as they were when they came from the machine.

EYE SPLICE

By far the most-used splice is the common eye splice. The end is turned back and spliced into the standing part. The technique is the same whether the eye is actually a very long loop or just the smallest possible circle. The eye may be a free loop or it may fit closely around a metal or plastic thimble. It could be around a toggle or other wooden shape, but except for the need to work to an exact size, the method of splicing is the same.

Bend the prepared rope end into a loop of the size required, with two end strands laid across the standing part so they point across the lay and the third strand out of the way behind (Fig. 17-1A). This arrangement is important. It is possible to prepare the rope with two strands on the other side so they go across the standing part in the direction of the lay. Have two strands across the lay and regard that as the front of the splice.

Open a space in the standing part by lifting a strand ready for tucking. This will probably have to be done with a spike, but with small rope it is often possible to twist the rope open by holding each side of the position and twisting the hands in opposite directions (Fig. 17-1B), although a spike may have to be pushed through to hold the gap. Usually it is possible to withdraw the spike just before tucking and insert the end quickly before the gap closes. If this is impossible, the end has to be tucked alongside the spike.

Take the central end strand under the main strand that has been lifted (Fig. 17-1C). There is no need to pull much through at this stage. Note where the end strand comes out. The other front strand, on the loop side of the one just tucked, has to go in that space. Lift the next main strand, keep the spike on the side of the tucked end strand towards the loop and tuck the other end there (Fig. 17-1D).

There are now two end strands under two main strands, so there must be a main strand without an end strand under it. Turn the splice over and locate this main strand. The remaining end strand has to be tucked under it across its lay in the same direction around the rope as the other two tucked strands. It is this tuck that is more often wrongly done by beginners. Lift the main strand and take the end in so it points across the lay (Fig. 17-1E).

If tucking has been done correctly there will now be one end strand projecting from each space in the standing part (Fig. 17-1F). Pull through in turn until all the strands have been brought up with the same tension and the temporary seizing is close to the standing part. Get all of the ends emerging from about the same plane around the rope. They should all be at the same level and with equal tensions before going further with the splice.

Each end strand now has to go under the next main strand and under the one after that. Do this in turn. Lift a main strand and take the appropriate end strand over the adjoining strand and under that one (Fig. 17-1G). Move around to the next space and do the same again with the second end strand. Be careful that these tucks are all made at about the same level and the end strands do not cross each other. Tuck the third end strand in the same way. Keep the tucks as close to the first ones as possible. It is very easy to tuck so the end strands are almost pointing along the rope, which is wrong. They should be going around the rope at about the same angle as the lay, but in the opposite direction.

Make a third round of tucks, with each end strand going over and under one main strand again (Fig. 17-2). In natural fiber rope this is sufficient and the tucks made so far are described as *whole tucks*. For synthetic rope it is advisable to make another one or two whole tucks.

Sometimes a splice is left at this stage, but for neatness and strength it is wise to make a further tapered tuck. This is done by scraping away some of the fibers in each strand with a knife. Do this mostly on what will be the inside when the splice is finished and remove fibers at different levels so when more tuck is made only

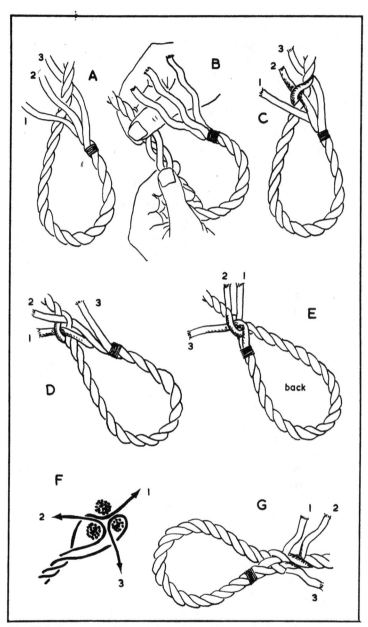

Fig. 17-1. An eye splice in three-strand rope has the ends tucked so they come in each space of the standing part: (A) three strands; (B) twisting in opposite directions; (C) central end strand under main strand; (D) lift next main strand; (E) lift main strand again; (F) one end strand projects; and (G) again, lift main strand.

Fig. 17-2. An eye splice with the end strands tucked three times.

about half the thickness will be nipped under the next main strand in each case. It may help to rub wax on the tapered fibers to keep them in place. Tuck all three tapered ends as tightly as possible. The effect of making paper tucks is to avoid the abrupt change of section that there is if the splice finishes with full tucks. It is an engineering principle that an abrupt change is a weak point and the tapered end of the splice has a better appearance as well.

Cut off any surplus ends that are left, but do not cut too close. Natural fibers may be left as cut, but if it is a very hairy type of rope there will probably be many stray long fibers projecting from the splice. They can be burned off carefully with a match or other small flame. The cut ends of synthetic rope may be fused with a flame, but be careful that no part of the spliced rope is melted.

That is the usual way of finishing an eye splice, but where the utmost strength is required and appearance is of less importance, the splice may be given five or six whole tucks and no taper tucks. The projecting ends are then *dog-knotted* together. Each end is halved and the fibers drawn out straight. Half from one end is then seized to half from its neighbor (Fig. 17-3) in turn around the rope. If the ends are long enough it may be possible to take a few fibers and twist them together to form a line for seizing, but it will be more likely that separate whipping line will have to be used.

256

Older knotting books, primarily intended for seamen say that a splice should be rolled underfoot to get it into a good shape. That may have been satisfactory at sea and a long distance from shore grit and dirt, but it is inadvisable in most circumstances ashore, as grit rolled into rope would weaken it. An alternative is to roll the splice between two boards.

EYE SPLICE WITH THIMBLE

If the eye has to fit tightly around a thimble, toggle or other solid object, the method of splicing only differs in the need to make the first round of tucks in the right place for the splice to draw up tight.

Prepare the rope as before. Wrap it around the thimble with the temporary seizing brought close to the standing part of the rope. Tuck the central strand under the nearest convenient main strand close to the thimble. If the splice is large enough, the strand can be lifted in position and the end tucked, but if it is a small splice or the object has deep grooves, note where the end strand will have to go and take the thimble out so the end is more easily tucked. Try the assembly with that end strand pulled close. If the fit is reasonable, continue tucking the other end strands. If the fit is not as you want it, the solitary strand can be slid closer or further away from the thimble before the other end strands are tucked. Adjustment after they are tucked is not so easy.

All three end strands can be tucked without the thimble in place. See that they all project in the same plane around the rope, as described for the open eye splice. Draw them tight around the thimble (Fig. 17-4). If this is satisfactory cut away the temporary seizing and tighten the tucks finally. From this point, tuck each end strand over and under one main strand in turn, as already described, and continue to complete the splice in the same way.

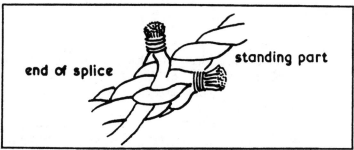

end of splice   standing part

Fig. 17-3. Ends dog-knotted prevent tucked strands from slipping.

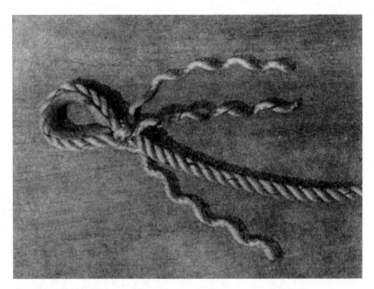

Fig. 17-4. An eye splice around a thimble with each end tucked once.

An eye can be left as described, but it can be made neater and given some protection if the last tucks are served over. The whole tucks are left exposed, but the part of the last whole tuck, the taper tuck and a short distance on the unspliced part of the rope are served over. Before doing this it is advisable to tension the rope. A splice does not move much internally under load, but the rope should be stretched for a short time before serving and the serving is most conveniently put on while the rope is under tension. The method of serving is described in Chapter 2. Use sail twine or other thin line, preferably of the same material as the rope.

A useful application of the eye splice in both forms is a *toggle line* (Fig. 17-5) where the open eye allows the toggle to pass when endwise and the whole thing is useful for securing a coil of rope or any other bundle.

BACK SPLICE

A back splice is an alternative to whipping the end of a rope or relying on sealing it with heat. The strands of the rope are tucked back into itself to provide the locking against unlaying or unraveling. Once made, there should be no fear of a back splice coming undone. However, there is one disadvantage. The action of splicing thickens the rope, due to the strands going back into the rope. This means that a back splice should not be used if the rope has to be threaded

Fig. 17-5. A toggle line has an eye splice to fit over a toggle.

through a block or any small hole. If the increased thickness will not matter, the back splice is a good way to finish the end of a rope.

Prepare the rope in the same way as described for the eye splice, including a temporary seizing at the limit of unlaying. The back splice is started with a *crown knot,* which is an interlocking of the separate strands, taken around so they finish pointing towards the rest of the rope in a direction across the lay. The most convenient way of making the crown knot for this purpose is to hold the rope in one hand with the temporary seizing level with the thumb

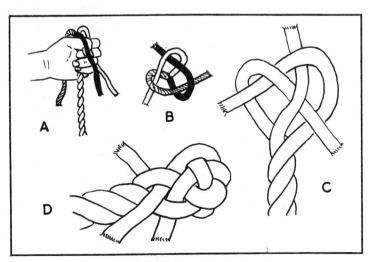

Fig. 17-6. A back splice is started with a crown knot: (A) arrange three-ends evenly; (B) take each strand anti-clockwise; (C) remove temporary seizings; and (D) lift main strands.

and the three ends arranged evenly over the hand (Fig. 17-6A). For the usual right-handed rope, take each strand in turn anti-clockwise, when viewed from above, over its neighbor: 1 over 2, 2 over 3 and 3 over 1, and down through the loop already there (Fig. 17-6B). Pull this tight and evenly so the ends finish ready for tucking and the knot rests flat across the end of the rope. Remove the temporary seizing (Fig. 17-6C).

The ends will be seen to each point across a main strand. Lift the main strands in turn and tuck the ends over and under as was done for the eye splice (Fig. 17-6D). Be careful when doing this not to distort the crown knot. Get all three end strands tucked before tensioning all of them.

Continue tucking. Three whole tucks should be sufficient in any material, as this is not a load-bearing splice and additional tucks in synthetic material are not required. Make a taper tuck for neatness. Four-strand rope can be back-spliced in exactly the same manner—the only difference being the four-part crown knot with its extra tuck.

SHORT SPLICE

The economic way of joining two ropes end to end is with a short splice. It uses less rope than most joining knots and it makes a stronger joint. It thickens the rope so there is a similar problem to the back splice if the rope has to pass through a small space. If ropes have to be joined without increasing their thickness there is the long splice (described next), which uses up a considerable amount of rope.

Both ends should be prepared in the same way as for the two previous splices and a similar amount will be required for tucking each way. Temporary seizings are advisable even with natural fiber rope as there is a tendency otherwise for the center of the splice to become elongated and slack.

Bring the two ends together so each end strand is opposite a space in the other rope (Fig. 17-7A). Push the ropes tightly together (Fig. 17-7B) so the whippings are as close as possible.

Splicing is done one way at a time. Put another temporary seizing over the three ends over the rope in one direction (Fig. 17-7C). Each of the other end strands has to be tucked in turn over and under main strands in the other rope against the lay. Do this at first over the temporary seizing on the other rope. When all three ends have been tucked, remove the temporary seizing and work the tucked ends close back to the meeting of the ropes (Fig. 17-7D).

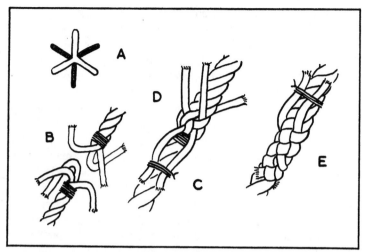

Fig. 17-7. In a short splice the ends are fitted together and tucked: (A) bring two ends together; (B) push ropes tightly together; (C) temporary seizings; (D) remove temporary seizing; and (E) turn the splice around.

In natural fiber ropes there may be two whole tucks and a taper tuck in that direction. For synthetic ropes it would be better to have four whole tucks. In both cases, for maximum strength the ends may be dog-knotted together instead of tapered.

With the tucking completed in one direction, turn the splice round (Fig. 17-7E) and do exactly the same in the other direction. When removing the temporary seizings and doing the first tucks in the second direction see that the center of the splice is completed without a gap there. The tucks in the second direction should follow those the other way closely. The complete splice may be rolled and should look symmetrical.

LONG SPLICE

This splice can be made so the completed joint looks only slightly different from a continuous piece of rope. It is not a tucked splice like the others described in this chapter. A joint without an increase in thickness is only achieved at the expense of wasting a considerable amount of rope. If the need to make a joint without any increase in thickness is essential, this has to be accepted. If a gain in thickness is acceptable, the short splice should be chosen.

The long splice is started like a short splice, but with much longer strands unlaid. How much depends on the strength required and the material from which the rope is made. For natural fiber rope the absolute minimum to be unlaid from each rope is seven times the circumference (22 times the diameter), but this is better increased to 12 or 14 times the circumference (38 or 45 times the diameter).

For synthetic fiber ropes this should be increased by at least a further 50 percent. As an example, a ½-inch diameter synthetic fiber rope will require both ends to be unlaid at least 29 inches. This makes a total of about 5 feet to be deducted from the overall length of the unjoined ropes.

Unlay the ropes for the required distance. Seal the ends of the strands. Temporary seizings at the limits of unlaying may be used, but they will have to be removed soon after starting splicing. Bring the two ropes together, with the long ends through the opposing spaces (Fig. 17-8A) in a similar way to starting a short splice.

Without disturbing the other strands or upsetting the natural kinks in the strand, start to unlay one strand and at the same time lay in its adjoining strand from the other rope. Try to put the new strand in with the same twist in the fibers. It should conform to its original kinks so it takes the place of the strand being withdrawn exactly. Continue doing this until you are within a short distance of the end of the strand.

Go back to the center and do the same in the other direction with another pair of mating strands. Let the other pair of strands remain at the center (Fig. 17-8B). It is helpful at this stage to have the rope under a moderate tension, so it is held straight and it can be examined to see that all of the laid strands fit properly into the rope.

There are several ways of locking the meeting strands at the three widely spaced positions along the rope. The meeting ends can be tapered slightly and joined to each other with an overhand knot twisted in the direction that brings the ends across adjoining strands (Fig. 17-8C). Taper more if necessary and tuck each end under the adjoining main strand and cut off what is left. Another slightly more complicated way has the two ends each divided into two groups of fibers which are twisted together with the aid of wax. Tie two of these with overhand knots (Fig. 17-8D). Tuck the other half strands under the adjoining main strands (Fig. 17-8E). Taper the projecting ends and wrap each once more around the strand it is already under. Taper the ends of the knotted half strands and take them over the adjoining main strands, then under and around the next main strands.

An overhand knot between the meeting ends is advisable, but if bulk has to be kept to the minimum, the ends can be tapered and crossed without twisting. This can be done whether the ends are

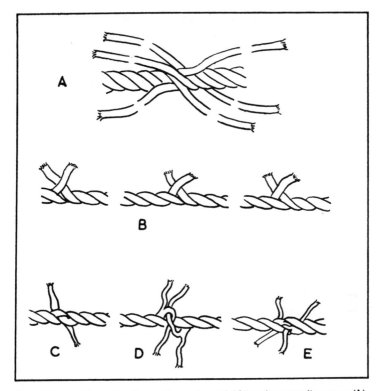

Fig. 17-8. In a long splice the mating ends are laid into the opposite ropes: (A) bring two ropes together; (B) let one pair of strands remain at the center; (C) ends go across adjoining strands; (D) tie two overhand knots; and (E) tuck the other half strands under the adjoining main strands.

kept singly or divided into two groups. In both cases, tucking is the same as described to follow knotting the ends. There will be some settling down in a long splice and it is best to stretch the rope before finally trimming ends and sealing synthetic material. Rolling at each meeting place should make the splice very difficult to detect.

If four-strand rope has to be spliced, the method for short splicing is the same as for three-strand rope, but for a long splice there has to be a greater amount unlaid. The distance suggested for three-strand rope should be increased by at least one-third. The ropes are brought together and a pair of meeting strands are worked with. You unlay one and lay up the other in its place until only a short piece remains.

In the other direction do the same with a pair that are diametrically opposite the first pair. This leaves two pairs of end strands at the center. To get their final positions measure the distance between the crossings of the final meeting place of the first two pairs and divide this by three. Mark these distances on the rope. Unlay and lay up one pair as far as this and do the same with the other pair the other way so the four sets of meeting parts are equally spaced along the rope. From this point deal with the ends in the same way as described for the long splice in three-strand rope.

Other Eye Splices

18

The common eye splice is thè one to use if an eye is needed in three-strand rope, unless there is a special reason for using a different splice. There are a great many other eye splices. Users of ropes in widely different parts of the world have devised different ways of splicing. In most cases the tucks are over and under as in the common splice, but some initial tucks are arranged differently. In fact, the common eye splice brings the parts together with the least disturbance of lay, so the final splice is neat and with the minimum of uneven projections. Some other ways of starting the tucks give a more clumsy pattern at the base of the splice.

Other methods of starting the tucks are mostly comparable in strength with the normal method. Unless there is sharp kinking of strands at the start, the further over and under tucks are the strong part. If there are enough of these the splice will hold. One excuse for poor splicing is that it does not matter how you tuck, as long as you get in enough tucks, but obviously it is better to follow a good pattern that results in a neat splice.

GERMAN EYE SPLICE

This is one variation of starting the tucks in an eye splice. It uses a *lock tuck*. There may be no special advantage in this with fiber rope, but in several methods of wire splicing, the ends are arranged with two around one main strand in opposite directions as a lock tuck, probably because that is a good way of holding on to the springy wire which may be resisting tucking.

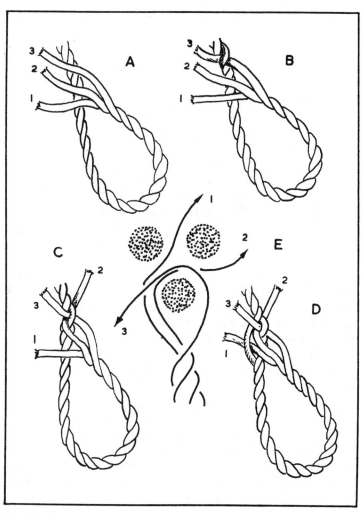

Fig. 18-1. A German eye splice has two ends tucked around one main strand: (A) prepare the ends; (B) tuck the end under a main strand; (C) take next end in the same space; (D) take remaining strand under the next strand; and (E) one end should emerge from each space.

The ends are prepared and laid across the standing part in the same way as for a common eye splice, except that all three ends are on the front and crossing the lay of the main strands (Fig. 18-1A). Tuck the end furthest from the eye under a convenient main strand (Fig. 18-1B).

Take the next end in the same space, but going around the same main strand the other way below the first one tucked (Fig.

18-1C). Take the remaining strand into the same space, but under the next strand (Fig. 18-1D). There should now be one end emerging from each space (Fig. 18-1E), but unlike the common splice there will be one main strand without an end strand under it. Manipulate the ends so they are brought to the same level in the standing part and tuck from here on in the same way as in a common eye splice, going over and under main strands against the lay.

FOUR-STRAND SPLICE

Putting an eye splice in four-strand rope differs from a similar splice in three-strand rope only in the way the first tucks are made to get the ends emerging from each space in the standing part.

Start by preparing the rope as for a three-strand splice, but put three ends across the front and one behind (Fig. 18-2A). Make the first tuck with the front end strand furthest from the eye. Tuck the next end below it, going in where the first end came out and under the next main strand. These two tucks are the same as for working with three ends. It is the tucking of the strand nearest the eye that so it comes out in the next space.

Turn the splice over and find the main strand with nothing under it. Tuck the last end strand in the same way as when making a three-strand splice. That end will be going in where the end that

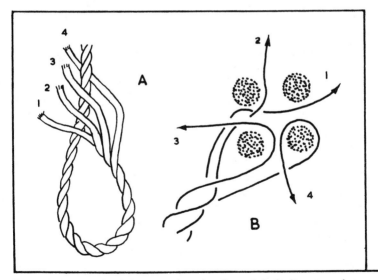

Fig. 18-2. An eye splice in four-strand rope has the ends tucked to emerge from separate spaces of the standing part: (A) put three ends across the front and one behind and (B) tucking.

goes under two strand comes out and the tucking should finish with one end projecting from each space (Fig. 18-2B). Draw up the ends and bring them all to the same level in the rope, then continue to tuck in the same way as for a three-strand eye splice.

SAILMAKER'S EYE SPLICE

In some sails the end of a bolt rope sewn around the edge of a sail may have to finish with an eye. A bolt rope is sewn on by hand with stitches that go over the strands of the rope, with the spacing of the stitches the same as the turns of the rope. If a normally-tucked eye splice was included at the end, this would complicate continued sewing as the sequence of stitches would be upset by the woven form of the strands. Instead of using a common splice a sailmaker tucks the ends with the lay. The effect is to keep the lay formation all the way to the eye. However, tucking in this way is not as strong as a normal splice, but as the stitches through the splice and the canvas support the ropework, this eye splice is acceptable for this purpose. The sailmakers' eye splice should not be used in a free rope where it has to bear a load.

With the ends prepared in the usual way, they are laid across the standing part with two in front and one behind, but arranged so the two are in line with the lay (Fig. 18-3A), instead of against it, as in all other tucked splices. Tuck the middle end strand under a convenient main strand (Fig. 18-3B). Tuck the end below it into the space it comes out and under the next main strand (Fig. 18-3C). Turn the splice over and tuck the remaining end under the remaining main strand (Fig. 18-3D). The arrangement of tucks will be seen to be the same as for a common eye splice, except they go the other way around the rope. There should be an end strand emerging from each space.

From this point, the ends are not tucked over and under strands, but each is wrapped around the main strand it is already under (Fig. 18-3E). For neatness a sailmaker may start tapering after only one full tuck, but that leaves the eye splice weak and dependent on the strength of stitching through it. For natural fiber rope there should be two or three full tucks before tapering and there should be two more in synthetic rope. Tapering may be by scraping away fibers, but a method sometimes used in this splice is to cut off one end after completing the full tucks. Then tuck the other two ends more and cut one off, leaving the third end to tuck again. When rolled, there is then very little difference between that splice and one made with scraped tapers.

268

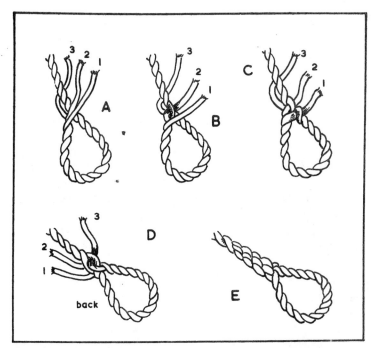

Fig. 18-3. In a sailmaker's eye splice the ends are tucked with the lay of the standing part: (A) two ends in line with the lay; (B) tuck middle end strand under a main strand; (C) tuck end under next main strand; (D) turn splice over; and (E) each end is wrapped under a main strand.

EYE SPLICE WITH COLLAR

The majority of eye splices taper from the eye, which is satisfactory in all conditions except if the part with the eye has to be drawn close to a block or fairlead. For these circumstances there has to be enough strength built into the splice as close to the eye as possible. This can be done by working a collar with the ends around the rope. The effect is also decorative and this splice may be used as an alternative to others for the sake of its appearance. Strength should be as good as a common eye splice.

Start by tucking the ends exactly as for a common eye splice, but it is convenient for drawing then through the collar if they are kept longer than for an ordinary splice, although the amount left in the collar at the end is probably very little different. Pull the first tucks tight and get them all to the same level with the ends projecting equally-spaced around the standing part. The collar described here is actually a *manrope knot* and there are others equally suitable if the aim is to produce decoration.

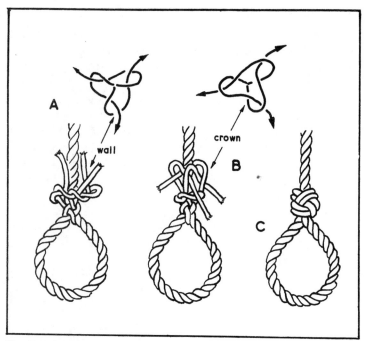

Fig. 18-4. An eye splice with a collar keeps all parts close to the eye: (A) take each end up through the loop; (B) draw parts tight; and (C) do not cross turns.

Take each end under its neighbor and up through the loop formed (Fig. 18-4A), going around the rope to the right. This action is called a *wall knot* and is tucked the opposite way to the *crown knot* that was described for the start of a back splice.

Draw the parts of the wall knot moderately tight and even, then continue above it to make a crown knot by going around the same way, but this time go over the strands and down through their loops (Fig. 18-4B). Draw this to the same tension as the wall knot, which brings the crown on top of the wall, with its ends angled downward.

Each end will be alongside a turn of the wall knot. Tuck each end alongside a turn of the crown knot. Take it in alongside that turn. The result will be to bring the two knots together with doubled strands as if a three-part plait had been worked around the rope. Use the point of a spike to draw through the slack until the surplus can be pulled up by the ends. Work each part from where it emerges from the splice a little at a time to its end. See that turns do not cross and the final collar shows parallel strands all around (Fig. 18-4C). When the collar has been worked as tightly as possible, cut off the ends.

CHAIN SPLICE

A rope may have to be spliced to the end of a chain to lead it through a narrow space or hole, such as the hawse pipe for the anchor chain of a ship. Because the clearance is no more than is needed to pass the chain, there may be little space for a normal splice in a rope stout enough to do the job. The chain splice is a way of joining a rope into the end of a chain so its bulk is kept small.

The chain splice uses only two of the three strands through the chain. Consequently that is a weak part, although it reduces bulk in the doubled part of the eye. This means that a chain splice may be strong enough for this particular purpose, but it is unsuitable for normal load carrying.

Unlay one strand for a greater distance than will be needed in the eye. Keep this out of the way and bend the remaining two strands into the eye through the end of the chain. Tuck one end between the two strands to make the eye (Fig. 18-5A). Take the other strand that has formed the loop and put it into the space left by the unlaid strand. Retain its shape and see that it fits in with the same amount of twist in it as the other strands. Take it some way along the rope and join it to the unlaid strand by one of the methods described for a long splice (Fig. 18-5B). Cut off those ends.

Where the other end has been tucked near the eye, treat it as an end for normal tucking. Taper it and tuck it over and under against the lay two or three times (Fig. 18-5C). Roll the splice to get its shape even.

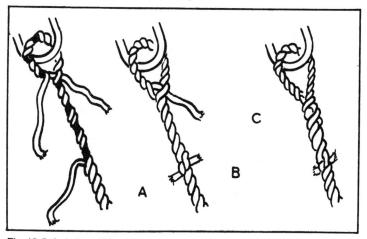

Fig. 18-5. A chain splice is kept narrow to follow a chain through a hole: (A) tuck one end; (B) join as far along splice; and (C) taper it.

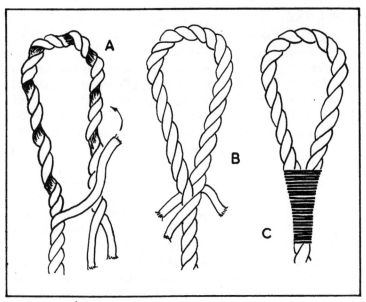

Fig. 18-6. In a grommet splice strands go opposite ways around the eye: (A) bend two strands into the eye; (B) lay up single strand; and (C) serve over.

GROMMET SPLICE

This may also be known as an *artificial eye*. It has a family resemblance to the chain splice, but all three strands form the eye and its strength should be very little less than a common eye splice. As there are no tucks at the neck of the eye, this finishes with a slimmer taper.

Unlay one strand for a distance greater than that around the intended eye. So far as possible let the strands keep the kinks they have acquired during making the rope. Do not straighten or pull them. Bend the two strands into the eye (Fig. 18-6A). Lay up the single strand in the space it was taken from, but going around the other way (Fig. 18-6B). This puts the rope back together around the eye and leaves the three ends projecting towards the standing part of the rope.

Separate the yarns of natural fiber rope or the filaments of synthetic rope. Use some of them to worm around filling the gaps between strands. Wax may help to make the material manageable and then thread can be used to half-hitch along the rope and hold the worming in place. Any parts left over can be laid straight along the rope and tapered. Finally, serve over, starting from close to the eye (Fig. 18-6C). It would be possible to tuck the ends as in normal

272

splicing, but this would increase bulk and the splice would not be as good as a common eye splice.

If a grommet splice has to be made in four-strand rope, start as for three-strand rope. Unlay one strand and form the eye, then lay up that strand in its place around the eye, but note which other strand comes opposite it in the rope formation. Unlay that end as far as the neck of the loop and lay it up in its space the other way, so the eye finishes with two strands around the loop in each direction.

DOUBLE-ENDED EYE

If a rope has to be spliced to something so both its ends can be used, none of the normal splices are suitable. This occurs with sails that have double-ended sheets, such as most sails forward of the mast in a modern yacht. One way of dealing with the problem is to pass the rope through the grommet or make it into an eye, then seize the parts of the rope together. Another way is to pass the two parts of the rope through each other. This may be called a *brummell splice* or *guy-line eye* from its use in joining rope to tents.

In stranded rope lift one strand near the eye and pass the other side of the rope through the gap. Do the same a little further along the part that has just gone through it (Fig. 18-7A). It is possible to do this with braided rope, providing it is not too tightly laid. A spike or fid can be pushed through the center of the rope to make a hole large enough for the other part.

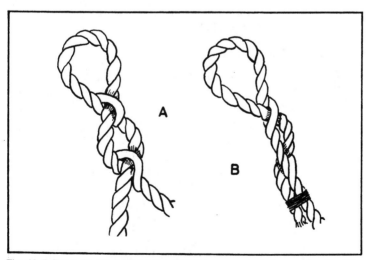

Fig. 18-7. For a double-ended eye splice the rope goes between strands: (A) pass first part through and (B) seize the end.

The two crossings can be worked together to lock the splice and give a neat appearance, and they can be covered with a seizing for the best finish.

A variation is sometimes used to make a quick splice in the end of a rope. For the best results the main part is passed through what will be the end, far enough back for that to be tucked, then the end is passed through the main part. Sometimes the splice is made by tucking the end twice through the standing part. That is not as strong and it is advisable to seize the end to the standing part (Fig. 18-7B).

FLEMISH EYE

This may be called a *spindle eye* and it may be confused with the grommet splice by also being called an *artificial eye*. The only place where the Flemish eye would be preferable to the other splices would be where a very small eye was required. It is possible to make an eye that is little further across than the diameter of the rope. Construction is tedious and not justified except in the particular circumstances.

Have a short length of rod or tube of the same size as the inside diameter the eye is to have. Put a whipping around the rope at a distance from the end that allows enough length in what is left to go around the eye and some way along the rope. The whipping can stay there inside the splice, so it need not be treated as a temporary seizing.

From the whipping to the end open the strands into their separate yarns or groups of filaments. Twist these into small lines with wax.

The eye will be made around the center of the rod or tube. To keep it in place there may be some turns of spare line wrapped around to make humps on each side of where the eye will come. They will have to be cut away later to get the eye off (Fig. 18-8A). The humps are not essential. Fasten short lengths of yarn along the rod at fairly close intervals, going over the humps if they are used. Either hold the yarns down with a few turns around them or use adhesive tape. These yarns will be later used as stops around the parts making the eye (Fig. 18-8B).

Divide the yarns of rope into two equal groups and position them on each side of the tube. Take a pair of yarns and join them over the tube with an overhand knot (Fig. 18-8C). Repeat this with all the yarns, staggering the knots as much as possible to avoid forming lumps anywhere around the circumference. Do not cut off any yarns.

274

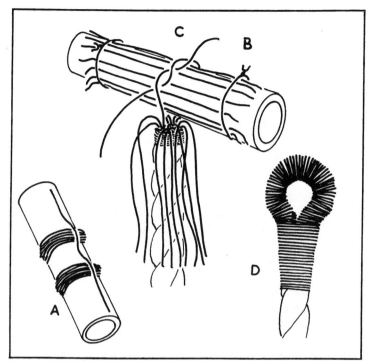

Fig. 18-8. In a Flemish eye a small eye is made from yarns of the rope over a former: (A) turns of spare line; (B) yarns used as stops; (C) overhand knot; and (D) serve over the eye.

When all of the rope yarns have been knotted, free the yarns laid along the tube and use them to draw the knotted yarns together to form a round section in the eye. Cut off the ends of these yarns. This leaves the eye in shape and the ends of the yarns that made it hanging down the rope.

If it is a stranded rope, use some of the ends hanging down straight and some to worm around the spaces between the strands. If it is braided rope lay all the ends along the rope. Taper by cutting the ends to different lengths. Use thread to half-hitch over to keep the parts in place.

Serve over the eye completely and further serve the tapered ends along the rope (Fig. 18-8D).

EYE SPLICE VARIATIONS

The method of tucking a common eye splice can be adapted to other unions between ropes or its parts, although the assembly does not finish as an eye in every case.

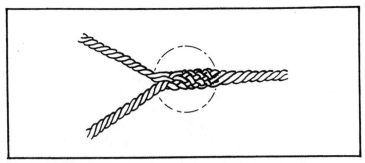

Fig. 18-9. A fork can be made by joining ropes with a branch splice.

If one rope has to branch off another, as when making a double towing bridle, one rope may be spliced into the other in a *branch splice* exactly as if it was the end of the first rope brought around to it (Fig. 18-9).

An eye can be arranged in a rope with a *cut splice* (Fig. 18-10A). The rope is cut and the two parts unlaid for splicing, then overlapped by the amount needed for the eye. Each end is then tucked into the other standing part in the same way as eye splicing.

The two sides of a cut splice need not be the same length. If one side is allowed to curve outward while the other side is quite short, this could be used as a double-ended splice as an alternative to that shown in Fig. 18-7. Unequal parts might also be an advantage in a place like the line used to hook over a boat tiller. It could also serve as a hand grip along a rope. When made with unequal parts this may be called a *horseshoe splice*.

The parts could be strengthened by serving over (Fig. 18-10B). It could be done when the loop goes over a spar, as when making shrouds for the most of a small boat.

The traditional way of making a joint in a ship's log line uses a variation on the cut splice. In the *log line splice*, start as for a cut splice and make the tucks at one end, then twist the ropes together in the opposite way to their lay and make the tuck at the other end (Fig. 18-10C). Apart from its original use, this splice could be used to make a thickened hand grip along the rope or it could be an indication of the amount of rope let out when the rope slides through your hand.

If it is preferred to not cut the rope, a loop similar to that of a cut splice can be made by splicing in another piece. This could be a projecting loop from a rope under tension, and be any size from a hand grip to a considerable length. This is a *cringle*, but there are some alternative ways of making cringles described later. In this

276

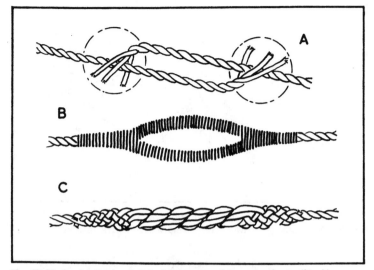

Fig. 18-10. A cut splice is made by joining ropes into each other as if tucking eye splices: (A) cut splice; (B) serving over; and (C) make tuck.

case, the new piece of rope is prepared and its ends tucked into the continuous rope in the same way as for eye splicing (Fig. 18-11).

It is possible to make an eye splice in the body of the rope without using any ends. It may be regarded as a trick although some practical uses are claimed. With most three-stranded rope it is possible to grasp a section of rope between your two hands and twist in an unwinding direction (Fig. 18-12A) so the opening strands start to twist back on themselves. Once the twisting of the strands starts, more unwinding of the main rope will cause the strands to

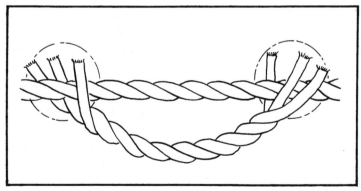

Fig. 18-11. A cringle can be added to the side of a rope by splicing in the same way as for an eye splice.

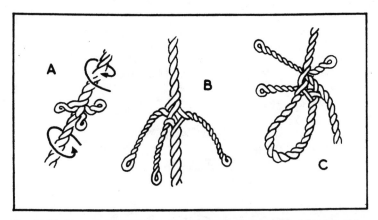

Fig. 18-12. An eye splice can be made in the body of a rope by twisting it back t coil strands for tucking: (A) twist in unwinding direction; (B) long spirals; and (C) twisted ends.

wrap into long spirals (Fig. 18-12B). These will be the ends for tucking, so continue until they are long enough.

Form the rope into an eye, and commence tucking exactly as if making a common eye splice, but using these twisted *ends* (Fig. 18-12C).

278

Other Splices in Stranded Rope

19

Although eye splices are most commonly used and have produced the largest number of variations, there are other splices and types of ropework using splicing techniques that are sometimes needed when the basic splices are not appropriate. Besides joints between similar ropes there is sometimes the need to join three-strand rope to four-strand rope, or to wire rope, which is dealt with in Chapter 21.

KNOTTED SHORT SPLICE

One problem when making a short splice is keeping the two ropes closely into each other so the finished splice is without a slack part at the center or a different angle of the strands there. Knotting the strands helps to keep the ropes tightly linked while the strands are tucked each way. Although this is a help in making the splice, the result is weaker than a conventional splice, which is generally preferable.

The opened ropes are brought together with each strand in a space of the other rope, then an overhand knot is made with each pair of strands (Fig. 19-1). With the usual right-handed lay, each strand is knotted to the one on its right and this brings each end out in the correct direction to be tucked over and under in the usual way. Make sure the knots keep the ropes tight. It is possible to finally adjust them when changing direction to tuck the second way.

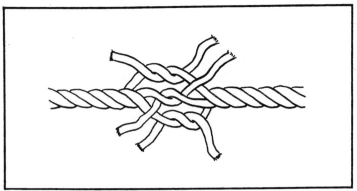

Fig. 19-1. A short splice can be knotted at the middle to hold the strands before tucking.

SHORT SPLICE

There is no satisfactory way of splicing four strands into three strands without altering the make-up of one rope to match the other. This means that the three-strand rope can be made four-stranded for the length needed for splicing, or the four-strand rope can be reduced to three strands for the same length. In the final strength there is probably little to choose between the two methods. There has to be a certain amount of unevenness in the finished splice, in any case, but making four strands into three is probably the neater of the two splices.

To make a three-stranded rope into four, unlay for a distance that will make the ends long enough for tucking and a further distance slightly further than the other rope is expected to tuck. With synthetic rope seal the ends of the strands and put on a temporary seizing at the limit of unlaying. This will also be worthwhile with many natural fiber ropes to prevent uneven disturbance of the strands at the next stage (Fig. 19-2A).

Take one of the strands and divide it into two equal parts. Twist these together to form thinner strands. Wax may help to keep the fibers or filaments in place while doing this. This makes four strands for the total length unlaid (Fig. 19-2B). Lay up the two whole and two half strands into a four-strand rope for the distance the other rope will have to tuck (Fig. 19-2C). In most ropes it is advisable to put on another temporary seizing at this point.

Prepare the other rope in the usual way. Bring the ropes together and make an ordinary short splice, with two full and two taper tucks each way in natural fiber rope and up to four whole and two taper tucks each way in synthetic rope.

280

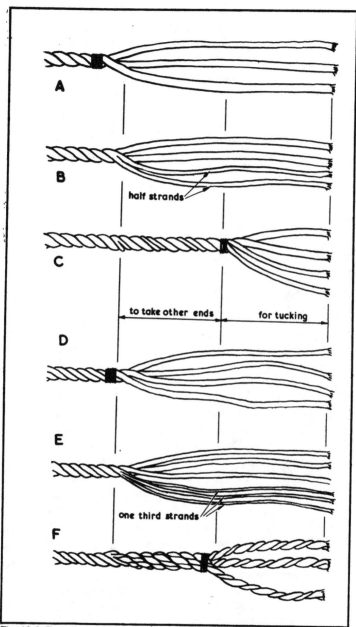

Fig. 19-2. To splice ropes with different number of strands, one rope has to be converted to the same number of strands as the other: (A) prevent uneven disturbance of the strands; (B) four strands; (C) lay up strands; (D) unlay the ends; (E) divide one strand into three; and (F) lay up the combined strands.

For the other method the three-stranded rope is undisturbed, but the four-stranded rope is reduced to three strands. Unlay the end of the four-stranded rope for a distance sufficient for tucking into the other rope and a further distance slightly greater than the other rope is expected to tuck (Fig. 19-2D). Seize at this point. Divide one of the strands into three (Fig. 19-2E). Slightly open the fibers or filaments of each of the other strands so one-third of the divided strand can be laid in and wound around it.

Lay up these combined strands for the distance the other rope is expected to tuck (Fig. 19-2F) and put on a temporary seizing. Prepare the other rope in the usual way and tuck it in the same fashion as suggested for the other method.

SHROUD KNOTS

In the days of fighting sailing ships, almost all of the rigging was made of natural fiber ropes. Since those days improvements in the manufacture of wire ropes has brought the use of wire for most standing rigging for yachts and the remaining sailing ships.

A shroud is one of the major supports for a mast. If a fiber rope shroud was shot through it had to be repaired quickly and safely. One problem was the fact that it could not be shortened very much and any of the usual splices would use up more rope than was acceptable. A type of splicing called shroud knots was devised. There are several variations, but all of them make a secure joint between the meeting ends, while using up less rope than any other splice or knot. The original purpose may have disappeared, but a shroud knot may be the best choice in other circumstances where a joint has to be made with the minimum shortening.

The most common form of shroud knot is a form of interlocking *wall knots*. The rope ends are unlaid for a short distance and fitted together in the same way as for a short splice (Fig. 19-3A). With the strands of one rope make a wall knot around the other, going around the opposite way to the lay. Each end goes under its neighbor and up through the loop that is formed by it (Fig. 19-3B). Pull the knot tight by drawing up the ends in turn. Get an even tension to leave the ends projecting along the rope.

Do exactly the same the other way with the strands from the other rope (Fig. 19-3C). Get the two knots as tight as possible so their turns fit against each other (Fig. 19-3D).

It is the interlocking of the two knots that provides the strength when the ropes come under strain, but to prevent them from loosening and to make a neat finish, separate and taper the strand

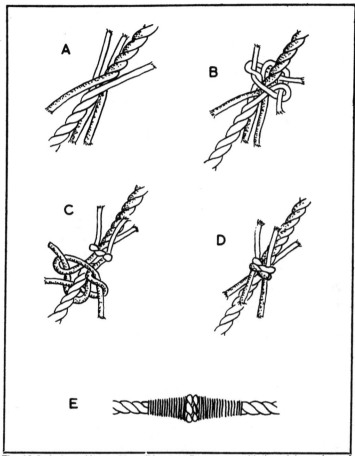

Fig. 19-3. A shroud knot with wall knots splices ropes with the minimum loss of length: (A) rope ends unlaid; (B) each end goes up through the loop; (C) repeat; (D) get the two knots tight; and (E) serve tightly.

ends. Use some of the fibers to worm around between the strands and lay any remaining fibers straight along the rope. Serve tightly in both directions from close to the knots to past the ends of the laid down fibers (Fig. 19-3E).

Another shroud knot uses slightly more rope, but makes the joint with crown knots instead of shroud knots. It is probably very slightly stronger. This may be called *French shroud knotting*.

Bring the ends together (Fig. 19-4A). With the ends from one rope make a crown knot around the other rope. The difference between this and the first method is in putting each end over its neighbor (Fig. 19-4B) and down through the loop it makes, instead

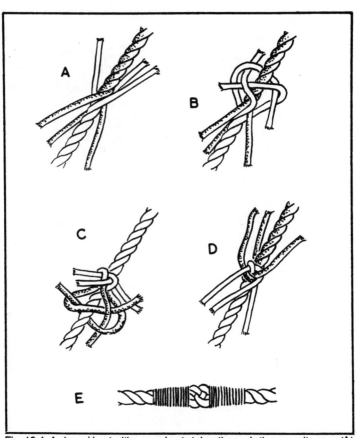

Fig. 19-4. A shroud knot with crown knots takes the ends the opposite way: (A) bring ends together; (B) put each end over its neighbor; (C) repeat; (D) pull knots tightly; and (E) taper and serve.

of working upwards. Work this knot tight around the other rope, but be careful of pulling it too far down. A seizing on each rope will prevent this. If it is made with fine line it can be left inside the finished knot.

Do the same the other way (Fig. 19-4C). Pull the knots tightly close together so the strands come between each other and point back over their own ropes (Fig. 19-4D). Finish in the same way as for the first method, worming and tapering before serving both sides (Fig. 19-4E).

In another method the knot is served on only one side and the rope the other way is clear right up to the knot. This would be an advantage if the knot had to come as close as possible to a block or a small hole in a fairlead.

Bring the parts together (Fig. 19-5A)and make a crown knot with the ends of one rope around the other (Fig. 19-5B) in the same way as in the previous example. When this has been drawn tight, make a wall knot the other way (Fig. 19-5C). Pull the knots close together. The effect of using the two different knots is to bring the ends out pointing in the same direction (Fig. 19-5D). Arrange them equally around the rope, then finish in that direction by worming, tapering and serving, the same as for the other methods (Fig. 19-5E).

CRINGLES

A cringle is a rope loop. It can be on the side of a sail or canvas cover. It may be at the side of a rope edge to a net or cover. One method of splicing the cringle to the other rope has been shown (Fig. 18-11), but the more usual methods form the cringle from a

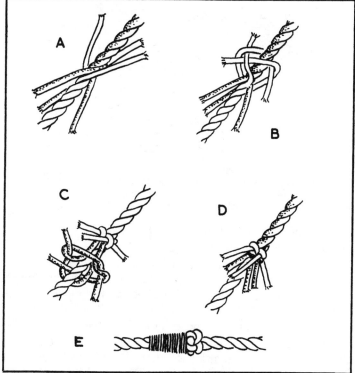

Fig. 19-5. A shroud knot with wall and crown knots takes all ends one way: (A) bring parts together; (B) crown knot; (C) wall knots; (D) ends point in same direction; and (E) taper and serve.

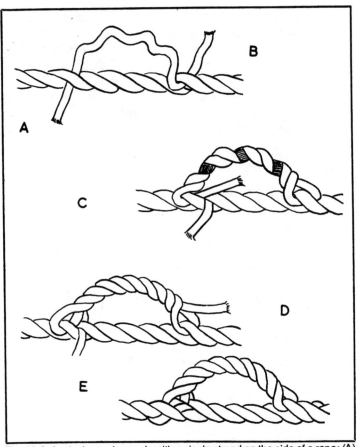

Fig. 19-6. A cringle can be made with a single strand on the side of a rope: (A) tuck one end into the rope; (B) tuck under another rope strand; (C) tuck the working end; (D) lay it back into the cringle; and (E) taper both ends.

single strand of rope. This means that one length of rope will produce the strands for three cringles.

To make a cringle on a rope, unlay one strand longer than three times the length around the cringle. Try to keep it in the shape it was in the rope, preserving the kinks and wavy form as much as possible.

Tuck one end into the rope, going under a strand against the lay as if for splicing (Fig. 19-6A). Leave enough projecting for two or three tucks. Take the remainder around the shape the cringle is to be and tuck under another rope strand (Fig. 19-6B). Open the rope wide at that point so the strand can go through with the minimum disturbance of its shape.

Lay the working end back around itself, keeping the lay as accurate as possible and twisting the fibers in the strand you have opened. At the other end of the cringle, tuck the working end under another strand of the rope (Fig. 19-6C) and lay it back into the cringle to make that three-stranded (Fig. 19-6D). Work the three parts neatly into each other so the cringle makes an even rope, then tuck the working end under a main strand in a direction across its lay. Taper both ends and tuck them as for splicing into the rope (Fig. 19-6E).

There is a variation if the cringle has to be made through eyelets or grommets instead of into a rope. The strand has to be

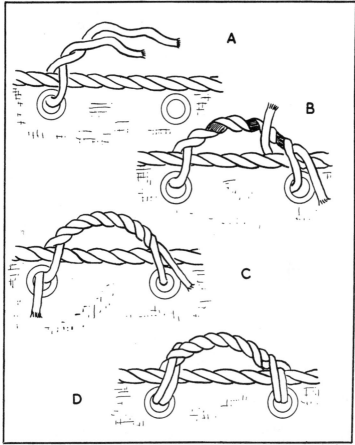

Fig. 19-7. A cringle can be made through eyelets with a single strand tucked on itself: (A) pass the strand through one grommet; (B) fit the two parts into each other; (C) lay it back into the cringle; and (D) pass ends through the grommet.

287

about the same length as for the first method and it is just as important to keep it in its natural form if possible.

Pass the strand through one grommet (Fig. 19-7A) and keep one part about twice as long as the other. Fit the two parts into each other, going around in the natural lay that they had in the rope they came from and pass the longer part through the grommet at the other end (Fig. 19-7B). Lay it back into the cringle to make that into a three-strand rope. Coax this into a good shape (Fig. 19-7C). Pass the ends through the grommets and turn them back on the cringle and tuck them over and under as for splicing (Fig. 19-7D), tapering for a neat finish.

Another way to finish this type of cringle is to leave more at the first end, then only bring the working end back to near the middle of the cringle and take the first end around the space to meet it, then the two parts are joined and finished in one of the ways described for dealing with meeting ends in a long splice.

GROMMET

A grommet is a continuous ring of rope. It is made from one strand, so one length of rope will make three grommets. It would be possible to make a grommet any size, but in practice it is better to splice the ends of a piece of rope together if a large loop or sling is needed. The name is sometimes used for a metal ring fitted into canvas or leather, but that is better called an eyelet. A small grommet may be used instead of the metal eyelet and it would then be sewn into the canvas. Another use for a rope grommet is in forming the strop of a traditional type of block. The method is also used for making rope quoits for various ring games.

To make a grommet use a single strand about three and one half times as long as the intended circumference is to be. As with making cringles, leave the lay undisturbed if possible. Bend the strand into a circle of the required size and commence twisting the parts together, following around the lay (Fig. 19-8A). It does not matter if this is done with one long end or with both ends in opposite directions. Continue until the parts meet (Fig. 19-8B), then follow around once more, filling the spaces between these pairs of turns so as to make a three-strand rope. Where the ends meet, join them in one of the ways described for joining the ends of a long splice (Fig. 19-8C). It will probably be satisfactory to leave the joint at that, but if a seizing would not interfere with the use of a rope grommet, there could be a few turns of seizing over the meeting ends.

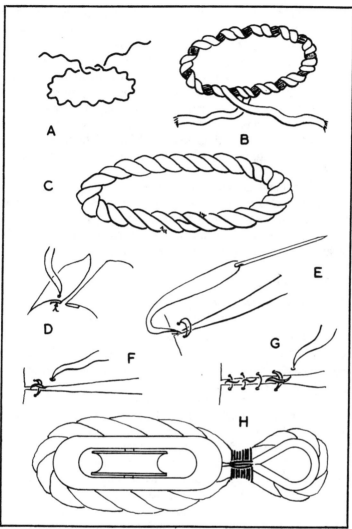

Fig. 19-8. A grommet is a continuous rope made from one strand. It may go around a block. Its joint can be covered with canvas: (A) bend the strand; (B) continue until parts meet; (C) join ends as if for a long splice; (D) pass thread up; (E) needle should come up through space on left of stitch; (F) pull tight; (G) start next stitch; and (H) allow for tightening with a seizing.

Another treatment of the joint is to cover it with cloth or canvas. If the grommet is to be used as a quoit in a game, the color of the canvas would identify it. To get the canvas tight around the rope, its edges are turned under and the seam is made by sewing with a herringbone stitch.

Use double thread in a needle, with its ends knotted together. Bend the canvas into place with a slight gap between the meeting folds to allow for tightening. Pass the thread up through the far side at the left, so the knot is under (Fig. 19-8D). Come across and down through the near side, with the needle coming up through the space on the left of the stitch (Fig. 19-8E). Pull tight and go over the stitch and into the space so the point can go up through the far side again (Fig. 19-8F). That is a complete action. Come back to the near side to start the next stitch (Fig. 19-8G). Pull each stitch tight as it is made. At the end, use the needle to half hitch back around the last stitches.

If a grommet is made to go around a block, it usually encloses a thimble as well. The length will have to be arranged to suit, but allow for tightening with a seizing between the two parts (Fig. 19-8H). The meeting ends can come at the bottom of the block and be arranged between the rope and the wood.

PUDDING SPLICE

If only one strand of a piece of three-strand rope becomes damaged by wear or accident, it can be cut out and replaced with a new strand (Fig. 19-9). Ideally, the replacement strand should be cut from a piece of rope that has had similar use and may have stretched about the same amount. If new rope has to be used, it should be worked and stretched before cutting a strand from it.

The new strand is put in in a similar way to dealing with a long splice. Its length should be about 40 times the rope diameter, or more. The best way to lay in the new strand is to let it follow as the damaged strand is unlaid so the other two strands are undisturbed and the rope keeps its shape. Join the ends of the strand in one of the ways described for a long splice. See that the new piece is properly bedded in place before tensioning its end tucks.

If there are two damaged strands and the third one is still sound, it is possible to put in two new pieces with pudding splices, but it is advisable to fit one in completely before dealing with the

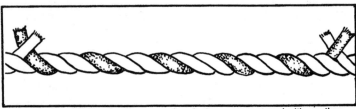

Fig. 19-9. A pudding splice is a way of replacing a worn strand with another.

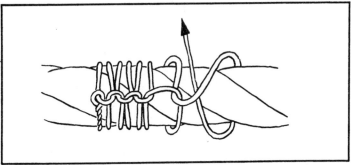

Fig. 19-10. Cockscombing is a method of serving with the directions of the turns alternating.

other. After that, the second one is fitted in the same way, but the meeting points have to be staggered. Each of the new pieces should be longer than if only replacing one—a length of about 60 times the diameter would be appropriate. Let the overlapping joints of the parts come at about mid-length positions of each other. This means that after the first strand has been put in, one end of the second strand should come about midway between its ends.

COCKSCOMBING

Splices may be served over, either in their entirety or over their ends. Eyes are sometimes served all around. A snag with ordinary serving is that if chafe wears through it at one point, a considerable length of it will soon unwind and its value as protection will be lost. One way of locking the turns is to half hitch them as they are made, but the crossings of the half hitches will stand above the serving and may chafe through. Close half hitches cannot be kept in line around the outside of an eye and some of them will come inside and be a chafing risk.

The alternative for serving around an eye is cockscombing. If a part is damaged, very little of the rest of the turns are likely to be affected. The serving is arranged around the eye with alternate half hitches on the outside (Fig. 19-10). The direction of the turns is reversed each time. Besides being a safer way of half hitching, cockscombing is also a decoration.

Braided Rope Splices

20

Braded rope has its outer casing made by a pattern of interwoven fine strands around the rope in opposite directions. This makes a smooth exterior which is pleasant to handle, easy running and with little tendency to kink. The outside of most of these ropes are in the form of a round plait, with several parallel fine strands each way, but the inside construction varies. There may be a core of straight and parallel yarns of filaments sufficient to fill the outer casing. There may be a second plaited cover inside the first and then a parallel yarn core. Another form has an inside which is a normal three-strand rope filling the plaited outside casing.

Of course, none of the usual tucked splices suitable for stranded rope can be used and there have to be special ways of dealing with braided rope and these vary according to the construction of the rope. Very tightly-woven braided rope cannot be treated in any way that could be regarded as a splice and joints have to be made by knotting or sewing and seizing. For other more loosely-made ropes there are special splices. Fortunately, synthetic braided ropes are of a much looser construction, so the casing and core can be manipulated to allow tucking and burying the working part of a splice to give a strong neat finish.

TOOLS

Some other tools are needed besides the knife and plain spike—the only ones needed for splicing stranded rope. Thread or

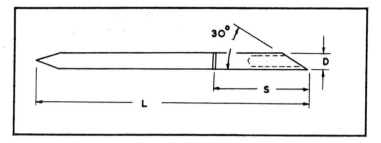

Fig. 20-1. A special fid leads strands through braided rope.

twine has to be taken through the rope in some splices. This is best done with a sailmaker's needle. It has a triangular point larger than the parallel round part next to the eye, so it forces a gap large enough for the double thickness of twine to go through. Needles are graded by a gauge thickness—the higher the number, the thinner the needle. For ropes up to about ¾ inch thick, sizes between 12 and 18 gauge should be suitable. For the small amount of sewing in an occasional splice it will be satisfactory to force the needle through with a piece of metal, such as the side of a knife, or by pressing the eye down on the bench, but for much sewing it is better to have a *sailmaker's palm*. This is a leather strap to fit over the thumb and across the palm of the hand, with a metal pad to thrust against the needle.

In some braided rope splices the end of the rope has to be pulled through. It could be tied to a piece of twine in a needle that does the pulling after a spike has opened a space. For small ropes there could be a bodkin, as used for domestic needlework. A better tool would be an awl in a wooden handle with an eye end (Fig. 20-2A), such as is used by leatherworkers and for making some types of rug. In some splices part of the rope has to be tucked along another part. For that it is necessary to have a special fid and pusher. The end of the piece to be tucked goes into a hole in the end of the fid and the pusher holds its there and thrusts the fid through (Fig. 20-1).

Recommended sizes for the fids are shown in Table 20-1 as suggested for their ropes by Samson Cordage Works. One pusher size should suit all sizes. It should be a metal rod, up to 3/16-inch diameter, in a handle. There will have to be some briefly held temporary seizings and these are most conveniently made with adhesive tape. In some splices, positions have to be marked on the rope. A wax marker is better than an ordinary pencil.

Table 20-1. Recommended Fid Sizes.

Recommended Fid Sizes.			
Rope diameter	Fid diameter (D)	Fid length (L)	Short section (S)
¼	7/32	5½	2 1/16
5/16	¼	6¾	2½
⅜	5/16	7¾	2⅞
7/16	⅜	9½	3 9/16
½	7/16	11	4⅛
9/16	½	12¼	4¼
⅝	9/16	14	4½
¾	11/16	16	4¾
⅞	13/16	19	5
1	15/16	21	5¼

FLEMISH EYE

Of the splices already described for stranded rope, the only one adaptable to braided rope, without alteration is the blemish eye (Fig. 18-8), but the method described there should only be used for quite small eyes. If the eye is larger (more than about three times the diameter of the rope), there is no need to open the rope around the eye.

For the usual soft-laid synthetic braided rope, allow a length of 15 to 18 times the diameter from the end and put on a temporary

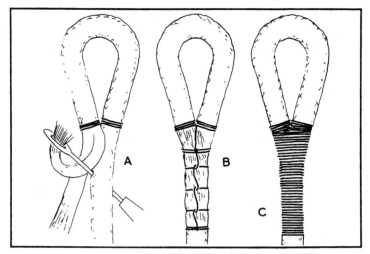

Fig. 20-2. A bodkin pulls through ends in making a Flemish eye splice: (A) temporary seizing; (B) use twine to half hitch; and (C) serve.

294

seizing (Fig. 20-2A). Unlay the casing and core back to this point to make a collection of straight yarns. It may be advisable in some ropes to also mark the other limit of the eye with a seizing.

Pass half the yarns through the rope if possible, close to where the neck of the eye is intended to be. How many can be taken through depends on the hardness of the construction of the rope. Open a space with a spike and use a needle or an awl with an eye to pull through the yarns as tightly as possible. Lay all the yarns down the rope. Trim them to different lengths to provide a taper. Use thread or twine to half hitch and hold them in place (Fig. 20-2B). Finally serve a short distance up the sides of the eye and for the length of the laid-down yarns (Fig. 20-2C).

Another way of getting a similar result has the parts of the rope sewn together. This can be done as an alternative to the first method with any braided rope, but with hard-laid rope that would resist opening for the first method, sewing is the only way. Some natural fiber braided rope with straight yarns for the heart is very hard and intended for use in window sashes.

Bend the rope back to the size of eye required and allow enough of the end to rest against the standing part. There should be a section which is kept undisturbed (about 10 times the diameter) and a further length that is unlaid into straight yarns (about 5 times the diameter). These yarns or filaments are cut to different lengths to make a taper (Fig. 20-3A). Draw the neck of the eye together with a temporary seizing.

Have doubled sail twine in a needle. Rubbing wax on it helps to make the stitches stay put as they are formed. Sew the two solid parts of rope together with large stitches through their centers. Go along the joint one way and come back with more stitches crossing them (Fig. 20-3B), sewing as tightly as possible. Spread the tapered yarns around the standing part of the rope and half hitch twine over them (Fig. 20-3C). Tension the rope so the parts settle and finally serve over everything (Fig. 20-3D).

LOCK TUCK SPLICE

With single braided rope, having a casing around a core of straight yarns, it may be possible to make a neat splice with the end buried in the rope, but this depends on the looseness and flexibility of the casing. It should be possible if a piece of rope is taken between the hands. The casing can be slid along the core and the hands brought towards each other so the pattern of braiding bunches and can be shortened.

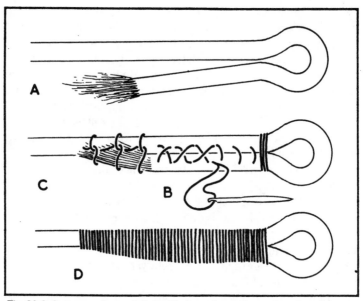

Fig. 20-3. An eye can be made in braided rope by sewing and serving: (A) make a taper; (B) go along joint one way and come back with more stitches crossing them; and (C) spread the tapered yarns.

Use a marked fid, as shown in Table 20-1, with a pusher. Temporarily seize the end of the rope with adhesive tape and measure back from it two fid lengths. Mark this position and the other limit of the eye (Fig. 20-4A). For as far as the first fid length, pull and cut out some strands to produce a taper and secure the end tightly with tape to make a pointed tail (Fig. 20-4B).

Force the tapered tail into the hole in the fid and use the pusher to force the fid through the rope at the third mark (Fig. 20-4C). Take the rope through so mark 2 reaches mark 3. Be careful not to twist the rope while doing this. From this crossing measure and mark about three diameters along the standing part. This is the second insertion point. From this, measure about one and one-fourth fid lengths further to another mark.

Push the fid with the rope in its end into the second insertion mark and straight along the core so its end comes out at mark 4 (Fig. 20-4D). Pull the end hard to tighten the locking tuck at the neck of the splice. The casing will almost certainly have gone out of shape and bunched up. Bring it to a reasonable shape, but do not pull it along the rope at this stage. Cut off the end close to where it emerges.

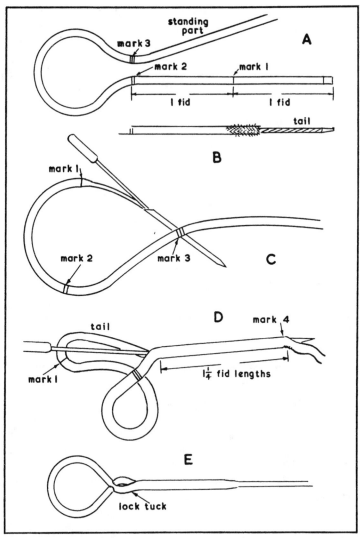

Fig. 20-4. A lock tuck splice in braided rope has the end pushed through the standing part and then along it: (A) mark the position; (B) secure the end tightly; (C) force the fid through the rope at the third mark; (D) pull the end out at mark four; and (E) cut end disappears inside the rope.

Milk the casing away from the eye by stroking along with the hand tightly around it. The effect of this will draw the casing back to something like its original form and cause the cut end to disappear inside the rope (Fig. 20-4E). That completes the splice.

There are possible variations at the locking tuck. One tuck, as described, should be sufficient to make a strong eye in small ropes, but in larger ropes (upwards of ⅝-inch diameter), the end could be taken through the rope a second or third time before burying it along the rope. Each tuck should be drawn as tight as possible, as it is made and only the last one pulled up by the buried end.

THREE-STRAND CORE SPLICE

Some flexible loosely-braided synthetic rope is actually three-strand rope with a casing formed around it. Usually the casing is sufficiently flexible to be worked back from the end to expose the three-strand rope far enough for a small eye to be spliced in it. Even if it will not push back far enough, some of the casing can be cut off to expose the core rope, but enough casing must be left to draw back over the tucks of the splice.

Prepare the core for splicing in the usual way for a basic eye splice (Fig. 20-5). Splice in the normal way, but give the tucks a good taper, possibly with no more than one full tuck, followed by several more taper tucks. Work the casing back over the rolled splice and put a short length of serving over it near the neck.

KNIGHT'S EYE SPLICE

The knight's eye splice is one method of making an eye splice in single or double braided synthetic rope with the casing loosely woven over the core. It cannot be used in older hard natural fiber braided rope. As with many other splices in this type of rope it is necessary to limit the distance the outer cover is allowed to slide along the core by putting a temporary knot in the rope further along than the splice is expected to reach (Fig. 20-6A).

Allow what is needed to make the eye with a further short length for tucking. At the point where the eye is to close, work back

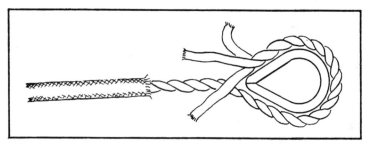

Fig. 20-5. If the rope is braided around a three-strand core, the cover can be moved back to allow the core to be spliced.

298

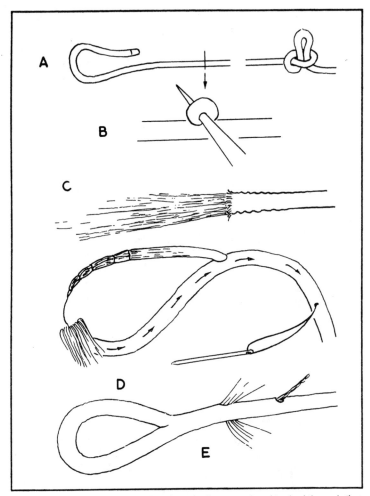

Fig. 20-6. In a Knight's eye splice the core is tapered and tucked through the standing part: (A) temporary knot; (B) gap; (C) get the end to a point; (D) use needle to lead the pointed core through; and (E) emerging yarns.

the pattern of the casing with the point of a spike so there is a big enough gap for the whole core to be hooked out (Fig. 20-6B). If it is double braided rope, pull out the inner casing as well as the core it encloses. This leaves the outer case quite loose, but be careful that it keeps its shape and does not unlay.

Taper the core. If there is an inner casing, it can be worked back to expose enough core for tapering. Wax will help the tapered part to keep its shape, but seize around it with fine thread, half hitched. Get the end almost to a point (Fig. 20-6C). Unlay the yarns of the outer casing for about 3 inches. Attach the end of the tapered core securely to a length of twine on a needle.

The tapered core has to be drawn through the casing the other way and further along the standing part of the rope. It will go into the open part of the casing easily as far as where it has been pulled through the side, but after that it has to go in alongside the existing core. The casing can be worked back a little to loosen it, but a spike may be pushed along the core to make space. Use the needle to lead the pointed core through (Fig. 20-6D) until the casing has closed against its own standing part and formed the eye. Depending on how tightly made the rope is, it should be possible to work some of the end of the casing into the rope. Tighten by pulling the end.

Any lumpiness where the end is cut off can be reduced if some of the yarns are drawn out through the casing further back. Some of the yarns from the end of the tucked-out casing may be drawn through by opening the weave. The point of a needle can be used to draw through others of the tucked end of the core, so there are some yarns emerging at places back from where the end is (Fig. 20-6E). Cut off what is left of the end. Milk the rope by stroking from the eye along the standing part. Undo the knot further along. The tucked ends should disappear inside and the finished splice should show little evidence of how it was made.

SAMSON EYE SPLICE

This is the eye splice recommended by the makers for double braided synthetic rope. The result is a strong neat splice that has all

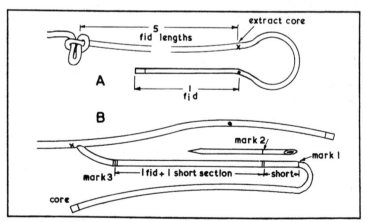

Fig. 20-7. For a Samson eye splice the core is extracted and lengths marked: (A) temporary knot and (B) short section marks.

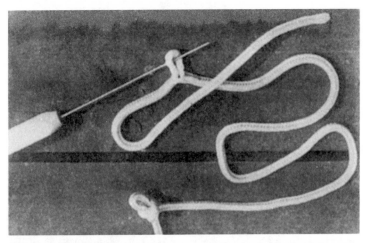

Fig. 20-8. The first step in making an eye splice in double-braided rope is extracting the core.

its construction hidden. A marked fid of the appropriate size for the rope is essential for this splice.

Prepare the rope with one fid length to a mark, then allow the amount needed for the eye and mark its end. Go about five fid lengths to a temporary knot to restrict movement of the casing (Fig. 20-7A). At the second mark make a gap in the weave of the cover and extract the core from there to the end (Fig. 20-8). Smooth the cover from near the knot to check that there has been no slipping. Note the position on the core where it emerges from the outer casing. Slide the cover back from this point about one-third of the fid length and make a mark on the core. Make further marks from it along the core at a distance equal to one fid and its short section, then another short section (Fig. 20-7B).

Push the fid into the core at mark 2 and pass its point through so it just emerges at mark 3. This can be accomplished by bunching the core casing back on to the fid. Put the end of the outer casing in the hole in the fid and jam the end of the pusher into it (Fig. 20-9). Push the fid and the outer cover through until the first mark on the outer cover almost disappears into the core. Remove the tools and leave the end projecting.

In the next stage the core has to be pushed through the cover. Enter the point of the fid at the first mark in the cover and push it through to emerge at the mark indicating where the end of the eye is to be. If the eye is to be quite large loop, and much further around than the length of the fid, take the fid and its following core out

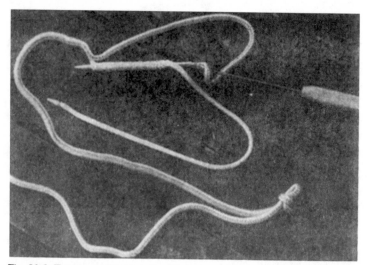

Fig. 20-9. The cover, fitted into the fid, is passed through the core of double-braided rope with a pusher.

through the casing at any convenient point. Pull this much through and re-insert the fid in the same place to go on at a further stage (Fig. 20-10A). Pull the core end through until it is tight and handle the casing to get its tension right and the crossover tight in both directions.

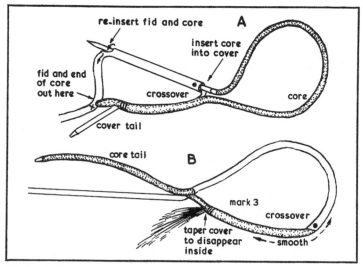

Fig. 20-10. The two parts are tucked through each other with the aid of a fid: (A) re-insert the fid and (B) unlay and cut the yarns.

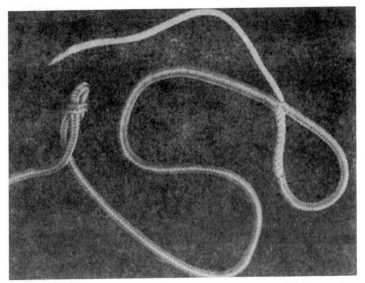

Fig. 20-11. With the cover buried in the core the splice is ready for the final stage.

The next step is to make the end of the cover disappear inside the loops. Unlay a short distance and cut the yarns to different lengths to get a tapered end (Fig. 20-10B). Smooth both sides of the loop away from the crossover and these tapered cover ends will disappear into the rope at mark 3 (Fig. 20-11).

The cover now has to be drawn over the core and crossover. Hold the rope tightly at the knot and *milk* the cover by gripping and stroking tightly away from the knot (Fig. 20-12). This action will cause the cover to work around the loop. Continue until the whole eye is enclosed in the cover. Smooth the eye towards the core tail. Cut that off reasonably close to the cover, but there can be a short piece left. Pull at the top of the eye and the end should disappear into the rope. Untie the knot and even up the cover pattern by smoothing and stretching the whole rope to get the final shape (Fig. 20-13).

New double braided rope should give no trouble in making this splice. If used rope seems tighter than desirable for making this splice, soaking in water for a few minutes will loosen and lubricate the fibers.

If the eye is to be made around a thimble, it should be inserted after the core and casing are fitted into each other, but before the loop is drawn to size. Excessive tightness at this stage should be

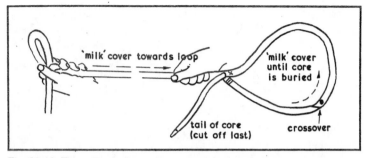

Fig. 20-12. The splice is drawn into its final shape by milking the cover.

avoided as the casing has to be drawn around the loop over the thimble in the final stage.

BACK SPLICE

As with stranded rope, the usual end treatment for a braided rope is sealing with heat and a whipping. For most purposes this is the best way, but it is possible to make a back splice that finishes with little evidence of being spliced (Fig. 20-13). There is some thickening of the end when back spliced, but this is not as great as when three-strand rope is back spliced

Temporarily knot some distance from the end of a double-braided rope to prevent the casing from moving too far. Measure one fid length from the end and make a mark (Fig. 20-14A). Open the cover there by moving back some of the weave and extract the whole of the core through this point. Tape the ends of the core and the casing to prevent them from unlaying.

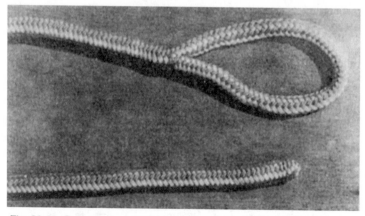

Fig. 20-13. Completed eye and back splices in double-braided rope.

Mark the position of the core where it emerges from the casing after checking that the rope is still normal up to that point. Slide the cover back from this mark on the core to expose enough of the core to make more marks on it equal to the short distance on the fid back from mark 1, then another distance equal to a full fid and a short part (Fig. 20-14B). Push in the fid at mark 2 and out at mark 3 by bunching the core back along it. Jam the end of the cover into the fid and use the pusher to take it through (Fig. 20-14C). Besides pushing, the braid can be milked back over the fid to help it through. Pull the end through and remove the tools.

Remove the tape from the end of the cover. Smooth the core from mark 2 towards mark 3 and the tucked cover end will disappear. When this happens, hold at mark 3 and smooth the core from there towards mark 2 until all excess is eliminated (Fig. 20-14D).

Hold the knotted part of the rope and milk the casing back towards the splice. The cover will slide over marks 3 and 2 and then mark X. Carry on milking for the bump at X to go inside the cover (Fig. 20-14E). Cut off the projecting core close to the cover. Work a little more of the cover over the end to hide this and complete the splice.

SINGLE BRAID END-TO-END SPLICE

If two ropes of the same size made with a braided cover over a straight or twisted core are without an inner braiding, they can be joined with a splice that comes between long and short in size and finishes· with a slight bump at the center. Prepare both ends by taping their ends and marking at 1, 2 and 3 fid lengths from the end (Fig. 20-15A).

At mark 1 count 16 pattern crossings towards the end and pull out each group of marked strands (Fig. 20-15B). This will remove all the strands tucked one way and leave only those going the other way. Tape the now thinner ends and overlap the two ropes ready for splicing (Fig. 20-15C).

Push the fid into mark 2 so it emerges from mark 3 of one rope. Put the end of the other rope in the fid and push it through (Fig. 20-15D). Pull the rope through and remove the tools. Continue pulling the rope through until mark 2 is buried.

Put the fid into the other rope and enter it a short distance from the first insertion point—a distance about the same as the diameter of the rope should be sufficient. Take the fid and the other rope tail through to mark 3 (Fig. 20-15E). Pull through until that rope is buried to its mark 2.

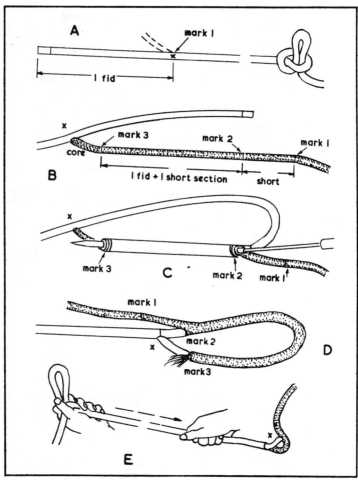

Fig. 20-14. To make a back splice in double braided rope, the core is extracted and the parts tucked back on each other: (A) mark one fid length from the end; (B) full fid and a short part; (C) jam the end of the cover; (D) smooth until all excess is eliminated; and (E) continue milking.

Smooth the outer cover in both directions from the crossover until most of the slack has been removed. Cut off the projecting tails at an angle to produce a slight taper, then smooth out more of the casing until the ends disappear (Fig. 20-15F).

DOUBLE BRAID END-TO-END SPLICE

Double braid ropes of similar size can be joined end to end with their parts buried in a similar way to that used in a samson eye splice.

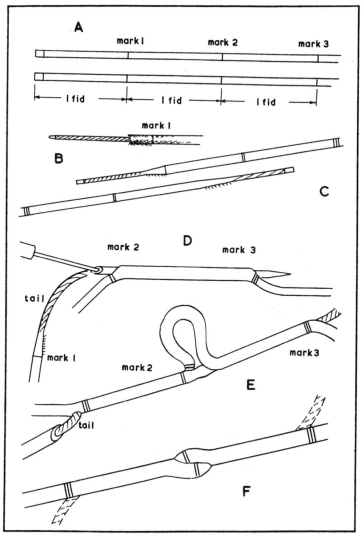

Fig. 20-15. Single-braided rope may be joined end-to-end with a slight thickening at the center: (A) prepare both ends; (B) pull out marked strands; (C) tape the thinner ends; (D) push the fid into mark 2; (E) then into mark 3; and (F) cut off projecting tails.

When joined closely there is a small gap at the center. The same method could be used to make a larger loop there as a form of cut splice.

Prepare the ends of both ropes by knotting about five fid lengths back and taping the ends. Make a mark one fid length from the end and another equal to the short distance on the fid (Fig. 20-16A). Open the weave of each rope and extract the core through the space at the further mark. Tape the ends. Stroke the casing along to get the exact point at which the core of each rope emerges, and make a mark there (Fig. 20-16B).

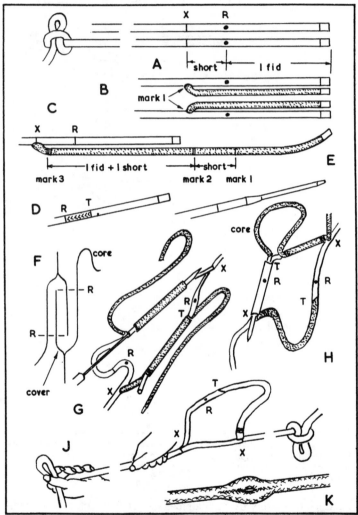

Fig. 20-16. Double-braided rope may be joined end-to-end by tucking the parts to leave a small eye at the center: (A) make fid length marks; (B) casing; (C) be sure mark positions match; (D) left-twisting strands; (E) taper the ends; (F) overlapping covers; (G) pull ends through; (H) cut off each core; and (J) continue until slack cover has been taken up.

308

Push the covers back to expose much more core, then make more marks: mark 2 at one short fid distance from mark 1, then mark 3 at a distance of one whole fid and one short distance from that. Check the two ropes against each other to see that the mark positions match (Fig. 20-16C).

The covers have to be tapered in the following way. At mark R count seven patterns towards the end. At that point make a mark all around the rope. From mark T continue marking towards the end, making a mark at every second right-twisting set of strands for a total of six. Do the same with left-twisting strands (Fig. 20-16D). Remove the tape from the ends. Starting with the last marked set of strands, cut them away and pull them out completely. Do this with the marked strands up to mark T. This tapers the end, which should be taped again (Fig. 20-16E).

Bring the ends to each other with the covers overlapping up to marks R and the extended cores on the outside (Fig. 20-16F). Push the fid into one core at its mark 2 and out at mark 3. Put the tapered cover in the end of the fid and push it through. Pull the end through until its mark T meets mark 2 on the core, then do the same the other way (Fig. 20-16G).

Now get the core of each piece into the cover, entering at T and emerging at X, leading through with the fid. Pull in both directions to get the crossovers tight. Remove the tapes from the ends. Hold the crossover and stroke the braid smooth on each side of it. The tapered cover should disappear. Cut off each core close to mark X (Fig. 20-16H).

Milk each cover in turn from its knot towards the splice. The cover will slide over the surplus core. Continue until all the slack cover has been taken up (Fig. 20-16J). This should leave the small gap exposed at the center (Fig. 20-16K). Untie the knots and rub the casing even.

JOINING THICK TO THIN ROPES

Two braided ropes can be joined so a thin one acts as a tail for the thicker one. The thin one need not be braided, but could be three-stranded. The neatest effect is obtained if the smaller rope is the same size as the core of the larger one, but the method can be used if it is smaller.

Knot the larger rope some way back from the end to prevent undue sliding of the cover. Slide back the cover from the end and cut off the core at a distance equal to about 25 times the diameter of the rope (Fig. 20-17A).

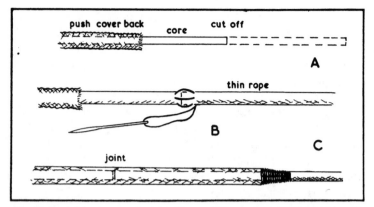

Fig. 20-17. A thin rope can be joined into a thicker rope so the cover hides the meeting with the core: (A) cut off core; (B) join the ends; and (C) lengthwise turns.

Bring the end of the thin rope up to the cut core. If they are both synthetic ropes, they can be heated with a flame and fused together when they become molten. The joint can be rolled so the joined part is made the same size as the core. Whether this is possible or not, the ends should also be joined with a few stitches arranged through each part (Fig. 20-17B). Smooth the cover over the joint and along the thinner rope.

Put on a few turns of a whipping (West Country is appropriate) a short distance back from the end of the cover to hold it to the thinner rope. Open the end of the cover and arrange a taper by cutting back some of the strands to different lengths. Continue to whip over this until the strand ends have been passed.

Although a normal whipping around the rope may be satisfactory, a secure attachment is made by having the whipping line through a needle, then after the turns have been put on there can be some lengthwise turns over the others and through the rope (Fig. 20-17C).

Wire Splices  21

Wire rope has been in use for a long time. It has several advantages over fiber rope. It is of greater strength, has a much greater diameter and for sailing craft, it offers much less wind resistance due to its smaller size. In recent years there have been developments that have changed many of the characteristics of wire rope, therefore older publications containing information on dealing with wire rope are not necessarily relevant today.

At one time iron rope was used for situations where the rope would not have to flex very much. Once it was in position it remained under tension. This was so with the standing rigging of ships where iron wire became common for masts supports. Steel was used where the wire had to be flexible and might have to pass around drums of windlasses and similar things. If the wire had to pass around a sheave, that could not be too small a diameter or the strands of the rope would soon break.

There was no satisfactory stainless steel that could be used for rope and most iron and steel ropes were protected by galvanizing (coating with zinc). The protection did not last very long and rust was an ever-present problem, so wire ropes had to be further protected with grease, varnish and serving. It is only in the years since World War II that stainless steel of a high enough quality has been available to make into ropes. This has taken over for most situations where wire rope is used, although galvanized steel rope may still be met. There is little use today for iron rope. A few other metals are made into ropes for special purposes, but their splicing should be the same as steel ropes of the same formation.

Wire ropes have always been made with more strands than fiber ropes. The next step is a geometrical arrangement of circles that will touch and keep their shape is from the fiber rope three up to seven. Six circles around a central one of the same size make a pattern that cannot be pushed out of shape (Fig. 21-1A). The next step up with similar characteristics is 19. Many modern flexible stainless steel ropes have this formation. The greatest strength where flexibility is not required is a single strand and this is sometimes met on a yacht as *rod rigging*. The seven-strand construction is a good compromise between strength and reasonable flexibility, but for the flexibility required in the running rigging of a yacht, nineteen-strand is more commonly used.

Traditional galvanized iron and steel ropes were seven-stranded, but in many of them the heart strand was fiber (Fig. 21-1B). The straight natural fiber strand was often soaked in oil during construction so it lubricated and protected the metal around it. Of course, the fiber strand was only there to provide shape and it did not contribute to the strength of the rope. Where maximum strength is required, the heart strand is the same metal as the surrounding laid strands. In splicing, the fiber heart strand can be cut away, but a wire heart strand should be tucked.

There have been a very large number of wire splices described. The greatest need is for eye splices, and with these the saying, *different ships—different splices*, had some truth in it. Many of these splices included one or more locking tucks, with two end strands going opposite ways around one main strand. Some traditional wire splices were tucked with the lay. Wire is easier to manipulate that way and that way may be the reason for them. This is comparable to the fiber rope *sailmaker's splice* and is not as strong as tucking against the lay.

Modern wire splicing is almost entirely restricted to making eye splices in seven-strand rope. There is no satisfactory way of tucking nineteen-strand rope. For both types of wire rope there are other ways of making eyes or attaching fittings to their ends, and for many purposes these are preferable. In some of these the end fitting has a hollow into which the wire ends are spread and held by lead or solder melted in. Several more recent types have a combination of screw and wedge, so the wire ends are spread and gripped by internal and external cones squeezed together. Both of these types make neat ends in line with the wire and with no projections. Other

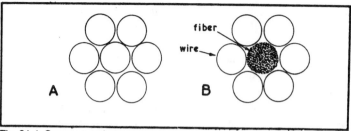

Fig. 21-1. Seven-strand wire rope may have a wire or fiber core: (A) six circles; and (B) fiber heart strand.

types use clamps tightened with screws across the rope. The doubled-back end that forms the eye is clamped to the standing part. In some devices the screw action compresses plates on the wires. They may be shaped to kink the wire for a better grip. One popular type is U-shaped and a crossbar is forced down by nuts on the ends of the U. All of these fittings have to be matched to the wire for size, then they make strong joints, although some can only be considered ugly when in position.

WIRE EYE SPLICE

Seven-strand rope may be turned back on itself, either as a free eye or around a thimble and spliced in a way which is comparable with the common fiber rope eye splice. A major difference between splicing wire and fiber is in keeping the former under control. Learning where the ends have to be tucked is easy, but making the wires go as you want can be difficult. Wire is also hard on the hands and most workers cannot get through their first splice without drawing blood. Iron wire is easiest to handle. Steel galvanized wire and most stainless steel wire is quite springy, due to the tempering it has been given. Some preformed wire holds its shape, but much wire will unlay itself for a considerable distance if nothing is done to restrain it. A loop around a thimble is easier to keep in check than a free loop, so use a thimble for a first eye splice.

If the wire has to be cut from a longer length, put a safe seizing on each side of where the cut is to be. How the wire is cut depends on available tools and its thickness. Wire cutters with a plier action are convenient, but they need to be large to cut any but the smallest wire. A cold chisel can be used with a hammer on an iron block (Fig. 21-2A). From the end go back a sufficient length for tucking. As with fiber rope, this needs to be ample as making the last tuck with a short end is difficult. A length of about 9 inches for a ¼-inch diameter wire rope should be satisfactory. Put on a seizing at this point and another to make the distance around the thimble (Fig. 21-2B), although that one is not so important. The seizings have to stay in place on a slippery surface. Use thin line and wax it just before use. West Country whippings make good seizings on wire.

The ends of the strands have to be prevented from unlaying. Leave them in the end seizing until withdrawing as you are ready to deal with them. One way of dealing with each end is to withdraw it from the seizing with a pair of pliers gripping a short distance from the end. Continue to hold with these while using another pair of pliers to twist the projecting ends around each other in the direction of their lay (Fig. 21-2C). Whether this is successful or not depends on the springiness of the wire, but with most wire it is possible to get a tight twist that will hold for the duration of tucking.

Another way of sealing the end is to have a small amount of solder molten in a can over a flame and another container of flux nearby. Dip the end into the flux and then into the solder briefly. Hold it until the solder goes dull, indicating that it has set. If the wire is greasy, wipe it before soldering.

There could be a wrapping of electrician's tape on the end (Fig. 21-2D), or a temporary whipping of fine line could be put on (Fig. 21-2E). Both would be rather clumsy on fine wire and the thickening of the end would be a nuisance, but they can be used satisfactorily for larger sizes.

The wire has to be held tightly around the thimble right from the start. The first tucks must be close to it. If there is slackness around the thimble, later working may cause further loosening, possibly so much that the thimble comes out. There are special wire splicing vises that are almost essential for large wire ropes, although much can be done with an ordinary vise and some ingenuity. For the smallest flexible steel wires, it is usually possible to get the wire tight by hand.

Put a tight seizing around the top of the thimble (Fig. 21-2F). Bring the two sides together closely into the thimble and hold them with a figure-eight seizing (Fig. 21-2G). If the wire rope resists being bent around, tapered wood blocks in a vise will pres it into shape (Fig. 21-2H) and hold it while the figure-eight seizing is put on. The splice might be held in the vise until some of the tucks have been made, but it is a help to be able to move the splice about during later tucking.

A more portable splicing vise might be made from a rigging screw where the eye goes between its sides and the screws are used to push blocks of wood or plastic against it (Fig. 21-2J). A nail

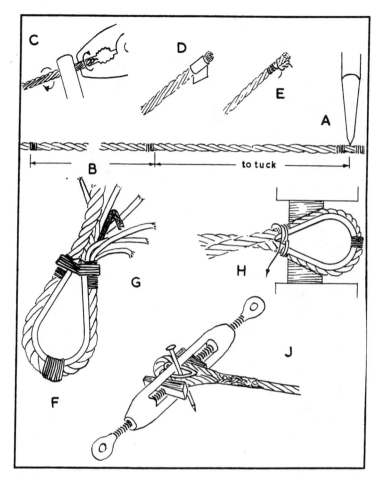

Fig. 21-2. Preparation of wire for splicing is important: (A) cold chisel on an iron block; (B) put on a seizing; (C) twist the projecting ends; (D) tape wrapping; (E) temporary whipping; (F) tight seizing; (G) figure-eight seizing; (H) vise; and (J) portable splicing vise.

through the thimble will prevent the splice from slipping back and out of the grip. This arrangement can be kept on until much of the tucking has been done.

Splicing can be done with an ordinary pointed steel spike, but with springy wire, the ends have to be tucked alongside the spike in position. If the spike is withdrawn, the wires close too quickly for an end to be entered. Some spikes are made flattened behind the point so they can be pushed in and turned on edge to leave a sufficient gap for the wire to enter. A better arrangement has a groove along the

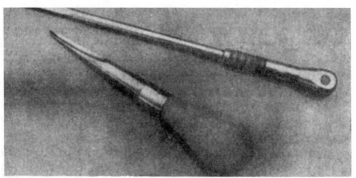

Fig. 21-3. For wire splicing it helps to have the spike grooved.

spike (Fig. 21-3). This can be made on an ordinary spike by grinding along with the edge of a stone. There are other spikes available that are deeply grooved with a section like a woodworking gouge. For small wires it is possible to use a screwdriver, pushed in with its end flat, then turned on edge to open the gap for tucking.

Fiber rope can be opened by twisting between the hands or by a direct thrust with the spike. It is unlikely that wire rope will untwist enough to open much. The spike, of any sort, is better put in along the lay (Fig. 21-4A) and twisted to bury its point under the adjoining strand to finish across it (Fig. 21-4B). Be careful that only the outer strand is lifted as it is possible to dig into the heart strand and lift a few wires or fibers from that.

If fiber rope tends to kink, its flexibility will usually pull the fibers straight and they will settle into place. With wire it is possible to let the wire kink back on itself as it is being tucked (Fig. 21-4C). If the tuck is continued and the wire pulled through, the kink may become a tight angle in the wire that will not pull straight. If this happens, twist the end of the wire in the direction that will unwind the kink while there is still a lagre curve yet to be pulled in. A combination of untwisting and pressing should keep the wire in shape (Fig. 21-4D).

If there is a wire heart, besides its position, it can be identified by being straight, where the other strands show the waviness due to having been laid up around it. For the best eye splice a wire heart end should be retained and buried in the center of the splice as it is tucked. There is no need to do this with a fiber rope heart which can be cut off. For a less important eye using rope with a wire heart, that could also be cut off.

All of that may seem a lot of preparation before actually tucking any ends, but having everything ready and amenable is very important. Arrange the ends so three are across the lay. Regard this as the front of the splice. Have the other three outside strands on the other side of the standing part. If the heart is to be tucked, bend it back temporarily between the two groups of three ends. Lift a convenient strand and put the upper end under it (Fig. 21-5A). Do not have this too close to the thimble at this stage as the other two ends have to be tucked below it.

Take the end nearest the thimble in the space where the other one comes out, but go under two strands against the lay. Arrange the remaining front end strand to go in at the same place, between the two that are tucked and only under one strand (Fig. 21-5B). Use the spike and pliers to work these three tucked ends close down to the thimble.

Turn the splice over. Keep the heart strand out of the way. Note where end number 3 goes in. Take end number 4 under the next main strand so it comes out where number 3 goes in. Tuck the other strands in turn in the same way, each going under one main strand (Fig. 21-5C). There will now be one end strand projecting from each space in the standing part. In most wire ropes the standing part will now have opened to a sort of cage. Do not be in a hurry to close it. Note a space where the heart strand comes opposite and press a part of it in so it goes alongside its own standing part in the center of the rope and projects from the rope higher up (Fig. 21-5D). It will help to avoid confusion between the many strands if the heart is laid along the rope and temporarily seized to it out of the way of further tucking of the laid strand ends.

Get all of the projecting ends brought down as close as they will come to the thimble and draw them tight with pliers in turn around the splice. It is helpful in tightening to have a large screw eye in the

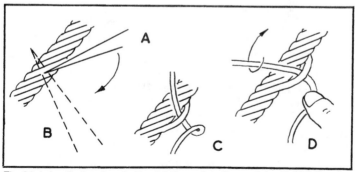

Fig. 21-4. A spike is entered with a twisting action. Be careful not to kink the wire: (A) spike; (B) twist to bury the point; (C) let wire kink back on itself; and (D) combination of untwisting and pressing.

bench and pull through that (Fig. 21-5E). So far as they will, get the ends in the same plane around the rope (Fig. 21-5F).

If the wire has opened very much it will help to get it back into a more compact form before continuing tucking. This is sometimes done with a hammer on an iron block, but that is rather harsh and may damage the wires. It would certainly damage galvanizing. A wooden mallet on a wooden block may not have enough effect and the best way is to use a lead mallet on a lead block, rotating the splice between hits.

Further tucking is done in the same way as for fiber rope splicing: over and under one main strand in turn. Try to tuck at about the same angle around the rope as its lay the other way. It is very easy to get the tucks too elongated so they go almost straight along the rope. After going all around tucking each end once, bury the heart a stage further, pushing it into the center of the splice at the space where it emerges. The heart strand does not go over any of the laid strands. After tucking all around, draw the ends to the same level and get them tight. Knock the splice into shape again if necessary.

It is common to tuck a total of four times with all ends, burying the heart at each stage. After these whole tucks the heart can be cut off and pushed into the middle. Wire cannot be tapered like fiber rope, but the splice can be given a taper by taking alternate ends and tucking them once more. The other three should be kept out of the way. Some workers prefer to tuck the last ends over one and under two.

At this stage, stretch the splice and hammer it into shape. Do this more than once if necessary to get a good shape. Do not cut off the ends until the splice is in shape, then cut the ends close to the splice and hammer again.

Oldtime wire splices were usually parcelled and served with tar or other waterproof preservative included, mainly as a protection against rust. With stainless steel this is not a problem, but the projecting ends may scratch hands, so it is still common to protect part of the splice. For small wire, the parcelling can be a few turns of electrician's tape. Leave the first two or three turns of tucks exposed. Cover the rest of the splice and a short distance on to the plain rope. Follow this with serving.

SHORT SPLICE, FIBER TO WIRE ROPE

A soft fiber rope tail may be needed on a wire rope. This often happens where the wire rope has to carry the load in use, but when

318

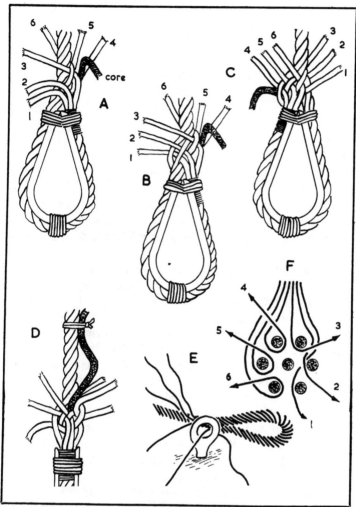

Fig. 21-5. Ends are tucked so as to have one emerging from each space of the standing part: (A) lift a convenient strand; (B) arrange remaining front strand: (C) tuck other strands; (D) heart strand; (E) large screw eye; and (F) get ends in same place around the rope.

out of use the wire is allowed to run out and a fiber rope remains attached to a cleat. It is done with some sail halliards. The fiber rope is easier to handle, but the wire rope is pulled on to the cleat when the sail is hoisted. Usually, the fiber rope is only there to provide a moderate pull and need not be very large.

For a short splice, the heart is cut out of the wire rope and the outer strands are paired. They can be temporarily seized together.

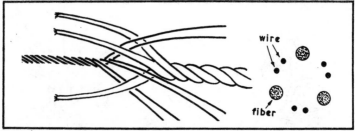

Fig. 21-6. For a short splice between wire and fiber ropes, pairs of wire strands fit between the fiber rope strands.

Although not shown, put a temporary seizing on the wire rope where it is divided and make sure the ends of the strands cannot come unlaid by using one of the treatments suggested for the eye splice. Seal the ends of the strands of the fiber rope and put on a temporary seizing where the strands divide if it is the sort of rope that will unlay unintentionally.

If the wire and fiber ropes are not very different in size, taper the fiber strands before making any tucks. Bring the ends together with a pair of wire strands in a space in the fiber rope (Fig. 21-6). From this point tuck the wire into the fiber rope in the usual over and under way, treating each pair of wires as a single strand. Having done that, tuck the fiber rope ends into the wire, but this time going over two and under two each time. It should be sufficient to make three whole tucks each way. Cut one wire of each pair and tuck the other once more to give a tapered effect.

Whether that method is possible or not depends on the type of wire and the relative thickness of the wire and fiber ropes. If the wire is much thinner than the fiber rope, the fiber rope ends cannot be tucked into the wire without excessive tapering. A better way then is to do all the tucking with the wire.

Unlay the fiber rope for some way—12 inches on a ½-inch diameter rope would be about right. Taper each strand for this full length. Scrape away fibers, mostly from the insides of the strands and use wax to keep the remaining parts in place. Lay up the tapered ends again so the end that will meet the wire rope is about the same size as it. Leave just a short distance at the end unlaid.

Prepare the end of the wire rope into three groups of two, but have these ends about twice as long as the tapered part of the fiber rope. Bring the parts together as before and start tucking the pairs of wire ends over and under one into the fiber rope. Continue past the tapered section. Reduce to single wire strands for two more tucks. Cut off the projecting ends of both ropes.

It is possible to bury the wire ends and sew them inside the fiber rope. The rope is twisted open and a few stitches are used around the wire inside to hold it there.

LONG SPLICE, FIBER TO WIRE ROPE

This splice is preferable to a short splice when there is much difference between the sizes of the wire and fiber ropes. It differs from the short splice in using the six wires individually by arranging to tuck into the fiber rope at two places. The heart is cut out.

Unlay the fiber rope for a greater distance than would be needed for an ordinary short splice. Taper the strands. Unlay the wire rope for a much greater distance—up to 150 times its own diameter (about 36 inches for ¼-inch rope). Use seizings where necessary to keep both ropes in check. Take three alternate wire strands and lay them together as a three-strand rope, using up about half their length. Keep the other three out of the way and mate the ends of the twisted strands with the fiber rope (Fig. 21-7A). For compactness in illustrating, the parts of the splice are shown much closer than they would be in practice. Put a temporary seizing over this junction.

Lay up the fiber strands around the three-strand wire part, as far as the other three wire ends and arrange these with the ends fitting into each other (Fig. 21-7B). Tucking is now done with the wire ends in the manner used in a sailmaker's splice. Each end is

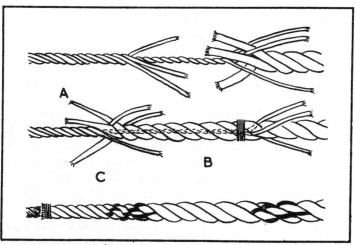

Fig. 21-7. For a long splice between wire and fiber ropes, tucking is done at two positions: (A) mate ends of the twisted strands; (B) ends fit into each other; and (C) lay up remains of fiber strands.

wrapped around the adjoining strand, not over and under across the lay. Tuck in this way four or five times at each position. Cut off the wire ends or sew them in, if preferred.

Lay up the remains of the fiber strands around the wire rope and seize the ends (Fig. 21-7C). There could be seizings over the whole splice or only over the tucked parts.

LONG SPLICE, BRAIDED FIBER ROPE TO WIRE ROPE

Double-braided rope is used for many purposes on yachts and the rope tail for a wire halliard may be braided rope and not stranded rope, therefore, a different method of splicing has to be used. This splice is comparable in size to the splice for three-strand rope. The sizes given should suit the usual yacht ropes and would have to be increased for very large ropes. The wire rope is about the same size as the heart of the double-braided rope.

Knot the fiber rope about three feet back from the end to limit the amount of movement of the casing during splicing. Slide back the casing and cut off about 10 inches of the core (Fig. 21-8A).

The wire rope does not have to be tucked. It can be sealed permanently, but this should be done so the diameter is not increased. If there is a wire heart, the outside strands could be cut back so the heart projects a short distance to give a tapered effect. This should be sufficient tapering, but for a further stage, alternate wires could be cut back. Electrician's tape could be used to hold the wires, although a good way to seal the ends is with solder. They may be filed round so there are no projections.

Unlay about 5 inches of the inner braided sleeve, picking it into its separate fibers. Push the wire end into the core. If the rope core is very tight, it may be necessary to unlay more of the inner sleeve to reduce the pressure. Make sure the wire goes in centrally (Fig. 21-8B).

Tape around the braided core that has been picked apart. Divide these ends into three groups and twist them into strands with the aid of wax. Taper their ends (Fig. 21-8C). The ends have to be tucked into the wire. The method can be used with seven strand or 19 strand. Tucking is done under pairs of wire strands. This uses all the laid strands of seven-strand rope, but the pairs should be selected equally around 19-strand rope.

Tuck under two strands, then go back around the pair again (Fig. 21-8D). Do this with each fiber strand under a different pair of wire strands. Pull tight, then either continue around the same pair of strands or go over two wire strands and do the same again at the

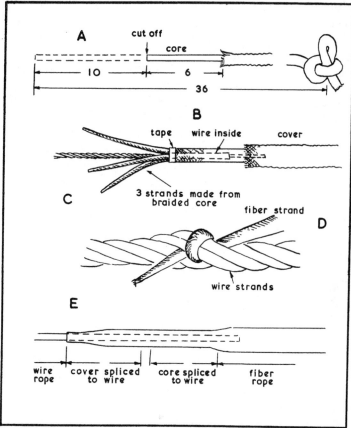

Fig. 21-8. When wire rope is spliced to braided fiber rope the wire goes inside the cover. It is made into strands for tucking: (A) slide back the casing; (B) make wire go in centrally; (C) taper the ends; (D) tuck under two strands; and (E) tucked fiber rope.

next two wire strands. This should be sufficient, although there can be a further set of tucks. Cut off the ends.

Work the cover over this part of the splice and take it along the wire until all slackness has been taken out. Put a temporary tape around the cover about 5 inches from the end and unpick from there. Make what has been unpicked into three strands in a similar way to what was done with the inner sleeve. Tuck these into the wire in the same way as was done there. The wire then has the fiber rope tucked into it in two places (Fig. 21-8E).

This completes the splice, but there may be a serving over its end. The other parts are covered by the casing. The casing should be smoothed after releasing the knot. The total length of the splice is not important providing there is a short length of untucked wire rope between the places where the fiber rope ends are tucked.

With single braided rope the core is proportionately thicker as there is no inner sleeve. The outer fibers of this will have to be kept out and used for twisting into tucking strands, but otherwise a splice can be made in a very similar way. If the core is a three strand rope, the wire can be spliced into it in one of the ways described for a short splice, then the cover drawn over it. If the wire to fiber core splice is adequate, the end of the cover can be seized to the wire rope, but if more strength is needed there, its end could be divided into three parts and tucked into the wire, as described for the other splices.

Lashings  22

Ropes are lashed when they are bound tightly around a solid object, usually to hold something closed or to bring things tightly together. Lashings may join poles together when making a temporary structure, such as scaffolding or staging, sheer legs for lifting tackle or even a bridge. Other lashings are used around chests and large packages.

The material used depends on the sizes of the parts being lashed, but if there are sliding loads it is important that the ropes are not very big in relation to what they have to hold. A large number of turns of comparatively fine line will produce more friction to resist slipping than fewer turns of stouter line. Obviously, whatever rope is used must be strong enough for the purpose, particularly if what is being assembled has to support a considerable load and failure could be serious. In the days before the general use of tubular steel scaffolding, poles were lashed to provide builders with staging to ever-increasing heights and the poles and lashings used were not individually very strong, but by designing the scaffolding on engineering principles so loads were shared, the structure was built up from parts that were easily handled.

If four poles or anything else are joined at the corners with anything but absolutely rigid joints the whole structure can be pushed out of shape (Fig. 22-1A). If there are only three parts, the structure is a triangle. It keeps its shape, even if the joints are not rigid (Fig. 22-1B). This means that when designing an assembly of

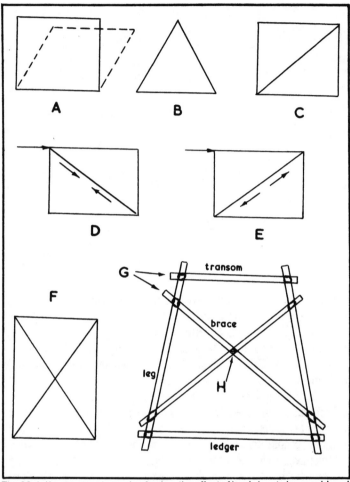

Fig. 22-1. If a structure is made of poles, the effect of loads has to be considered and lashings made accordingly: (A) whole structure pushed out of shape; (B) joints are not rigid; (C) diagonal; (D) diagonal will bend; (E) load will try to stretch the diagonal; (F) two diagonals; and (G) lashings at the ends; (H) diagonal lashing.

parts lashed together it will be better if it is built up of triangles. A four-sided assembly can be converted by putting in a diagonal (Fig. 22-1C). If this assembly is pushed at one corner, the stresses in the diagonal depend on which way it is loaded. If it is the end of the diagonal that is being pushed, there will be a compression load in the diagonal. If the load is sufficient, the diagonal will bend (Fig. 22-1D). If the diagonal is the other way, the load will try to stretch it (Fig. 22-1E).

326

In some structures it may be sufficient to have a diagonal one way on a four-sided assembly, but the common four-sided trestle is usually given two diagonals which are joined where they cross (Fig. 22-1F). This means that whichever way a corner load may come, the diagonal that gets the tension locks the one that is compressed and prevents it from bending.

To make this type of assembly there are two types of lashing. A *square lashing* is used where two poles cross and the loads on them may tend to make one slide over the other. This applies whether the poles cross squarely or at some other angle. In the standard trestle, these are the lashings to use at the ends of all the poles (Fig. 22-2G). Where poles cross there could be a bending load in one of them in some circumstances and the other would have to resist it. The lashing used is a *diagonal lashing,* therefore this occurs at the centers of the braces in the trestle (Fig. 22-1H).

If legs have to be spread after lashing, that is a place for a *sheer lashing*. It can also be used if overlapping poles are to be lashed to make a greater length. Variations on the three lashings cover most needs.

SQUARE LASHING

In most circumstances one pole will be more upright than the other. It is common to start lashing on the more upright pole below the other, mainly for convenience, as this means that the first turns support the other pole. Any of the knots for attaching a rope to a spar could be used, but it is usual to make a clove hitch and twist the end around the standing part after drawing it tight (Fig. 22-2A). The rope is then taken squarely around both poles (Fig. 22-2B), putting on the maximum tension at every turn. It would be unsatisfactory to

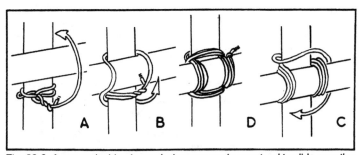

Fig. 22-2. A square lashing is used where one pole may tend to slide over the other and is tightened with frapping turns: (A) twist the end; (B) rope is taken squarely around both poles; (C) change to turns; and (D) finish with a clove hitch.

327

go loosely around both poles and then pull tight. Draw the rope tight each time it goes around a pole.

For average conditions its goes around completely three times, but this depends on the relative sizes of the spars and the rope. It could be four or five times. Try to avoid crossing the rope. If new turns are added outside the existing ones on one pole and inside them on the other, the turns will come neatly together without crossings.

When sufficient turns have been put around the two spars, change to turns between them (Fig. 22-2C). These are *frapping turns*. Their purpose is to tighten the main turns by squeezing them between their wraps. As with the main turns, get as much tension as possible for each half turn and be careful that one turn does not ride up on another so it might slip later and reduce the total tension. Three frapping turns are usually enough. Finish with a clove hitch on the second spar, so start and finish are on different ones (Fig. 22-2D).

How the final clove hitch is formed will control the lasting tension in the lashing. It is important that the crossing part of the hitch comes as close as possible to where it takes the pull from the frapping turns. If the crossing is further around the spar the load on the lashing will cause it to turn on the round surface, so some slackness develops in the lashing. Put on one half hitch and pull it around so its crossing is close to the pull (Fig. 22-3A). Draw it tight and it will stay in place while you put on the second half hitch (Fig. 22-3B) and make it so its crossing is close to the first. If there is any spare rope, a bight can be half-hitched around a spar.

Tightening can usually be done by direct pull with the hand. It helps to have an assistant at the other side of a lashing, so alternate pulls can be taken by him. In some circumstances it is possible to put the feet against a spar and get help from the leg muscles when pulling the rope. It is important to hold on to any tension gained while another turn is taken, and an assistant may grip the lashing while the rope is being passed around.

Rope of moderate size will offer a good grip. Lighter rope may be given a turn around the hand, but it may be helpful to take some strains with the aid of a spike. This could be a proper marline spike or fid or just a piece of wood given a rough point. The knot needed is a *marline spike hitch* and it is useful to be able to make this almost single-handed each time a strain has to be taken. Put the spike across the rope and twist it with the point (Fig. 22-3C). Twist a little more so there is a loop over the spike (Fig. 22-2D). With the tip of

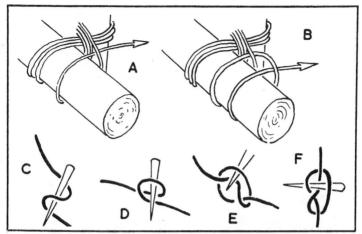

Fig. 22-3. A lashing is finished with a clove hitch. Tension can be taken with a hitched marline spike: (A) half hitch; (B) draw it tight; (C) twist the spike; (D) twist a little more; (E) pull standing part; and (F) lock spike across the sides of the loops.

the spike pull the standing part across the loop as if about to make an overhand knot with it (Fig. 22-3E), but instead of drawing the bight through, push the spike across to lock it against the sides of the loops (Fig. 22-3F). The spike then serves as a handle to grip and pull the rope. Form the knot so the pull comes against the twisted part of the knot. Besides using the marline spike hitch as a grip for a direct pull, it may sometimes be better to use the wood as a lever. Make the hitch fairly close to the lashing, so the end of the piece of wood can be levered against one of the poles.

DIAGONAL LASHING

Where two braces cross in a framework the ends where they overlap should be arranged so they cross as close as possible. In a four-sided framework this means the crossings at the square lashings are usually all on one side in three places and on the other side at one corner (Fig. 22-4A). Even then the crossing poles may not bear against each other before they are lashed. This means that the first action is to pull them close and the most suitable knot for doing this is a *timber hitch* (Fig. 22-4B). It does not matter which way this is done if the crossing is square, but if the spars cross at flatter angles, it is better taken through the more obtuse angles. Draw the timber hitch tight and put on three turns in the same direction as the hitch (Fig. 22-4C). As with the square lashing, there could be more turns.

329

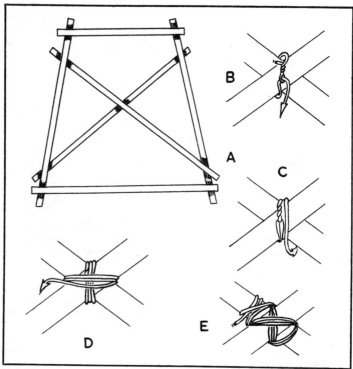

Fig. 22-4. A trestle is assembled so the parts are close and the center joint is made with a diagonal lashing: (A) crossings; (B) timber hitch; (C) draw timber hitch tight; (D) put on three more turns; and (E) clove hitch on a spar.

Change from that direction to the other way and put on three more turns there (Fig. 22-4D). Pull turns very tight at every stage, usually by tensioning at each half turn. When changing direction do it with the minimum of crossing lines. The best way is to go around the adjoining spar to the other direction, on its side nearer the other spar.

This lashing is also finally tightened with frapping turns, taken around between the spars and given all the tension possible at each half turn. Three should be sufficient, and the rope finishes with a clove hitch on a spar (Fig. 22-4E). The turns and hitch are shown open for clarity, but they should be tight with the crossing of the hitch close to where it takes the pull.

SHEER LASHING

If two poles are to cross and the load they have to take comes between them, the sheer lashing should be the choice (Fig. 22-5A).

330

This arrangement of poles may be called *sheer legs,* hence the name. A common arrangement has the lashing near the top, then lifting tackle is suspended between the legs. The crossing would be lower if the legs had to support a heavy rope under tension.

The lashing is started with the spars parallel and they are opened before completing it. Tension has to be arranged so the legs can be opened, yet the turns will be tight enough. Experience will show how much tension to put out on and how long to make the lashing, but the natural stretch of most ropes will allow a first moderately tight lashing to become even tighter. Making the lashing about as long as the combined thicknesses of the poles is a reasonable proportion for most conditions. Too long a lashing may not open enough.

Put a clove hitch on one spar and twist the end around the standing part. Put on turns around both spars (Fig. 22-5B), using a

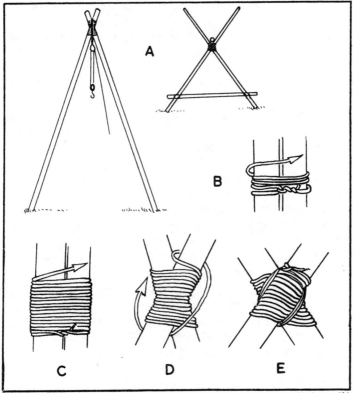

Fig. 22-5. A sheer lashing is used where poles are spread to make legs: (A) sheer lashing; (B) put on turns around both spars; (C) continue around the spars; (D) change to frapping turns; and (E) finish with a clove hitch.

moderate tension that is judged to be sufficient to allow opening of the spars later. Continue around the spars for a sufficient length (Fig. 22-5C). A minimum of 10 turns are advised and more than this if they are necessary to make up a length as great as the width.

Hold on to the tension while the legs are opened to near their final angle. Go around one spar and change to frapping turns (Fig. 22-5D). Opening the legs will have tightened the main turns, but the frapping turns will provide even further tightening and hold on to the tension gained. Finish with a clove hitch on either spar (Fig. 22-5E), again keeping the crossing close to the pull.

SHEER LASHING FOR LENGTHENING

Poles can be arranged to overlap to make up a greater length, either in scaffolding, or for a tall flag pole or some other structure (Fig. 22-6A). Two lashings are used at each overlap.

This lashing is very similar to the one for sheer legs, but as the poles will not be opened it is unlikely that frapping turns can be made. Put a clove hitch around one spar, usually near its end, and start taking turns around both pieces (Fig. 22-6B). The number of turns can be anything convenient and the lashing could be as long as the combined diameters or more. Allow sufficient length at the end for a clove hitch around both spars.

Take a half hitch with the rope (Fig. 22-6C). Draw this tight so its crossing bears on a spar and does not come over the space between the spars. Go around to make a second half hitch over it (Fig. 22-6D).

Make the other lashing at the other end of the overlap. How much to overlap the spars depends on circumstances. If the assembly will be part of a structure where other parts will keep this joint in shape, the overlap need not be very much, but if it is like a flag pole, where stiffness has to rely on the overlap, it will have to be more. The further the pair of lashings are apart, the more inherent stiffness there will be in the joint.

If the lashings have been put on tightly by hand tension, they may be satisfactory with no further treatment, but it is usual to get further tightness by driving wedges into the ends of the lashing at the gaps between the poles (Fig. 22-6E). They need not be carefully shaped wedges, but may be rough wood, pointed and driven in with a mallet.

TRIPOD LASHING

If three poles are lashed together so their feet can be spread as a triangle on the ground they may not need rope supports in many

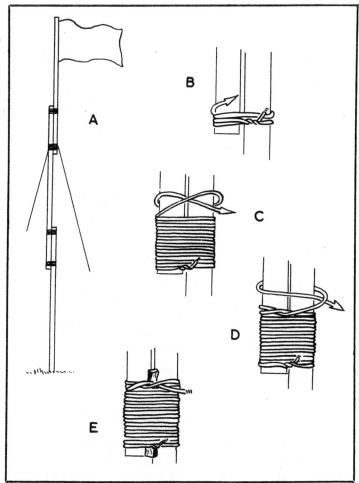

Fig. 22-6. Another version of the sheer lashing can can used to lash poles to make an increased length: (A) arrange poles; (B) clove hitch; (C) take a half hitch; (D) second half hitch; and (E) drive wedges into the ends.

applications. Three legs will stand firmly on an uneven surface, where a four-legged structure might wobble.

One way of making a *tripod* or *gyn* is to put the three poles together and parallel, then lash around where they are to be spread, using turns in the same way as for a sheer lashing, without the frapping turns. There can be a clove hitch finish and the tension of the turns have to be judged so they come tight when the legs are spread. A further tightening can be by frapping turns. The turns around the three poles are not finished with a knot, but one person

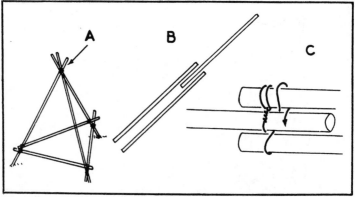

Fig. 22-7. In a tripod lashing the line is taken around the three poles in a figure-eight manner: (A) lower parts of legs; (B) figure-eight lashing; and (C) over-and-under manner.

holds the strain on the rope while the legs are opened, then frapping turns are put over the turns in two sets, going from the space between two poles to the space between them and the other poles.

A tripod built in that way may be suitable for many purposes, but if the tripod is to be used for supporting a heavy load, there is a stronger method. In any case, the lower parts of the legs should either be firmly lashed to stakes in the ground or be braced by other poles square-lashed to them (Fig. 22-7A).

The stronger three-leg lashing may also be called a *figure-eight lashing*. The poles are laid for lashing so one pole points the opposite way to the two on each side of it (Fig. 22-7B). The lashing starts in the usual way with a clove hitch around one pole and the end twisted around the standing part. The line then goes in an over-and-under manner around the spars (Fig. 22-7C). How many turns and how tight they are put on depends on the spars and rope, but it is advisable to experiment before making the final lashing. The middle spar has to be brought over so it and the other two can form a triangle on the ground. For a wide spread the lashing can be put on tighter than if the poles have to finish more upright.

When the center pole is brought over, this twists the lashing turns and the effect on tightness is similar to using frapping turns. The total distance the lashing goes along the spars has to be kept short enough for twisting to be possible, so the number of turns will be less than for a sheer lashing. This means that it may be better to use slightly thicker rope than would be used for other lashings on similar-sized poles to compensate in strength for the lesser number of turns. Frapping turns can be added if they are thought advisable, and these are put on in the same way as for the first tripod lashing after the parts have been pulled into shape.

CROSSED LASHING

The square lashing already described is the one to use in appropriate circumstances, and this has become accepted as the best way of making the joint, but battens lashed across the shrouds of sailing ships were fixed in a different way. Ropes across to form steps for climbing were called *ratlines,* but battens made firmer footholds (Fig. 22-8A).

A crossed lashing may have some advantages in attaching a light piece of wood to a thick rope, but even there a square lashing seems at least as good. The crossed lashing is almost the same as a diagonal lashing. As the parts are already touching, there is no need for the timber hitch and a start is made with a clove hitch around the shroud or vertical pole, then turns go diagonally over the joint, first one way and then the other. On shrouds the line used would have been finer in relation to the parts joined than would be the case in lashing spars, so more turns are needed for security—maybe 10 or more each way.

Usually all of the turns are put on one way before changing direction (Fig. 22-8B), but the lashings could be made by changing direction more than once—a few turns one way, then a few the other and a change of direction twice more before completing. The crossed lashing on shrouds was usually left at that, but it could be tightened with frapping turns if they seem advisable.

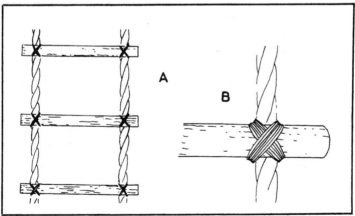

Fig. 22-8. A crossed lashing is used for lashing wood to rope: (A) ratlines and (B) all turns are put on before changing direction.

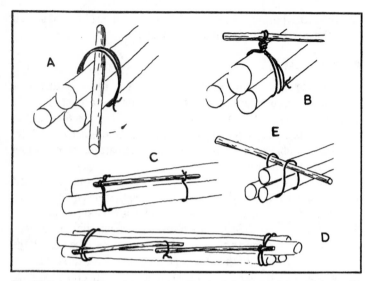

Fig. 22-9. Log lashings draw logs together by twisting rope around them: (A) pass a pole through the turns; (B) twist the rope; (C) rope around one of the logs; (D) secure the two poles together; and (E) tightening by pole through rope strap around logs.

LOG LASHING

Logs may have to be drawn tightly together, either for loading and transporting or to form part of a raft. Any lashing has to pull the logs against each other and secure them in that position. Groups of three are particularly suitable as three round logs will bed against each other without risk of later movement, but four or more may move to different relative positions later and the lashing will be loosened.

Take several loose turns around the logs. The ends can be joined with a *sheet bend,* although a *reef knot* would do if it finishes in a position where it bears against the surface of a log. Pass a pole through the turns (Fig. 22-9A) and start twisting. The effect of twisting the rope around itself will apply considerable pressure to the logs and get them together (Fig. 22-9B). Something has to be done to stop the pole from unwinding. There could be a rope around one of the logs further along to tie it down (Fig. 22-9C). Usually logs have to be drawn together at both ends, so two lashings are needed. It may then be possible to secure the two poles together to prevent unwinding (Fig. 22-9D).

Instead of the turns around the logs there could be a single or doubled rope strop made up and put around the logs so the tighten-

336

ing pole goes through its ends ready for twisting (Fig. 22-9E). The result is the same. Either method of tightening may be called a *Spanish windlass*.

LADDERS

Sometimes a ladder has to be improvised for use with a lashed structure. There could be two poles as sides and rungs made with lighter pieces of wood lashed across. If a ladder with rope sides is required, rungs could be made with battens lashed to rope with crossed lashings as they were on the shrouds of sailing ships.

For a temporary ladder it is possible to quickly attach rungs by using marline spike hitches. Two suitable ropes are laid down

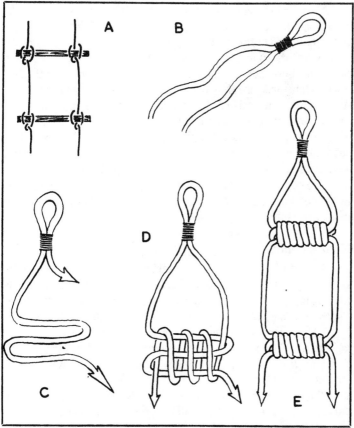

Fig. 22-10. Temporary ladders can be made with marline spike knots or by knotting the rope itself to make rungs: (A) spacing; (B) seize the bight; (C) S-shaped double bight; (D) projecting bight; and (E) tight assembly.

parallel and pieces of wood laid across. Each can be joined in without using the ends of the rope, in the way described for tightening a lashing (Figs. 22-3C to 22-3F). See that the spacing matches along the two ropes and arrange the hitches so the rung will press against the crossed part (Fig. 22-10A). If the load comes the other way, the hitches will be forced loose.

Another way of making a ladder forms the rungs as well as the sides from rope. The rungs may be only just wide enough for one foot at a time, but this makes possible climbing with a ladder that has very little bulk when out of use, and it can be made without the need to find wood for rungs.

For a single length of rope, fold it in half and seize the bight for an eye to support the ladder or lash it in place (Fig. 22-10B).

At a suitable distance for the first rung, bend one side across in an S-shaped double bight (Fig. 22-10C). Pass the other rope through the end of the upper part of the bight and take many turns around the three parts. The number of turns determine the width of the rung. There must be enough to build up sufficient width to get a foot in. Only three are shown for clarity, but there would have to be many more. When there are enough turns, take the end down through the other part of a bight projecting from inside (Fig. 22-10D). Adjust the S-shaped bight length by pulling at its ends and tighten the turns around it. The tighter this assembly can be made, the better will be the shape of the rung (Fig. 22-10E).

The next rung should be made by working from the other side, so the total amount of rope used up in making the ladder will be about the same each side.

STAKE LASHINGS

Many assemblies built up by lashing poles together have to be supported by ropes to stakes. Single stakes may be adequate in some places, but much depends on the size and length of the stake and the holding power of the soil it is driven into.

For a strong anchorage a log or a rock may be buried and the rope attached to that, but a strong arrangement of stakes is known as a *three-two-one holdfast*. The load is taken by a close group of three stakes. They have their tops lashed to a group of two, which have their tops lashed to a single stake (Fig. 22-11A). The angle of the group of three, as with any other arrangement of stakes, should be arranged so the pull comes at right angles to it or at a slightly lower angle than that (Fig. 22-11B). If the angle is too upright, the load-bearing rope may slide up the stake. If it slides down a stake

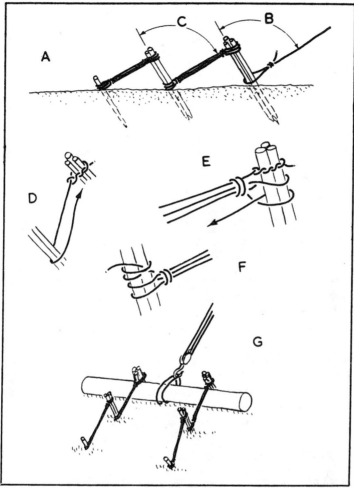

Fig. 22-11. Stakes can be given increased holding power by lashing groups to each other: (A) tops lashed to single stake; (B) angle of stakes; (C) lashing; (D) several turns; (E) go around the stakes again; (F) one or two turns around the lashing; and G) hold fast.

with a low angle, that does not matter as it will be stopped by the ground. In any case, the leverage tending to pull the stakes through or out of the ground is less, if the pull is as low as possible.

The angle of the group of three determines the positions and angles of the others. A lashing from the top of the group of three should be at about right angles to the stakes and go to the bottom of the group of two, which are driven parallel to it (Fig. 22-11C). The same spacing and angling applies to the single stake.

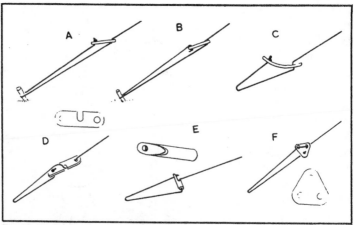

Fig. 22-12. Guy line runners take many forms and are used to adjust tension in a rope: (A) knotted end of rope; (B) reversing the knotted end; (C) curve; (D) standing part; (E) tubular type; and (F) tilt the plate.

To lash the stakes together, put a timber hitch around the tops of the group of three and get them as tight as possible, then follow with several turns to the next stakes (Fig. 22-11D). Get a good tension on these turns. At the top, go around the turns and pull them together, then go around the stakes again and back to the lower stakes (Fig. 22-11E). Put one or two turns around the lashing there and finish with a clove hitch on the stakes (Fig. 22-11F). Do the same from the top of the two stakes together and down to the bottom of the single stake.

This holdfast holds very well, but if even more strength is needed in an anchorage, there can be two or four sets driven and a log put between them to take the strain (Fig. 22-11G).

GUY LINE RUNNERS

With much lighter loads, as with ropes holding a tent up, there are usually some means of adjustment provided and these do not always hold well. The runner may be a piece of wood or metal with two holes through it. The closer the hole fits on the rope, the better it will hold. Usually the end of the rope is knotted at one hole and the hold comes by the friction through the other hole (Fig. 22-12A).

If a runner slips it can be made to put more of a kink in the rope and therefore grip better by reversing the knotted end (Fig. 22-12B). If a metal runner can be bent, a curve in it will have a similar tightening effect (Fig. 22-12C), which could be increased by turning the knotted end over.

A metal runner can be made to lock at any position if a notch is cut in its side. This need only be deep enough to take the diameter of the rope, so it does not weaken the metal. The standing part can be looped into the notch after the runner has adjusted the line (Fig. 22-12D).

Some other metal runners work in a way that may not always be obvious. A tubular type slides on the main part of the rope, but it gets a good lock by moving to right angles to the pull (Fig. 22-12E). Another type is a triangular plate with three holes. Two slide on the main rope and the end is knotted through the other. Tilting the plate so the knotted end is downward tightens it (Fig. 22-12F).

LASHING LOADS

Several knots for tying parcels have been described, but when large containers and bundles have to be drawn together and secured with rope, the techniques have to be suited to the heavier weights and stouter lines.

If a bundle has to be half-hitched around along its length, this can be done with it standing on end. A first loop goes on near the end that is upward, with a timber hitch or the end taken through a spliced eye. Form a hitch large enough to go over and drop it on (Fig. 22-13A). Draw this tight below the first noose, then do it again to get another half hitch further down and so on for the length needed (Fig. 22-13B). The end can then be continued lengthwise to twist

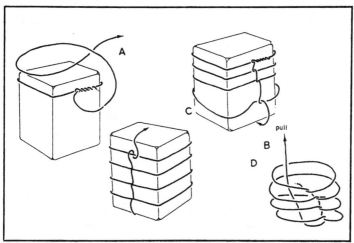

Fig. 22-13. Half hitches can be dropped around a load as the first steps in lashing it: (A) large hitch; (B) draw tightly; (C) continue the end lengthwise; and (D) pass lower end of the lashing up through the center.

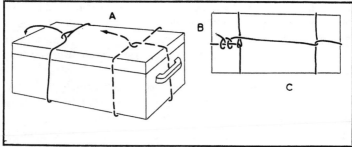

Fig. 22-14. A chest may be lashed in a manner that allows it to be opened without removing the rope: (A) rope taken over the end of the box; (B) half hitched handles; and (C) clove hitch.

into the turns at the other side (Fig. 22-13C) and finish by knotting to the noose.

Such marline hitches can be removed easily in one action. Drop the hitches to the floor and remove the bundle they were around. Pass the lower end of the lashing up through the center and pull (Fig. 22-13D) so as to draw the rope out without knots.

A chest or similar object can be lashed in that manner, but one method of securing a box with a lid in a way that allows it to be opened without removing the rope entirely has one end first surrounded with a noose and the rope end taken over the end of the box and underneath (Fig. 22-14A). If there are handles, the rope goes down through one and up through the other, then it is half hitched around the second end (Fig. 22-14B). When all the parts are drawn tight, the rope goes along the top and is tightened with half hitches to form a clove hitch on the other side of the noose (Fig. 22-14C). If the chest is to be opened, the knot is cast off and the ropes can be eased off the lid without undoing any crossing so they can be brought back and tied.

If a package is almost square it may be secured with lines arranged with two in each direction. For a parcel tied with string, this may be done with several knots and the string will be discarded afterwards. With rope it is better to do it with a continuous length so the rope does not get damaged and there is only one knot to undo to release the lashing.

The parts of the rope have to be bent around each other when they cross and this must be done tightly. Pull with both hands each time or have an assistant pulling one way while you pull the other way.

Work with equal parts of the rope. Put their center under the load and bring the ends to each other on top. Cross and turn them on each other (Fig. 22-15A) and pass one underneath in the other direction. Where it comes up, twist the two parts together again (Fig. 22-15B). The end that went underneath goes under again, so it comes up ready to meet the other part, which is following a square path on the top (Fig. 22-15C). Twist and bring the upper piece up to complete its square path while the other goes under for the last time. It can merely cross the rope on top or be twisted around it, then it meets the top end and is tied to it (Fig. 22-15D). How it is tied depends on the size. In light line on a small parcel, it could be a packer's knot. In rope it might be a reef knot or sheet bend. If tension has to be put on, there could be a bowline in one rope, with the other tensioned through it and finally secured with half hitches.

BOSUN'S CHAIR KNOT

A man may be hoisted up scaffolding or up the mast of a ship using a board suspended by four ropes through holes to an eye which can be attached to the hoisting rope or the hook of a tackle. This is usually called a *bosun's chair* from its use on shipboard. For security the supporting lines of the bridle are arranged as continuous ropes that cross under the seat (Fig. 22-16A). Even if the wooden seat broke, the man would still be supported by the ropes.

If the halliard is not attached with a shackle or other metal fitting, its end may be joined in with a *double sheet bend.* Hoisting

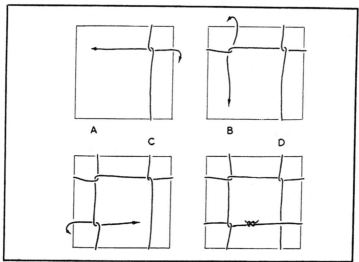

Fig. 22-15. Steps in lashing a package with a single rope: (A) cross and turn the ends; (B) twist the two parts together; (C) square path on top; and (D) cross the rope on top.

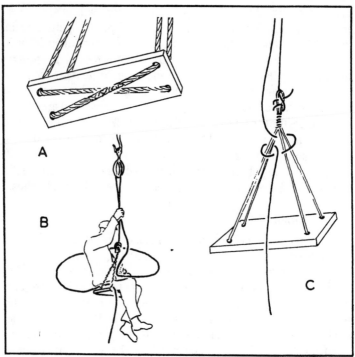

Fig. 22-16. A bosun's chair can be controlled with a bosun's chair knot made with the the hoisting rope: (A) supporting lines; (B) bight is drawn to pass over the body; and (C) projecting parts.

would usually be by men below, but then a special knot is used by the man in the bosun's chair to secure himself and adjust the height at which he works.

The parts of the line in front of the man are brought together and held with one hand. With his other hand he draws a bight of the hanging part through the bridle of the seat. Enough of the bight is drawn through to pass over the body (Fig. 22-16B), under his legs and up in front of the bridle. When the slack has been pulled through, it leaves the bight around the bridle with both parts projecting from the same side above it (Fig. 22-16C).

When tight this will hold the weight of the man, but if he draws up some of the slack and lets the line run around the bridle, he can lower to a new position safely.

Purchases

23

When effort is applied to a rope and the effect is to move a load greater than that applied, purchase has been gained. This is not something for nothing. If a small load moves a large load, the small load has to be moved a proportionately greater distance than it moves the large load. There are many engineering examples where levers are used or a small wheel meshes with or engages by belt with a larger wheel. One example applied to ropework is the winch drum, where a long handle revolves a small drum to wind the rope (Fig. 23-1). In this case, the longer the arm of the handle, the less effort is needed to wind in a given load, but the hand on the handle has to travel a greater circumference than does the rope around the drum.

There are several ways in which rope is used to apply a purchase without elaborate equipment. Twisting turns of a rope will exert a pull. It can also be very hard on the fibers of the rope and excessive twisting may break it. The amount of purchase cannot be calculated, but it can be considerable even though the amount of movement is slight.

A simple example is clamping the joints of a wooden framework while the glue sets. Several turns are put around and the ends tied. Scrap wood under the rope is advised to avoid marking the frame. A piece of wood is put through the turns and twisted (Fig. 23-2A). If the pressure has to be kept on, the lever can be put over an adjoining piece of wood or tied to the rope (Fig. 23-2B). A slightly

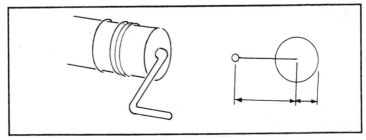

Fig. 23-1. The leverage on a rope around a drum depends on the length of the handle in relation to the radius of the drum.

different application of the same technique is seen in the *log lashing* (Fig. 22-9) where twisting the rope draws the bundle together. Frame saws, which are not quite obsolete, have their narrow blades tensioned by a twisted cord.

That method of tightening by twisting rope is sometimes called a *Spanish windlass*, but the name is more appropriate to a method of moving a load with the aid of two poles. The rope is attached at one end to a secure anchorage and at the other end to the load with some slack in the rope. A stout pole is held upright, preferably with its foot in the ground or otherwise securely held there temporarily to prevent it from lifting and moving.

A lighter pole is used as a lever. Twist the rope around it, then start moving the lever around the upright pole (Fig. 23-2C). This will draw up the rope from both sides of the upright pole, so the pole must be allowed to tilt towards the anchorage. The number of turns that can be given to the lever depends on the diameter of the upright pole. A long lever and a thin pole will move a very heavy load a short distance. In any case, two or three turns will be the maximum. The load should then be chocked and the rope released so it can be shortened, and another pull applied. The attraction of this method is that it allows a load to be moved without special equipment, other than rope and two pieces of wood, probably obtained locally.

Another useful method of using rope to gain a mechanical advantage is known as a *parbuckle* and can be applied to rolling a round object, like a log, either along the ground or up a slope. If there is a single object to serve as an anchorage, the middle of the rope goes around it and the ends are passed under the load and back to be pulled. Pulling the ends rolls and lifts the log (Fig. 23-2D). As the load rolls and the rope does not move over it, there is very little friction to be overcome and nearly all the effort applied is converted to movement of the log. For a long load there would have to be two or more parbuckles and they could be single ropes attached to stakes (Fig. 23-2E).

A method of getting a rope purchase was seen in the *rope tackle* (Fig. 9-7D), based on a sheepshank. Another application of the same principle uses a separate rope. A bowline or other loop is put in the end of the main rope. Another rope is attached to the anchorage and passed through the loop, then it is pulled to put on the strain and tied to the anchorage (Fig. 23-2F). The main problem with this arrangement and others that use rope sliding over rope is the amount of friction that has to be overcome. The effort needed to do this may be so much that the final result is very little mechanical gain.

DEADEYES

Rope sliding over smooth wood generates much less friction than when it has to slide over another rope. In both cases, much of the friction is due to the change of direction of the rope. If it is pulling around a rope no bigger than itself (Fig. 23-3A), the amount of

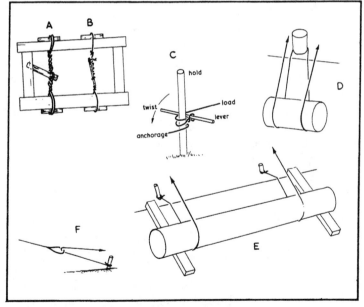

Fig. 23-2. Twisted rope will act as clamps or can be used to pull a load. Purchase can be obtained by doubling back the rope, as in a parbuckle: (A) twisted piece of wood; (B) lever can be tied to the rope; (C) move lever around upright pole: (D) pull the ends; (E) single ropes attached to stakes; and (F) another rope is attached to the anchorage.

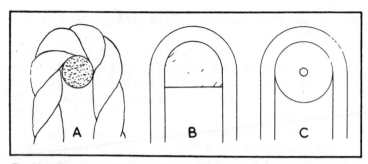

Fig. 23-3. There is less friction and wear when a rope goes around a large curve and is even less over a wheel: (A) internal stress; (B) pull comes around; and (C) wheel is substituted.

internal stress as well as the actual rubbing on the surface add up to considerable resistance to overcome before the remaining effort moves the load. If it is a larger smooth surface instead of the rope the pull comes around (Fig. 23-3B), and internal stress and surface friction are reduced, therefore friction losses are much less. They become even less if a wheel is substituted for the smooth round wood (Fig. 23-3C). Friction can never be completely overcome, but losses due to it can be reduced to an acceptable small amount.

An early attempt to overcome some of the friction was in the use of deadeyes. Deadeyes are blocks of wood with smooth holes through them. Very large numbers were used on sailing ships for setting up rigging (Fig. 23-4A). In a common arrangement a deadeye was made round with a groove in the outside to take a metal strap or the spliced eye in the shroud or other rigging. The number of holes depended on the intended purchase (Fig. 23-4B). The amount of theoretical purchase would be the same as when blocks of similar number of sheaves were used, as described in the next section. Against this would be more frictional losses than when wheels are used.

In using deadeyes one end of the lanyard being rove is knotted through one hole, then the end goes through the other holes in turn, at first loosely. Strain is put on with one part at a time, starting with that coming through the first hole from the knotted end. Final strain comes on the end, which can be finished with a clove hitch around the shroud (Fig. 23-4C). In a semipermanent set-up, as it would be on ship rigging, the end would be seized to one of the turns.

On a smaller scale the same idea is still used on yachts as an alternative to various types of screw-action tensioning arrangements. At the gunwale there is a metal fitting with a large eye, called a *shroud plate*. The shroud or other piece of standing rigging is

348

finished a short distance above it with an eye spliced around a metal thimble of about the same size as the eye of the shroud plate. The shroud is usually wire. A long fiber rope lanyard should be spliced or knotted to the thimble. Turns are taken through the thimble and shroud plate. As the lanyard has to share the same load as the wire shroud, enough turns should be included to allow for this. Six or more turns are likely. Besides sharing the load, these turns provide purchase—the more turns, the greater the purchase.

Tightening is by pulling through the lanyard in the same way as rope through deadeyes, then the end is finished with a clove hitch around the turns (Fig. 23-4D). Smooth synthetic cord produces minimum friction and this method of setting up yacht rigging is economical and satisfactory.

BLOCKS

The step forward from pulling rope around rigid wood is to bring in wheels, so most of the friction is reduced to that due to axles. Any assembly of this method of obtaining purchase is called *tackle,* which professional users pronounce *tayckle.* The wheels are not described as pulley wheels, but are more correctly called *sheaves* or *shivs.* What they are mounted in is a block, but not a pulley block in the language of the professional user.

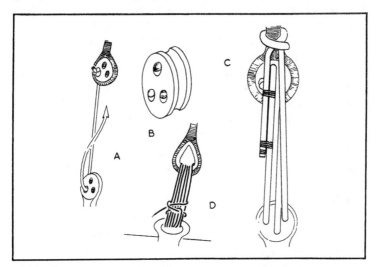

Fig. 23-4. Deadeyes were used for tensioning rigging and a similar method can be used with a lanyard through a thimble: (A) setting up rigging; (B) holes depend on intended purchase; (C) strain is on the end; and (D) tighten by pulling through the lanyard.

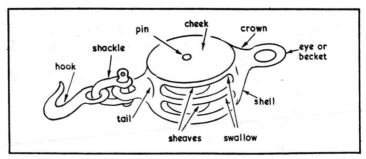

Fig. 23-5. A block contains one or more sheaves and is arranged to attach to other things at both ends.

Blocks have been developed from simple wooden pieces slotted to take one or more sheaves and bound with rope. Such blocks bound with a *grommet* are attractive in their traditional appearance, but modern blocks are metal. Sheaves may even be plastic and there may be wood added for the sake of appearance. The important part in reducing friction is the axle and bearing. There are still plain bearings, but some blocks have roller and other special bearings. The names usually applied to parts of a block are shown (Fig. 23-5). So far as possible, large sheaves are preferable to small ones as they distort the rope less and allow greater effort to go into useful work. However, there are usually practical limits, as very large blocks would be unacceptable. In the best blocks the grooves in the sheaves match rope of a particular diameter, so a greater part of the rope bears on the sheave.

Blocks are made in a great variety of patterns. All are designed to be used one way. The rope goes through the swallow. There would not be room for it at the other side of the sheave. There may be an eye or becket at one or both ends. Some blocks may have a hook or other fitting as part of the block. If a block can be opened at one side to put it over a rope, it is a *snatch block*. The pin, or axle, can usually be removed so the sheave may be serviced.

TACKLE

Blocks may be single-sheave or they can have an many as four sheaves. In most cases all sheaves are in line with each other, but there are some special cases. The use of rope through one block may be called a tackle, but this is more strictly correct when there are two or more blocks.

If a rope passes through a single fixed block (Fig. 23-6A), all that happens is that it changes direction. There is no purchase. If the action is a lift, the effort needed will be the same as the load, in theory, but actually a little more due to having to overcome friction.

If the same block is attached to the load and one end of the rope anchored, when the other end is pulled there will be a theoretical advantage of two to one (Fig. 23-6B). This would be a reasonable way of pulling a load horizontally, but obviously would not be satisfactory for an upward pull. In that case there could be another block at the anchorage to change the direction of the rope (Fig. 23-6C). It would not add anything to the purchase.

If that tackle was turned around there would be a gain, stepping up to an advantage of three to one (Fig. 23-6D). Again we have the problem of an upward lift. The problem could be taken care of with another sheave at the fixed end, either a separate block (Fig. 23-6E) or in a double block (Fig. 23-6F).

Checking on the theoretical advantage being gained is not as much of a problem as it may appear. All you have to do is count the number of ropes coming from the moving block, including anything fixed there. If there are three parts of rope at the moving block, the advantage is three to one. Ignore the number of parts at the fixed block.

This means that the advantage can depend on which way around a tackle is used as there will be one more part coming from

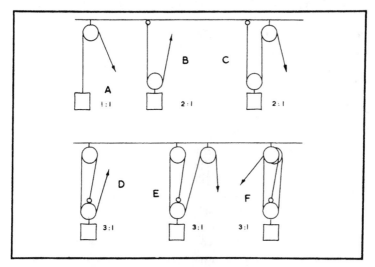

Fig. 23-6. The mechanical advantages of tackle depends on the number of sheaves and how they are arranged in relation to each other: (A) single fixed block; (B) theoretical advantage of two to one; (C) another block at the anchorage; (D) advantage of three to one; (E) separate block; and (F) double back.

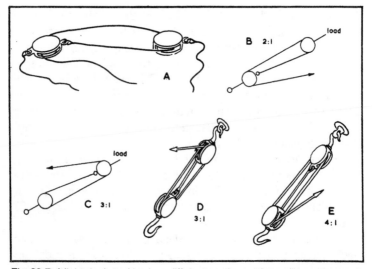

Fig. 23-7. A light single tackle gives different purchases depending on the way it is used, and having one double block increases the possible purchases: (A) beckets; (B) rigged tackle; (C) three to one; (D) purchase on three to one; and (E) reversed tackle.

the block at one end than the block at the other. Two single blocks are often kept for use when a temporary purchase is required and this tackle may be called a *handy billy* or *jigger*. There may be a lanyard at each end or beckets there for shackling (Fig. 23-7A), so the tackle can be rigged one way for two to one (Fig. 23-7B) or the other way for three to one (Fig. 23-7C).

Regular users of tackle may talk of *rigging to advantage* (meaning using the tackle in the direction that gives maximum purchase) or *rigging to disadvantage* (which is the other way around). It might be thought that rigging to get the greater advantage would always be preferable, but the lead of the end to be pulled has to be considered and the amount of movement required comes into calculations. For a purchase on three to one (Fig. 23-7D), three times as much rope has to be pulled through as the movement of the load. With the same tackle reversed the purchase goes up to four to one (Fig. 23-7E), but four times as much rope has to be pulled through as the movement of the load. Looked at another way, the load is not moved as far with the same amount of rope, but you use less effort.

Sailing ship seamen had special names for tackles and their parts. Many of these names have fallen from use, but in case they are met, here are some of them. A rope through a single block that changes its direction is a *whip*. If the single block is at the load, it is a *runner.* Two single blocks make a *gun tackle.* A single and a double block make a *luff tackle.* A double and a treble block make a *winding tackle.* Although the rope through deadeyes is a lanyard, that through blocks is a *fall.*

If one tackle is attached to the fall of another, as when a handy billy is attached with a rolling hitch to the much larger rope coming from a heavy tackle, the advantage at the fall of the handy billy is the product of whatever gain there is already on the heavy tackle and that of the handy billy.

A simple application is a *whip upon whip.* A second block is attached to the fall from a fixed block (Fig. 23-8A). Only one block is moving and there are two parts from it, so the advantage is two to one. The same applies to a double whip (Fig. 23-8B).

Sometimes the extra thickness of a normal double block would be a nuisance and one sheave is put below the other. It may be called a *burton* (Fig. 23-8C), but the effect of its use in tackle is no different.

The name burton also occurs in other arrangements. A *single burton* or *Spanish burton* uses two single blocks to get a three-to-one purchase with a downward pull on the fall (Fig. 23-8D). The

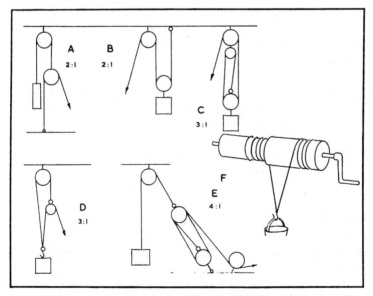

Fig. 23-8. Blocks can be arranged other than in pairs for special applications. Drums of different sizes will give considerable purchase: (A) second block; (B) double whip; (C) burton; (D) downward pull on the fall; (E) lead block; and (F) handle is turned.

normal arrangement of two single blocks gets a two-to-one advantage if there is to be a downward pull. However, the Spanish burton suffers from not having a very long lift.

Although a downward pull is preferable to an upward one, the amount of effort a man can apply is limited by his own weight. At that stage he is lifted off the ground. It is better to have a lead block (Fig. 23-8E) so the pull can be taken with the feet braced and additional help can be employed. In such a case, a helper should be at the tail of the rope, taking up slack at a secure point as the rope is pulled through so it cannot run back if the pullers relax.

Rope tackle based on blocks with a large number of sheaves has little use today. If such multiple tackle is met, the purchase can always be found by counting the number of rope parts coming from the moving block. One frequent problem with such tackles was the tendency to twist. Rope was rove in special ways to minimize this, but when parts of the fall rub and twist, friction can build up to a point where the tackle cannot be used. Lifts that would have been done with this multiple tackle are now made with chain hoists, usually power-driven.

There is one chain hoist with a continuous chain over wheels of different diameter that provides a good purchase. This is based on the same principle as a two-diameter windlass drum that was used for many purposes, but an example is that arranged to lift a heavy well bucket. As the handle is turned, the rope unwinds from one diameter drum and winds on to the other (Fig. 23-8F). With very little difference between the diameters, the weight that could be lifted a short distance is considerable. With an increased difference there could be a greater movement but the mechanical advantage would be less, although still a useful amount, coupled with a greater movement of the load.

If rope is to be rove permanently to a tackle, put an eye splice in the end, preferably around a thimble, and shackle this to the becket on a block. For a temporary attachment there could be a *round turn and two half hitches*. For a very small becket the end may only pass through once. In that case and preferably in the full knot, seize the end to the standing part after the half hitches. The free end of the rope should be whipped, but there should normally be an overhand or figure-eight knot in it to prevent it from running away.

Usually when tackle is used the end will be secured elsewhere, either knotted or held by a cleat or belaying pin. Sometimes it may be more convenient to secure the rope at the tackle, particularly if it is temporary and the fall will soon have to be pulled again. The

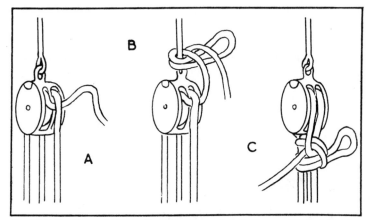

Fig. 23-9. Tackle can be locked by using its own fall: (A) free part of the fall under a turn; (B) temporary hold; and (C) clove hitch around parts between the blocks.

method of securing is called *choking the luff*.

To do this, the free part of the fall is put under a turn that would be pulling into the throat of a block if the load was allowed to run (Fig. 23-9A). That may be all that is needed for a temporary hold, but a bight of the fall can be used to put a half hitch above the block (Fig. 23-9B). It could be continued with a second half hitch to form a clove hitch in the bight.

A strong pull by the load could cause the part of the fall nipped under the turn through the swallow to pull in and jam, particularly if there is much clearance around the ropes there. An alternative to avoid this risk is to use the bight of the fall to make a clove hitch around the parts between the blocks (Fig. 23-9C). The first method locks the tackle exactly as set, and this may be important if the amount the load has been pulled matters. There would be a little backlash in the last method as the clove hitch pulls tight against the block.

24   Netmaking

If a net is examined, the joints will be found to be *sheet bends* in almost every case. This applies whether it is a small net with tiny meshes, a fishing net that extends miles or a cargo net made from substantial ropes. There are just a few other ways of joining the lines to make meshes, but in the vast majority of examples that is the knot used. Obviously it would be rather tedious to make the individual knots by tying in the usual way with the considerable length of line involved, so much of the technique of netmaking is directed towards ways of achieving results quickly and accurately. Netmaking is sometimes described as *braiding,* but that name is better used for one type of decorative ropework.

The line used has to be wound on a *needle* or *shuttle.* For large meshes it could be quite crude and open-ended (Fig. 24-1A). When fully wound, the overall shape is a ball. For smaller meshes it is better if the shuttle is long and narrow, preferably with a point, so it will carry a reasonable amount of line, yet be narrow enough to go through meshes. One type of shuttle may be brought in many sizes and may be metal or plastic (Fig. 24-1B). The ends are springy and the length is waisted slightly to reduce bulk.

Another popular type in many sizes is open at one end and pointed at the other (Fig. 24-1C). Loading this needle may not be immediately obvious. Take the line around the tongue or peg in the cut-out part, back down the same side, through the gap at the bottom, then up and around the tongue from the opposite side and

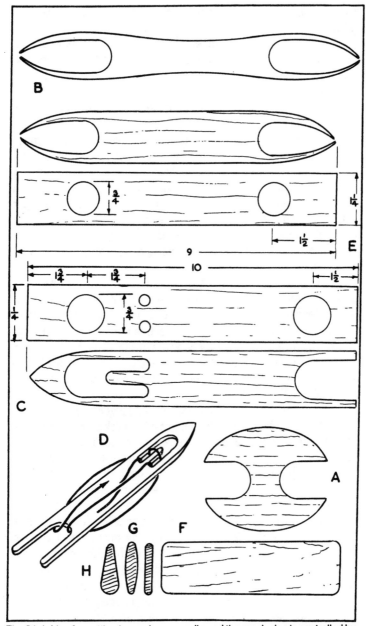

Fig. 24-1. Line for netting is used on a needle and the mesh size is controlled by a mesh stick: (A) open ended for large meshes; (B) metal or plastic shuttle; (C) open and pointed; (D) carry the line; (E) drill holes; (F) rounded corners and edges; (G) thinned edges; (H) thick lower edge.

357

down through the bottom gap to start the first side again (Fig. 24-1D).

Both types of needle can be made from wood. Suggested sizes are given to provide a guide to proportions, but these should be increased or decreased to suit requirements. Use hardwood as thin as you dare—say 3/16 inch thick for the sizes given. Start by drilling holes (Fig. 24-1E) and cut into them. Round the edges and taper towards the points.

If only a few meshes have to be made, as they might in a repair, it is possible to estimate their size or regulate them with the fingers, but for regular netmaking there should be a gauge to keep the meshes an even size. This is a *mesh stick*, but it may also be called a *spool, mesh gauge* or just a *mesh*, but the last name may confuse it with the rope mesh of the net. Its width is slightly less than one side or *bar* of a mesh. This means that there has to be a separate mesh stick for each size of mesh. As it is only a parallel strip, mesh sticks are easily made or altered.

The simplest mesh stick is a parallel strip of thin wood or plastic, preferably with the corners and edges rounded (Fig. 24-1F). Instead of being parallel in thickness the edges could be thinned considerably (Fig. 24-1G). Another section thins the edge towards the knots, while leaving the lower edge thick (Fig. 24-1H). For very small meshes it may be better to use a round rod as a mesh stick, as this gives more to hold. The controlling size of the side of a mesh is then half the circumference.

As a gauge the mesh stick need only be just long enough to go under the mesh being worked on, but it should be long enough for comfortable holding in one hand while the other makes the knot. As meshes are made they slide along the mesh stick and off the other end. Some workers prefer a length of only a few inches, while others prefer the stick longer. For a first attempt at netmaking a length of 8 inches will do.

Mesh sticks are usually wood, but they could be metal or plastic and even cardboard could be used for a small amount of work. Whatever the material, there should be no roughness anywhere. The upper left-hand corner (for right-handed working) could be rounded much more than the others to fit in the palm of the left hand.

There are no other special tools, but a knife will be frequently needed and there is sometimes use for a spike.

NET SIZES AND KNOTS

A net may have diamond meshes or square meshes. With diamond meshes the meshes have their sides diagonal to the outline

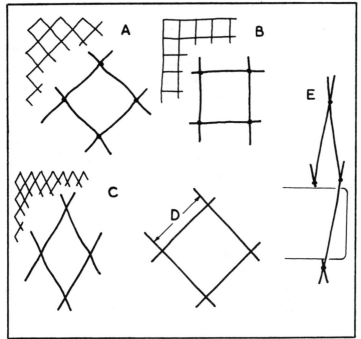

Fig. 24-2. Net meshes may be diamond or square and their size is quoted as the measurement of one bar: (A) diamond meshes; (B) square mesh; (C) taller and narrower meshes; (D) mesh size; and (E) mesh stick.

of the net (Fig. 24-2A). With square mesh the edges of the meshes are parallel to the sides of the net (Fig. 24-2B). The actual construction of the meshes is the same. Diamond meshes are usual, unless there is a special reason for using square meshes. With diamond meshes the overall sizes of the net can vary. If the sides are brought in, the meshes become elongated and the net becomes taller and narrower (Fig. 24-2C). Adjustment in this way is impossible with square mesh, so that is the method to choose when the net has to finish to exact sizes.

A net can be made with the meshes held squarely, but it is more usual and easier to let them hang almost upright. The mesh size quoted is the length of the bar at the side of the mesh (Fig. 24-2D). When hanging nearly vertical the mesh stick is kept enough under this size for it to regulate the length when knotting (Fig. 24-2E).

When determining the overall size of a diamond-meshed net it is advisable to allow the meshes to finish higher than they are wide, instead of pulling them square. Knots hold their shape better then.

BASIC NETTING

Making a net involves the repetition of knotting a new mesh to an existing one. This may run into hundreds of times, so the adoption of a routine that gets a true result quickly is important—the saving of a few seconds each time can make a great difference to the overall results, both in the ease of getting each knot right and the time taken. Consequently, the sequence of steps each time should be thoroughly mastered.

For a first net it is advisable to work to sizes that allow you to see easily what is happening. The line might be about ⅛-inch diameter and the mesh stick about 1-1½ inches wide. The needle should be narrower than the mesh stick. In many nets it is convenient to bunch the parts together, but for a first net it is better to have the meshes spread so their knotting can be observed without getting them confused due to an overlapping group.

Use a piece of dowel rod or a stout pole stretched as a bead for the net. Either arrange this so the net will hang vertically or have it along the edge of a table so you do the work towards you. Usually you work from left to right. As both hands are involved it does not matter if the worker is right-handed or left-handed, but if it seems more natural to work the other way, the whole process described can be reversed.

Secure the end of the line to the head rope, then make a series of loops along it, using the mesh stick to regulate their size (Fig. 24-3A). Clove hitches can be used at every point. The exact spacing does not matter, but for 1-1½-inch meshes the knots could be about 1 inch apart. The number of loops does not matter—10 or more would give good practice. Turn the whole thing over so the working end is brought back to the left.

Hold the mesh stick up to the bottom of the end loop and bring the working part over it so the needle goes through the loop (Fig. 24-3B). Hold the line to the mesh stick so it is tight around it. This is done with the left thumb and there are two possible ways of holding ready for making the knot by taking the needle behind the mesh. A part of the line can be gripped where it comes with the line ready to go around (Fig. 24-3C) or this loop can be turned over so there is a bight of the line to the left of the upper mesh (Fig. 24-3D). Either method is satisfactory. It is a case of deciding which you prefer. The second method puts the bight ready to bring the needle through as it comes forward (Fig. 24-3E). The first method does not involve as much line having to be looped and pulled through at each knot.

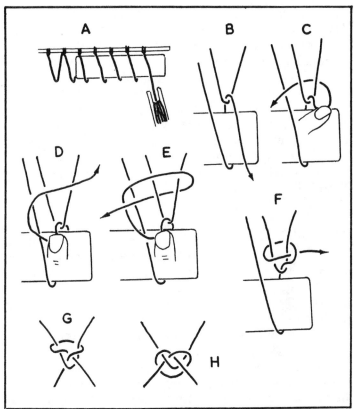

Fig. 24-3. First meshes are made along a rod and the knot is made by holding the line over a mesh stick: (A) mesh stick; (B) needle through the loop; (C) part of the line can be gripped; (D) turned over loop; (E) bring needle through; (F) sheet bend formation; (G) joining knot; (H) one part slips down.

Take the needle behind the mesh and across its front to make the usual sheet bend formation (Fig. 24-3F). Allow the part held under the left thumb to slip as the knot is tightened, so the knot pulls tight. Care is needed at this stage. The knot must close so it pinches the sides of the upper mesh and the arrangement of parts is the same as when the sheet bend is used as a joining knot (Fig. 24-3G). It is possible to let the part behind the upper mesh slip down (Fig. 24-3H). That leaves the parts so they can slide over each other. The mesh sizes would also be altered. This may happen at a later stage if the knot is not pulled really tight as it is made and before moving on to the next one.

After the first mesh has been made, slide the mesh stick through it to the next mesh. The working part of the line will be hanging in front of it, ready to make a new mesh on the next loop. Continue in this way across the net. As meshes build up on the mesh stick, let them fall off the end. At the far side reverse the net to bring the working end to the left and start across with a row of new meshes below those you have just formed.

The instructions in the last few paragraphs cover the important steps in making nearly every net. It is worthwhile to continue making this practice net until you have built up many rows of meshes and the actions become automatic working in a sequence that suits you and you are producing a net with uniform knots and sizes of mesh. You will then be ready to make many types of nets as the bulk of the work is usually routine meshing, with variations at the edges of the net.

JOINING NETTING LINE

A needle or shuttle will hold enough line for many meshes, but a point will be reached where new line will have to be joined in. One way is to tie the ends together with a sheet bend. This is less obvious if the knot in the bar of a mesh is kept close to one of the mesh knots.

Another way is to make a new knot over the top of the last one, then the ends are cut off fairly close. This is not as obvious or bulky as might be expected and is the usual way in making repairs.

The end of the new line can have an overhand knot put in it, then before the last knot in the old line is tightened, this is put through it (Fig. 24-4A).

Another inconspicuous way of joining in is to leave the last knot in the old line slack and pass the end of the new line around it. This is

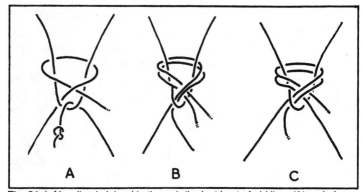

Fig. 24-4. New line is joined in through the last knot of old line: (A) end of new line; (B) both lines go into the knot; and (C) new line follows old knot.

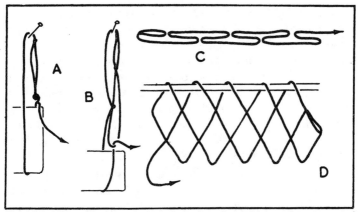

Fig. 24-5. A net can be started with a chain of meshes, which are then supported on a rope or rod: (A) make a mesh; (B) turn the chain back; (C) zig-zag course; and (D) support chain.

stronger if both lines go into the knots the same way (Fig. 24-4B), but distorting the mesh is avoided if the new line follows the old knot the opposite way (Fig. 24-4C).

CHAIN MESHES

If the net just described is wanted without a head rope, the knots around it can be slid off. That is quite a good way of making a net, but another way of starting is to make a chain of meshes for the first row. This leaves the first row of meshes knotted sideways in relation to the others, but that should not matter.

Make a loop in the end of the line as long as the width of the mesh stick. Hang this over a nail or peg. Hold the mesh stick up to it and make a mesh on it in the way just described (Fig. 24-5A). Withdraw the mesh stick and move it down to the bottom of the mesh just formed, but turn that over so the working end comes on your left. Make a new mesh there. Do the same again, but turn the chain back so you work from the left (Fig. 24-5B). The path of the line will be seen to be taking a zig-zag course (Fig. 24-5C). Continue in this way until you have made twice as many meshes as there are to be in the width of the net, as you are actually making the first two rows of meshes in this chain.

Turn the chain on edge. It will probably be advisable to support it for further steps on a rod (Fig. 24-5D) until you have gained some experience, but it would be possible to put all of the top meshes on each other in turn over a peg or nail, but care is needed as you work across making new meshes that you do not miss a mesh or twist it.

363

Selecting the correct mesh to work on becomes easier as the net gets longer, so even if a rod is used at first, the top meshes can be gathered up to one point as you have more net to handle. For a very long net, the rod or peg can be put into a lower row of meshes if it would otherwise necessitate pulling on a long length of net. It is always better to be able to tension the net as you form the meshes. It is possible to work without doing this and it may have to be done occasionally, but some sort of anchorage point is worth having.

STRAIGHT-EDGED NETS

A net made with ordinary meshes throughout has full meshes at the sides and ends, but if they are unsupported they become slack and the net has a loose uneven edge. One way of dealing with the ends of rows produces a net with normal top and bottom edges, but the sides are straight and doubled, so some extra strength is provided.

As the straight-edge part of the net will be narrower than the starting part, make a chain two meshes too long or have extra meshes along the supporting rod or rope. Work across the meshes in the usual way, but at the ends, let the knot take in the sides of the mesh being formed, as well as the one above (Fig. 24-6A). The effect will be to draw in the sides of the net after the first row (Fig. 24-6B).

If a diamond-meshed net is to have straight edges all around (Fig. 24-7A), the outer meshes have to be worked with three sides instead of the usual four. To get the sizes it is advisable to draw a mesh shape and measure its diagonal. If the diamond mesh is to finish as a square, the diagonals will be the same both ways, but if

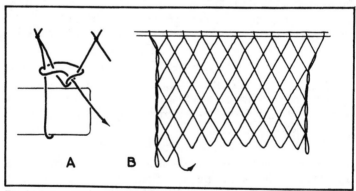

Fig. 24-6. The side of a net can be made straight by drawing in the end meshes: (A) let knot take in the sides and (B) draw in the sides.

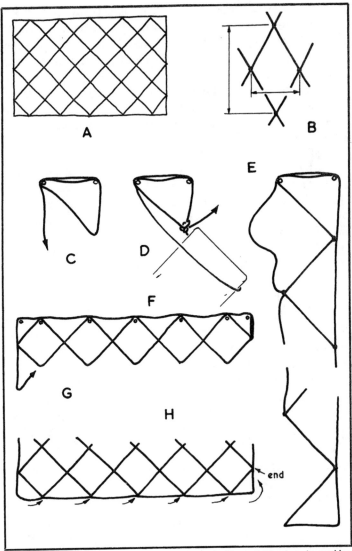

Fig. 24-7. A diamond-mesh net may be formed with straight edges by making triangular meshes: (A) straight edges all around; (B) diagonals; (C) hook over two nails; (D) tilt sideways; (E) bring the line upright; (F) support on row of nails; (G) new row of meshes; and (H) finish with triangles and a straight edge.

they are to be more upright, the diagonals across the top will be less than those down the sides (Fig. 24-7B).

Start by making a chain for the top edge. Make a loop in the line the length of a corner mesh and make a triangular mesh on that.

Hook this over two nails (Fig. 24-7C). Tilt sideways from that to make another mesh (Fig. 24-7D). Bring the line upright ready for another mesh (Fig. 24-7E). Make a chain of sufficient length with another triangle at the end to form the top of the net. Support this on a row of nails (Fig. 24-7F).

Have the working end on the left. Let the part come straight down as you make a new row of meshes (Fig. 24-7G). That edge will have a single line, but the opposite edge will be doubled as the line goes up the triangular mesh above and down to knot to a new triangular one before going back on a new row. Make a new knot on top of the one above (Fig. 24-8A) and come down to put a thumb knot around the mesh (Fig. 24-8B). Each time the line arrives at that edge it goes up and back on itself (Fig. 24-8C). Although shown at the right, the net may be turned over each time the line has to go back forming a new row of meshes.

At the bottom the line goes across the last row of whole meshes to finish with triangles and a straighter edge (Fig. 24-7H).

TAPERING A NET

A net can be made wider or narrower as it is formed. With decreasing or *bating*, the width is usually easier than increasing, or *creasing*. One way of tapering is to reduce the sizes of meshes as the work progresses by changing to narrower mesh sticks, but differing sizes of mesh may not be acceptable.

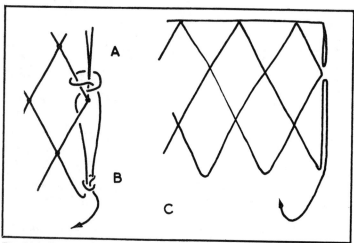

Fig. 24-8. Straight edges can be made by taking the line up to the next row of meshes at the edges: (A) new knot: (B) thumb knot; and (C) line goes up and back on itself.

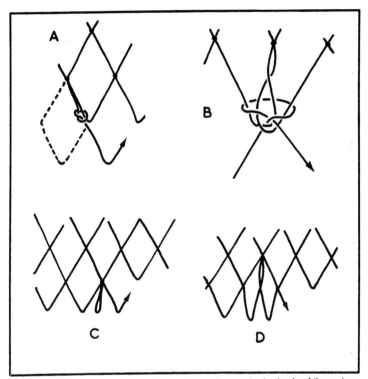

Fig. 24-9. A net width can be reduced at the edges or in the body of the net, or increased by making more meshes while working across: (A) tie back in the end mesh; (B) clove hitched meshes; (C) loop with similar knot; (D) two meshes.

One way of reducing the width is to tie back into the end mesh (Fig. 24-9A) so as to cut out one mesh. If this is done to every row the taper will be 45 degrees if the meshes are square. Cutting out meshes in this way need not be done at every row if less taper is wanted and it can be at one or both sides of the net.

Another way of reducing the number of meshes in a row is to pull two upper ones together when making new mesh below. The two meshes could be clove hitched with the working line or they can be overlapped and the usual knot formed (Fig. 24-9B). This produces some distortion, which is more obvious in a drawing than in a net. It is less obvious near the end of a line of meshes than in the body of the net.

One way of increasing the number of meshes in a row is to work a second loop. Make a mesh, then form a loop with a similar knot over the other (Fig. 24-9C). When the next row of meshes comes along, form a mesh on the top of the loop as well as on the meshes. Another way of getting a similar effect has the working end taken up to a mesh above, then brought down and knotted in line with the normal knots so two meshes are made in that line (Fig. 24-9D).

ROUND NETS

A truly round net has to be started at the center and worked outwards. In many cases an octagonal net might be just as satisfactory. If it has to be drawn up with a line through the outside meshes, the difference will not be very apparent.

To make an octagonal net the simplest way is to start with a row of meshes across the greatest width (Fig. 24-10A). It must be sufficiently built up to make the center area of parallel net, then the edges are tapered (Fig. 24-9A) to make one narrow edge (Fig. 24-10B). Turn the net around and support with a rod through the first line. Knot into the end mesh and work across what were the tops of this row of meshes, tapering the ends to match the further side (Fig. 24-10C).

A round net is started at the center with a ring of line or a grommet. Support this on a peg and work as many half meshes

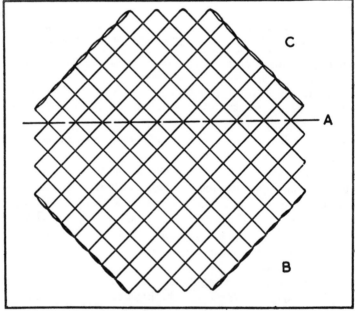

Fig. 24-10. An octagonal net is made by tapering both ways: (A) octagonal net; (B) narrow edge; and (C) knot into end mesh.

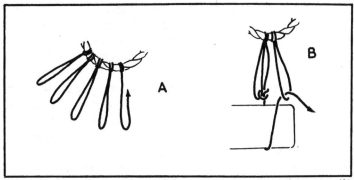

Fig. 24-11. A round net can be made by starting with a ring at the center: (A) clove hitches and (B) knot the line.

around it with clove hitches as can be fitted in (Fig. 24-11A). As further meshing progresses the later meshes become wider and better shapes will result if there are many meshes at the start.

Go to the bottom of the last mesh and knot the line there (Fig. 24-11B). Follow around all the loops, using the mesh stick to make meshes for a full circle. It might be possible to drop to the bottom of the last mesh in that circle and go around again, but the new meshes might be too broad. To correct this use one of the methods of increasing symmetrically for the sake of appearance.

If the circle has to finish flat lay it out on a flat surface as it progresses. Include increasing stitches as necessary so the added meshes keep a fairly uniform appearance. If the net has to finish in a more dished shape the need for increasing will not be as great because the new meshes can be arranged to pull the net into shape. If it is a deep net the later rounds of meshes will be in the form of a cylinder so they will all be the same shape. After each round of meshes the line goes along the side of the last mesh and is knotted to it, in the same way as when starting a circular net.

A net that is only part of a circle can be made in the same way. Meshes start at the center on a loop, but are only carried around as far as needed. As rows of meshes are made their limits are treated in the same way as a straight-edged net, so a straight line goes out from the center to the circumference and the result is a net that forms a sector of a circle.

A tubular net may be needed around a rigid frame for games or fishing. The first row of meshes may go through holes or around a rod. The method of working is very similar to that used when a flat net is made on a straight rod. Go around the circle making half meshes. When the start is reached, drop down to the bottom of the

369

last mesh and make a thumb knot there (Fig. 24-12A). Go around again and continue to make meshes for the length needed. Working in this way makes a parallel cylinder. If the bottom has to be closed it may be sufficient to put a line through the bottom meshes and draw them together (Fig. 24-12B).

A larger net cylinder may not draw together in this way very neatly. It would be better then to reduce the number of meshes in the last few rows by linking some together (Fig. 24-9B and 24-12C). This can be done evenly spaced around the cylinder and at different positions in each row, so the final row has very few meshes left to draw together with a line and the bottom of the net has a rounded shape. This is an easier way of making a closed net than to start at the bottom with a round net and change to cylinder.

SQUARE MESHES

A square-meshed net has exactly the same method of knotting between meshes, but the pattern may be regarded as having its top at one corner instead of along an edge. This means that rows of meshes are made diagonal to the shape of the net. The finished net will tension rigidly to size and this is particularly important in nets for some games. Square meshes are not so tolerant of uneven working as diamond meshes, so care is needed to keep the mesh sizes even or the lines of mesh sides may not follow neatly in both directions across the net. If there is no particular need for square meshes—

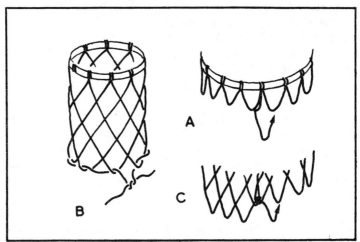

Fig. 24-12. A tubular net is made by dropping the line down to the bottom of a mesh after each round: (A) thumb knot; (B) draw lines together; and (C) link some together.

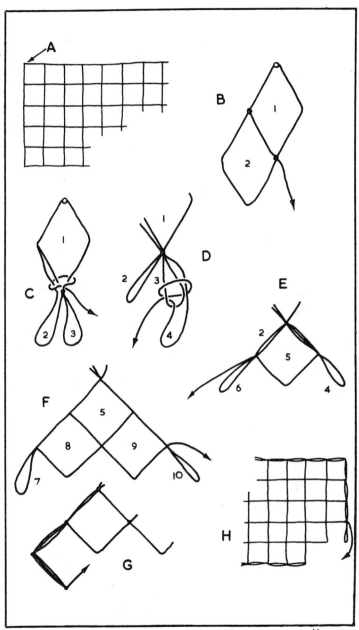

Fig. 24-13. Square-meshed nets are made by starting at a corner and increasing each row: (A) make the start; (B) hook loop over nail; (C) make another loop; (D) adjust by the mesh stick; (E) proper mesh; (F) two new meshes; (G) bottom corner; and (H) rows of meshes.

usually due to the need for rigidity of size—diamond meshes should be chosen.

Make a start at what will be the top left-hand corner (Fig. 24-13A). One mesh is made there and on it goes two meshes, which then build up to three and so on until another corner is reached, then that edge is reduced while the other edge continues to be increased.

The first method produces a net with doubled strands along the edges. This may be desirable for strength, but if the net will be attached to another rope, it would not matter and the second method could be used.

Make a loop of the size of the first mesh and hook it over a nail so its knot is at one side (Fig. 24-13B). Use the line to make another mesh to one side of it. Make a loop to the same length and use the line to draw in the side of the first mesh (Fig. 24-13C). The two loops hanging will actually form part of the border and the first mesh serves to hang the net while working and can be cut off later.

Make another loop, adjusted by the mesh stick on the bottom of one loop (Fig. 24-13D), then make a proper mesh across to the other loop (Fig. 24-13E). At that point make another loop, called a *false mesh*.

There are now three points where the line can be attached to go across. Bring the line down to the bottom of the nearest one and knot it there, then make a new false mesh below it and go across to make two new meshes (Fig. 24-13F). Although shown open for clarity, meshing can be done with the parts hanging from the nail. The numbers on the drawing indicate the sequence in which the meshes are made. From this point false meshes are made every time the end of a row is reached and full meshes are made across, so one more mesh goes into a row each time.

When a bottom corner is reached, take in two meshes with one knot the next time the working end returns to that side (Fig. 24-13G). This reduces the row by one mesh and turns the corner at right-angles. As more rows of meshes are added, treat the other side as before, but at the end of the line reduce meshes by one each time so the edge becomes straight and parallel to the top edge.

Continue in this way until the longer edge is the required length. Turn this corner in the same way as at the earlier bottom corner. From this point continue making rows of meshes, but reduce at both ends (Fig. 24-13H) until only one mesh is left.

The second method produces a net with alternate single and double edges to the meshes around the net. Make two meshes as if starting a chain, then make a third mesh in the side of the first mesh

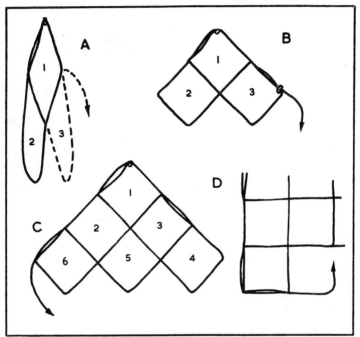

Fig. 24-14. Another method of making a square-meshed net has fewer lines along the edges: (A) third mesh; (B) knot it; (C) knot into its own side; and (D) turn corner.

(Fig. 24-14A). Hang the top mesh from a hook and take the working end down the side of the nearer mesh and knot it to it (Fig. 24-14B) diagonally in line with the other knots.

Work back across the two main meshes and make a third mesh by knotting into the side of the end one and come down to knot into its own side (Fig. 24-14C). Make a new row of meshes and continue bringing the line down the side of meshes at alternate ends, building up the pattern until the bottom corner has been reached. Turn the corner by omitting the final mesh in the following row (Fig. 24-14D). Continue reducing at that edge by tying into the side of the previous mesh each time. The other end is increased until the further corner is reached, then the rows are reduced at both ends until only one mesh is left.

REPAIRING NETS

Nets for sea fishing may need very frequent repairs. Other nets may suffer from chafe and require attention. Usually damage does not cover a very big area and it is possible to cut away and work in new meshes. For very large damage it may be better to make a new section of net, but for most repairs replacement meshes can be worked in with line-making meshes as you go.

Check which way up the net was made by examining a knot. Support above the damaged part by pushing a pole or rope through a row of sound meshes. If it is a square-meshed net this support will be diagonal to the outside of the net.

Cut off the damaged part fairly closely to the knots. With some upper and lower knots it may be possible to unpick the knots so plain loops are left, but elsewhere do not cut so closely that the knots are upset or the meshes open. It is usually best to trim so there is a straight row of meshes across the top of the opening, even if that means cutting sound meshes.

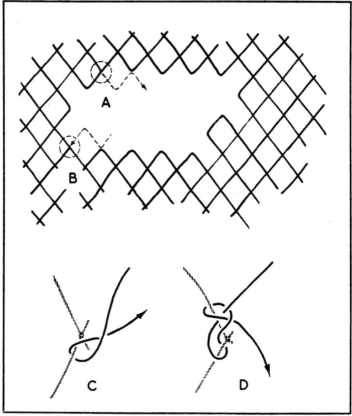

Fig. 24-15. A repair is made after cutting away to give the new line a regular path between the remaining parts: (A) one part of mesh missing; (B) three-legged mesh; (C) special knot; and (D) sheet bend.

Arrange a starting point at a *halver* or *three-legged mesh*. That is where the remains are a T-shape, with only one part of a mesh missing (Fig. 24-15A). Plan how the line will travel in making new meshes and try to finish on another three-legged mesh (Fig. 24-15B). If the passage of the line can be arranged suitably, it will go all the way singly, but otherwise there may be one or more places where it has to double back on itself. That may not matter except the double side to a mesh will show in the finished repair.

When the new line is worked in, use a mesh stick that matches the old meshes. Where the line goes across existing meshes above the opening, ordinary knots can be used. By turning the net upside-down they can also be used across the bottom. If you particularly want the bottom knots to look like the existing ones, each old mesh can be given a twist and the new piece worked through it to form the same shape as the upper part of a normal knot, but for most purposes the upside-down knots would be very difficult to identify.

Where new meshes have to be joined into existing meshes at the sides it would be possible to use normal knots, but they would then be at right-angles to the other knots in the net. That may not matter, but there is a risk that under strain they could slacken. At the side there will already be a knot in the old mesh and the new line has to be attached over that.

A special knot is preferable there. Take the end around below the knot (Fig. 24-15C), and put its standing part over the old mesh so the end can go around in a similar way to forming the ordinary sheet bend on a mesh (Fig. 24-15D). Draw this tight so the working end emerges pointing in the right direction.

Decorative Ropework

It is possible to work rope into very elaborate knots and other intricate forms that may have some practical value, but their object is mainly decorative. The peak of this skill came in the large sailing ship days when seamen looking for something to do in their limited spare time could only use what material was at hand. This material was old cordage, which was often teased out and laid up into new small lines and knotted or braided into objects that sometimes showed exceptional artistic as well as practical skill. Other examples might have served their purpose in occupying spare time, but the results were unlikely to be appreciated by anyone.

This sort of ropework finds expression today in more limited uses, but much modern cordage is far more attractive than the materials the oldtime seamen had to use. Quite pleasing things can be made with techniques that are often simpler and just as effective as the time-consuming knotting of those earlier days. Macramé work once meant close knotting in fine line, but the modern version uses larger cords and many of the knots and braids are those that were used by seamen.

Some decorative ropework is extremely complicated and any book instructions involve considerable illustration and description, but the more popular and satisfactory aspects of decorative ropework are based on some fairly simple processes. If these are mastered, it becomes possible to build up more elaborate constructions. This chapter covers the basic fancy knotting and braiding and it is suggested that these techniques be mastered. It should then be easy to move on to the more complex decorative works with cordage that are often multiplications of the basic steps.

TURK'S HEAD

This is a tubular knot that has practical uses, but it is mainly decorative. It is met in a large number of variations, all of which make a continuous sinnet that can be a free ring or could be tight around a spar or other solid object. There are also other knots made around rope with their own strands that have a similar finished appearance. One example is shown in the eye splice with a collar (Fig. 18-4). The basic knot is easily mastered and the other variations are elaborations on this.

The simple Turk's Head can be learned with a piece of cord about 1-inch diameter, working around the forefinger of the left hand with tucking done with the right hand and progress being held with the left thumb. Use a length of about 2 feet. The start is very similar to making a clove hitch.

Hold the short end with the thumb and second finger and put on a round turn (Fig. 25-1A), crossing the short part. Continue around the same way so the working end goes over itself and under the first turn (Fig. 25-1B). Leave this fairly slack so the further turns can be made easily. Ignore what is happening at the other side of your finger. Lift the second turn over the first and hold it there (Fig. 25-1C). Take the working end over the second turn and under the first (Fig. 25-1D). All the parts are now going over and under each other, one at a time.

Spread the crossings evenly around your finger and the long end will be in a position to go in alongside the short end (Fig. 25-1E). This actually completes a single Turk's Head, but that is not very decorative and it is common to double or treble it. Take the long end around the knot from where it has just entered, alongside the first part until it has gone around to the same point again. What you do with the two ends depends on the purpose of the Turk's Head. They have to be hidden under the turns that cross them (Fig- 25-1F). If the knot is to finish tight around a spar, it can be pulled up a little at a time so slackness is worked out towards the ends. The ends are finally cut off close and they should hold in place. If it is a free ring, the pattern is adjusted evenly, then the ends are either tied together with a little seizing of sewing thread or a needle is used to sew them together underneath the turns that will hide them.

To treble the knot, merely follow around again. In most materials this would hold its shape in a free ring, although varnish on colored cord might hold a three-part Turk's Head as a napkin ring. Trebling will spread a Turk's Head around a spar more attractively if the cord used seems too thin to look right after doubling the knot.

The Turk's Head, as described, suits many purposes, but if it is a fairly narrow band going around a large diameter, there have to be more tucks included. This can be done up to any size, so it is possible to make a sinnet of fine cord around a cask or other large item.

If the single Turk's Head, as made over the finger and single-tucked completely (Fig. 25-1C), is looked at from the other side, the long end will be seen to have gone from one side to the other and back again. The actions that brought it to this point can be repeated

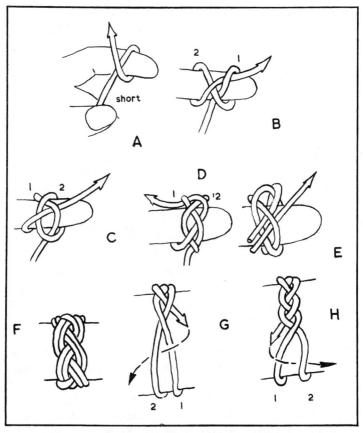

Fig. 25-1. A Turk's head knot may be worked around a finger: (A) round turn; (B) working end; (C) lift second turn; (D) working end over the second turn; (E) spread the crossings; (F) hidden ends; (G) slack; and (H) lift the first part.

as often as you need to make up a greater length, but you have to work complete sets of actions.

With the slack that has to be filled towards you, take the long end over the first part and under the second (Fig. 25-1G). Lift the first part over the second and take the long end over and under (Fig. 25-1H). This is another complete set of actions and the working end is back in position to do it again as often as necessary. Work the parts plaited further up so they are more compact to give you space for more tucking, even if the design will be spread more evenly later. This design can be doubled or trebled by following around and it is finished in one of the ways suggested for the simpler version.

A simple way of starting a Turk's Head knot is to first make a figure-eight knot, then put finger and thumb into the spaces outside the tucked ends (Fig. 25-2A) and pinch the middle part of the knot so the outside loops go downward and together. The formation will now be seen to be the same as when working around the finger (Fig. 25-1D). Take one end in alongside the other end and follow around.

Another way of picking up a Turk's Head is to lay out a loop (Fig. 25-2B) and loop one end over the other (Fig. 25-2C), then lift the lower loop partly through the first so the working end can be intertwined through the crossing (Fig. 25-2D). This brings it ready to go in alongside the other end (Fig. 25-2E) to follow around and make a normal doubled knot.

Although the Turk's Head is primarily a continuous sinnet around something or a free loop, it is possible to flatten it to make a mat. This is best done with more than the primary tucks. An example is a doubled knot which has been worked once more after the basic knot, so it can be carefully turned on edge and the parts adjusted to come flat (Fig. 25-2F).

MATTHEW WALKER

This name will almost certainly be mentioned in any discussion of knotting. Who Matthew Walker was seems to be lost in knotting antiquity, and he has been quoted as the only man with a knot named after him, but there are actually a few more, such as Hunter and Tarbuck. The Matthew Walker is a knot formed in the strands of a rope, that is finished as a knob around the rope, looking more like a stranded rope around than the sinnet appearance of a Turk's Head knot. In its simplest form it is used as a stopper, but elaborations build it up into a larger decorative knot.

However, although the knot had considerable use in the past it depended on the rope strands being laid up together again after the

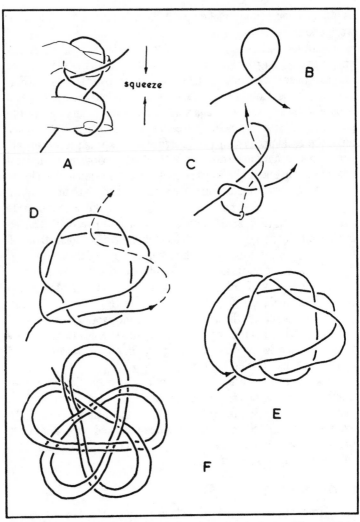

Fig. 25-2. A Turk's head can be made from loops interlocked and the complete knot may be flattened to make a mat: (A) starting the knot; (B) lay out a loop; (C) loop one end over the other; (D) lift the lower loop; (E) doubled knot; and (F) parts come flat.

knot had been completed. That was satisfactory with most natural fiber ropes, but with nearly all synthetic fiber ropes it is very nearly impossible to put the strands back together again so they fit as they did when they came off the machine. Consequently, the Matthew Walker knot is included here because you will certainly hear about it, but it is no longer of much real use.

Unlay the strands to the position where the knot is to come (Fig. 25-3A). A temporary seizing may be advisable to prevent further unlaying. Have the ends pointing upward. Take one end behind the other two (Fig. 25-3B). Take the next end behind and up through the loop of the first (Fig. 25-3C). Take the remaining strand around and up through the loop of the second (Fig. 25-3D). The ends should all be standing up. Draw the turns tight without disturbing the twists in the projecting parts. When the knot has been pulled tight, lay the strands back into each other, twisting each back into the form it was and laying the inner surfaces together again (Fig. 25-3E). Seal the ends and whip them.

This is the Matthew Walker knot, but if it has to be compared with other variations it may be called a single Matthew Walker. A double Matthew Walker makes a larger and more attractive knob. Have the three ends standing up. Take the first end around the other two and up through its own loop. Do this with each of the others, without crossing or tangling them (Fig. 25-3F). When pulled tight and the strands laid up again, there will be more bulk in the knot (Fig. 25-3G).

FLAT ENDLESS SINNET

Turk's Heads can be made in material other than rope and examples have been made in wire and leather thongs for scarf and napkin rings. There is a way of working a cut flat leather strip so both ends are closed, but there is a three-part sinnet between the closed ends. This could be a short length brought around and the ends joined as a scarf ring or a much longer piece as a strap or belt. Like the Turk's Head knot, there is a basic set of actions that can be repeated as often as necessary to make up the length. Even if there is no particular immediate use, a piece of leather braided in this way is an interesting project that will mystify other people.

Slit the piece of leather so there are three equal width parts between the closed ends. It is easier to work with supple leather, but the finished work looks best in reasonably stiff leather. A practice piece could have three strands no more than ¼ inch wide and an overall length of 3 inches is about the minimum that can be worked easily.

Cross the right part over the center, then lift the left part over it to the center (Fig. 25-4A). Hold the upper part in this position while you lift the whole of the bottom through gap 1, ignoring the twists that will develop. Push the bottom through gap 2 and the twists should come out (Fig. 25-4B). You should be able to knead the parts back into place (Fig. 25-4C).

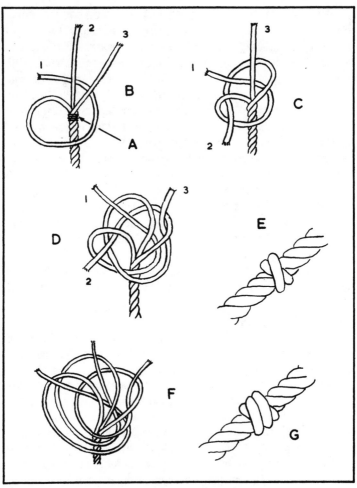

Fig. 25-3. The single and double Matthew Walker knots form knobs around a rope: (A) unlay the strands; (B) take one end behind the other two; (C) take end up through loop; (D) take remaining strand up through loop: (E) lay strands back into each other; (F) don't cross or tangle; and (G) pull tight.

For a short piece that is all you have to do. Notice that each part goes from where it was at the top to the same relative position at the bottom—the outside strands going to the other side and back, and the middle strands both ways. If you have to follow on, that must happen in each set of actions. Push the parts as high up as they will conveniently go. Hold them in place and regard the new start the same as the first start, so you go through two spaces in turn. For a long piece, push each set of crossing well up the strap to allow

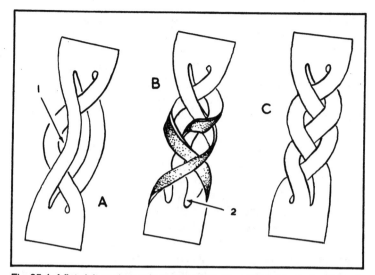

Fig. 25-4. A flat plait can be made in a strap with closed ends by passing the end through the gaps shown: (A) cross right part over center; (B) push bottom through gap; and (C) knead the parts.

plenty of space for working lower down, even if the pattern will have them spread throughout the length later.

FLAT SINNETS

Any number of strands more than two can be braided or plaited together in an over-and-under manner to make a flat woven pattern. The simplest is made with three parts, as may be done with children's hair. For a practice piece three lengths of line can be knotted together. It helps to be able to pull against something, so the knot can be hooked over a nail or, preferably, one of the ends can be taken through the knot as a bight so the projecting loop can go on the nail.

Each outside strand is brought to the middle (Fig. 25-5A), crossing the one that is already there and so bringing that to the outside. With each side crossed in turn, an even pattern is built up quickly. The only variations are in tightness. If the crossings are kept as far up the sinnet as possible as they are made, the finished work looks better and is tighter. However, if flexibility is important, the crossings are left further apart.

When made with more than three strands the result may be called *French sinnet,* although the French call it *English sinnet.* A start can be made with the ends tied together, but it is easier to see what is happening if they can be spread out, possibly by temporarily clamping between two pieces of wood, or hooking over closely spaced nails.

Start by crossing pairs. If there is an odd one, it comes in at one side in the next move and the one at the other side becomes odd. If the over-and-under arrangement is visualized, the formation can be followed (Fig. 25-5B). In the body of the sinnet, whatever its number, the strands go over and under, so those over in one line must be under in the next line. When strands reach the outside they are turned back (Fig. 25-5C). It is easy to allow the sinnet to finish with rather long angled parts. It looks better if the crossings are at about tight angles to each other, which means about 45 degrees to the side of the sinnet if the tucks each way are even.

Another way of arranging the strands takes the outer ones to the middle, whatever the number of strands. This is what was done with three strands, but with more than that the result is different from the simple over-and-under one arrangement of French sinnet. With five strands, for instance, they are arranged in two pairs, with a single strand outside (Fig. 25-5D). That is brought to the space between the pairs, then the outer one of the further pair brought over that (Fig. 25-5E). The one that is outermost at the other side

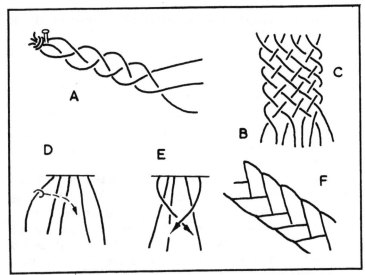

Fig. 25-5. Simple sinnets are made by crossing strands one or more times: (A) bring outside strand to middle; (B) over-and-under formation; (C) turn back the strands; (D) outside single strand; (G) outer one of further pair; and (F) outermost strand.

then comes in, and so on in turn from opposite sides (Fig. 25-5F). There is a snag with any sinnet that involves crossing two or more strands. This construction lacks some of the ability to hold shape that there is when only single strands are crossed. If a sinnet with too many parts is made by bringing the outer strands to the center, it may go out of shape after a little use. It is unwise to use this type of sinnet for more than seven strands.

As the number of strands increase, the variety of possible ways of plaiting become more. A simple way of plaiting an even number of strands is to use them in pairs, tucking them in the same manner as half the number of single strands. If kept flat and the strands riding over their partners avoided, this makes an effective belt or strap. Other patterns are obtained by going over two and under one, or some other uneven arrangement.

PORTUGESE SINNET

This may also be called *Boatswain's Plait* or many other names. It was popular at sea for knife and pipe lanyards. It is a good way to decorate line for something like a dog's lead and macramé enthusiasts use it for slings for plant pots and similar things.

The common arrangement is made with four strands—the center two forming a core. The core strands could be a different color from the others to show through as an extra decorative touch. The sinnet could be made on a single thicker line as a core. It could even be a rigid metal rod. A pair of plastic-covered wires might form the core. The outside could be made with similar material, providing it had enough flexibility to be worked, possibly with the aid of pliers.

There are two forms that the sinnet can take—flat or twisted—and the actions are the same. Twists come naturally and are not forced into the sinnet.

The core strands should be stretched for ease in working. They will be the length of the sinnet, but the outside working strands need to be considerably longer, depending on the relative thicknesses—upwards of four times the final length should be considered. A convenient arrangement for a practice sinnet is to use a continuous length, doubled back, so the center part is the length intended to finish, with a little to spare, then the turns are knotted together (Fig. 25-6A). The knotted loops can go on a hook and the looped end of the core strands may be hooked to your belt so they are tensioned.

Turn one of the outside working strands across the back of the core strands and hold it there (Fig. 25-6B). Put the other outside

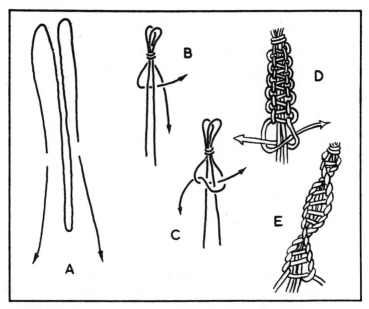

Fig. 25-6. Portugese sinnet can be worked to finish flat or twisted: (A) knotted turns; (B) working strands; (C) outside strands; (D) flat Portugese sinnet; and (E) twisted Portugese sinnet.

strand under it and across the front of the core strands to go down through the loop of the first part (Fig. 25-6C). What you have done is made an overhand knot with the working parts and included the core in the crossing. Making the sinnet is merely repetition of this. Pull that first stitch close up to the top.

Do the same again from the other side. Bend what was the second one used in the first stitch across behind the core strands, dip the other behind it and across the front to go down through its loop. Pull tight. If you examine what you have done with the two actions, you will see that you have tied a square or reef knot to enclose the core. If you continue making stitches on alternate sides and pulling them close on the tensioned core, you will get a flat Portugese sinnet (Fig. 25-6D).

If you continue to work from the same side with each stitch, two sets of actions will produce a granny knot and a succession of these will make a twisted Portuges sinnet (Fig. 25-6E).

LARIAT PLAIT

The lariat plait is a simple flexible plait of four parts. It gets its name from its use in putting thongs together to make a strong line

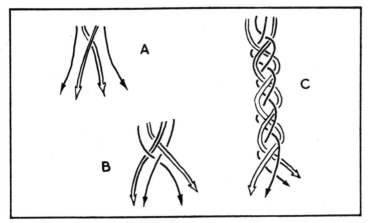

Fig. 25-7. A lariat plait is four-part and flexible: (A) cross one pair; (B) hold the crossing; and (C) make each crossing.

flexible enough for a lariat. It can be seen in some telephone cables. It may not be particularly decorative in itself, but it is a good plait to use near the working end of a lanyard or dog lead that has other stiffer sinnets higher up.

Pair the strands and be careful not to change pairing as the plait progresses. Cross one pair (Fig. 25-7A). Hold that crossing and cross the other pair between them (Fig. 25-7B). Both pairs must be crossed in the same manner. If the left strand of a pair goes behind the right strand, treat the other pair in the same way, and make every crossing as you proceed in exactly the same way (Fig. 25-7C). This is a sinnet where you do not necessarily bring the crossings as high as possible as you make them, unless you want a rather tight result. For flexibility let the parts take a natural formation.

MANROPE KNOT

The oldtime seaman knew a very large number of terminal knob knots to put on the end of a rope. Their purpose was both useful and ornamental. A rope forming a handrail would have a knob worked in the end to prevent it from pulling through a hole in a post. The end of the tiller lines might have elaborate knobs worked to impress seamen of other craft. Bell ropes had elaborately worked ropes terminating in knobs. The rope used on a gangway, and called a manrope, had knobs at its ends.

A manrope knot is a good general-purpose way of making a knob at the end of a three-or four-strand rope. There is no equivalent way of dealing with the end of a braided rope. The finished knot looks very similar to a tightened Turk's Head knot.

The knot is a combination of *wall* and *crown knots,* which are the same thing, depending on which way they are viewed. Unlay the end of the rope for much more length than is estimated will be needed. Put on a short seizing. It need not be removed later as it should be hidden in the finished knot.

Use the end strands to put on a wall knot (Fig. 25-8A) in the same direction as the lay of the rope. Note that each end goes up through its neighbor's loop. Pull this moderately tight above the seizing. Above this put on a crown knot (Fig. 25-8B), going the same way around. This time each end goes down through its neighbor's loop. Tighten this down on to the wall knot. The ends from the crown knot will be found to be alongside parts of the wall knot. Take each end into the wall knot alongside its partner there. Use a spike to open and coax the strands through. This will double

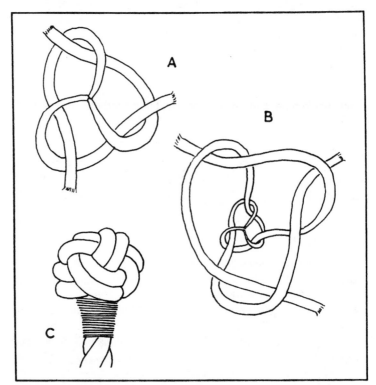

Fig. 25-8. A manrope knot is formed from a wall knot covered by a crown knot: (A) wall knot; (B) crown knot; and (C) serve over.

the wall knot and leave the ends pointing up alongside turns of the crown knot. Follow through so the outside pattern of the combined knot becomes doubled. Tuck the ends down through the center of the knot so they project back along the rope.

Use the point of the spike to draw through each tuck of each strand in turn so all slack is taken up by final pulls on the ends and the knob settles into a hard even pattern. It may be satisfactory to cut off the ends underneath the knot. If it has been drawn very tight there is a good resistance in the knot to prevent the ends from coming adrift. If the manrope knot has to be drawn close to a hole, finishing that way may be necessary. The alternative is to leave a short length of the ends to finish along the rope.

Separate the fibers of the projecting ends and cut them off to the limit a serving is to be. Taper them by cutting away to different lengths, but leave some full-length fibers to worm around between the strands. Use thread to seize down the tapered fibers, then serve over tightly from very close into the knot (Fig. 25-8C).

MATS

Rope mats have been made in a great many designs, some of them achieving their effect by being sewn through, but other mats are entirely knotted. If the mat is to lay flat, it should be made of a soft supple rope. Cotton was popular, but if synthetic rope is used, choose a soft loosely-laid type. One round type of mat has been shown as converted from a Turk's Head (Fig. 25-2F). If doubled or trebled and drawn tight so the spaces in the pattern are almost closed, this makes a compact mat hardly big enough for normal use on the floor. On board a yacht it could go around the eyebolt through the deck holding a block, which would otherwise rattle against and damage the deck. Ashore, it might serve as a coaster or pad on the table.

Larger mats have to be made by laying out the line and arranging it in a pattern that will give an over-and-under arrangement that can then be followed around, usually to treble the pattern. The design shown might be a mat inside a door or be fixed to a step to prevent slipping. Its decorative effect would then be incidental to its use.

Middle the rope and put it on the bench or floor with its center crossed in a ring and the ends crossed the same way near where the other end of the mat is expected to be (Fig. 25-9A). From this point bring the working ends back over in two crossing loops (Fig. 25-9B), with them projecting on each side of the first ring.

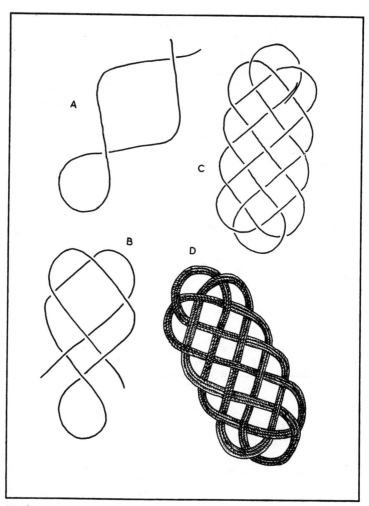

Fig. 25-9. A mat can be made by laying down the line so it builds up into an over-and-under pattern: (A) middle the rope; (B) two crossing loops; (C) make ring to match; and (D) ends follow around three times.

Without disturbing the pattern so far, take the ends into the end ring as shown, so they follow an over-and-under path back to the far end. You will probably need help to keep the pattern in shape, and it is best to do a little at a time with each end so you can see that there are no places that go wrong. At the far end, take one end around to make the ring to match the one at the other end (Fig. 25-9C). This will bring it alongside the other part and you have completed the pattern. Check that all the crossings are correct.

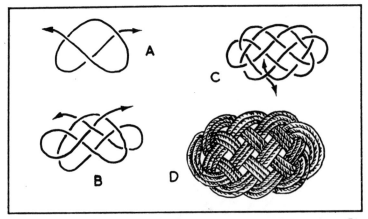

Fig. 25-10. Another mat pattern starts as a Napoleon knot: (A) turn a loop; (B) take ends around; (C) ends meet at bottom of pattern; and (D) treble it.

Use both ends to follow around three times (Fig. 25-9D). Sew through where the final overlap comes so it is hidden under crossing parts. Before doing this, manipulate the parts, take up any slack and get the adjoining turns to the same tension and laying flat. Try the mat on a flat surface. Turn it over and press it down. The overlapping joints have to settle slightly up and down.

Another mat gets a very similar result by starting with a *Napoleon knot.* Allow enough rope for trebling and again start with its middle. Turn a loop with the ends on opposite sides (Fig. 25-10A). Take the ends around again, but still on their own side of the loop (Fig. 25-10B), and interlocking where they cross at the center. Now go back through with each end, taking in the turns over-and-under one until they meet at the bottom of the pattern (Fig. 25-10C). That is the completion of the Napoleon knot. To complete the mat follow around to treble it in the same way as described for the first mat (Fig. 25-10D).

Either mat can be made larger by surrounding it with further turns of rope, which may continue from the pattern or be made from a new length coiled around. To keep the turns in place, use thread and a sail needle to sew through at intervals. The first coil should be sewn to the projecting parts of the pattern and further turns sewn at intervals to earlier turns. It may be possible to take stitches through several turns of rope so the whole thing becomes consolidated into a mat that can be picked up and moved about without coming apart. The end on the outside looks best if tapered and sewn to the previous turn.

391

GLOSSARY

adrift—A rope is adrift it if comes out of place. A knot is adrift if it spills or comes undone.

against the sun—Seaman's term for counterclockwise.

avast—Nautical instruction to stop pulling or working.

backhanded rope—Strands with a left-handed twist.

becket—A rope loop used as a handle or for attaching a hook or another rope. A rope handle.

belay—To secure a rope, usually by winding around a cleat or belaying pin.

belaying pin—A wood or metal pin through a hole in a rail, and projecting above and below, to which ropes can be secured.

bend—The knot used to tie two ropes together. The action of making such a knot.

bight—A loop in a rope, as when an end is turned back on itself.

bind—Seize spars together. Jammed turns of rope.

bitts—One or two upright posts projecting through a deck and used for securing hawsers or other large ropes.

bitt, to—Pass rope around bitts.

bitter end—The end of a cable or other rope opposite to the end that is being used for work. In an anchor cable it is the end made fast in the chain locker.

block—An assembly with one or more sheaves enclosed in a frame through which ropes run and their direction is altered. Blocks may be assembled to form tackle.

block-and-block—The term when two blocks in a tackle have been drawn together and no further movement is possible. May also be used in other situations to mean that limits have been reached.

bollard—A heavy device for attaching a rope, such as a post on deck or ashore. There may be a pair of posts and the term may be used as an alternative for bitts, but the name is now more commonly used for a large metal mooring point, often made in a form similar to a large cleat.

bolt—A roll of canvas. A bolt rope goes around the edge of canvas or a net. Less commonly a small mallet for pressing stitches into place.

bowline—Originally one of the ropes used to trim a square sail, but now the name of the knot that was used at its end.

bowse—To haul a rope tight around something or to haul it about with a tackle.

brace—A rope to trim the yard of a sail. The action of taking up slack in a rope.

braid—To make netting. To plait or interweave strands or cords to make a pattern.

brails—Ropes used to gather up surplus canvas in a sail when furling it.

bridle—A span of rope which has its ends secured.

bring up—To stop, usually when parts come into contact.

bull's eye—A piece of wood with a hole for a rope to pass through, which may serve as a fairlead.

buntline—Alternative name for brails.

cable—Strictly a large rope made by twisting three smaller ropes together, but may also mean any large rope or chain used for anchoring. Also a measure of length, originally based on the usual manufactured length of rope, but usually accepted as 100 fathoms (600 feet).

canvas—Woven fabric of natural or synthetic fibers, graded by number of relative weights. Afloat it is a general term for the sails.

capsize—In knotting, to pull a knot out of shape so it slips.

carry away—To break or go adrift.

cast off—Untie or cut a fastening so the rope becomes free.

casting line—A heaving line. The leader in fishing.

chafe—Wear away fibers. Chafing gear is protection to reduce chafing.

check—Slacken and hold alternately with a line around a bollard or other post while strain is being taken on a rope.

clap on—To put on a seizing or any means of nipping the parts of a rope.

clear—Remove twists and kinks from a rope so it runs freely.

cleat—In sailing ship days, a projecting piece of wood or metal for securing rope by twisting around its two horns. Modern cleats take various forms and may jam ropes without taking turns.

clew—An eye in the corner of a square sail. The aft bottom corner of a fore-and-aft sail.

clinch—Rope turned into a small eye and the overlaps seized together.

cockscombing—Half hitching around a ring or eye, as a form of serving which changes direction on the outside.

coil—A series of turns or rope, one on the other, for convenience in handling.

coir—Fibers from the outer husks of the coconut used to make rope that will float.

cord—Small line made from several yarns twisted hard together, but the term is commonly used for any smaller lines.

cordage—Comprehensive term for all kinds of line made by twisting fibers, from the smallest to the largest.

core—Heart, particularly the center strand of seven-strand rope.

cotton—Fibers of the cotton plant, used in making rope.

cow's tail—Unlaid or frayed end of rope.

crown—The top, but particularly a knot made at the end of a rope in its own strands.

earing—A short rope attached to the corner of a sail or at positions for reefing it.

end for end—Turning a rope around to equalize wear in it.

eye—A loop or bight of rope with the parts crossing. Spliced loop.

fag end—A ragged end.

fairlead—A wood, metal or plastic guide for a rope.

fake or flake—A turn in a coil of rope. The action of making a coil.

fall—The rope used with blocks to make a tackle. The hauling part alone may be called a fall.

fast—Secured. To make fast is to secure.

fiber—The smallest element of the construction of a rope. In synthetic ropes the fibers are more correctly called filaments.

fid—Tapered wooden spike used for opening rope strands.

filament—The smallest element of manufactured material that forms the fibers of synthetic rope.

flax—Fibers of the flax plant, used for rope and canvas.

fleet—Open tackle ready for another pull.

foul—Become entangled. In particular a foul anchor cable has become caught on something under the water.

fox—Yarns twisted together, usually by hand.

frap—Put on turns around others so they cross to tighten a lashing.

freshen—Move a rope so the bearing part is moved to minimize wear.

garland—A strop used for hoisting spars.

gasket—Usually a band of rope or canvas for gathering sails or other things together.

gear—Collective name for ropes, nets and other items, particularly for fishing.

grommet—Endless circle of rope, used as eyelets or block strops.

guy—A rope for steadying.

gypsy—The drum of a windlass around which rope is taken.

halliard or hallyard—Rope for hoisting sails, flags and similar things.

handsomely—Instruction to haul or lower carefully and slowly.

handy billy—Small tackle for temporary use.

hard laid—Tightly twisted rope.

hawser—Any very large rope, but particularly one for towing.

heart—A core strand.

heaving line—A light line with a weighted end intended for throwing and often used then to haul across a heavier rope.

hemp—Fibers of the hemp plant, once one of the most popular rope fibers before the introduction of synthetic rope.

hitch—A knot for attaching a rope to something solid or inert.

hoist—Lift by means of tackle. The hoist of a sail or flag is the vertical part next to the mast.

home—A rope is home when it is hauled tight.

Irish pennant—Frayed end of rope.

junk—Old rope unfit for important use, but useful for practice. On sailing ships it was taken apart to make into other things.

knot—Now the general name for all fastenings with rope, but strictly it was traditionally formed in a single rope.

lanyard—Small rope used for securing knives and similar things.

lash—Secure by binding with rope.

lay—The direction of the twist of the strands of a rope.

lay up—Restore the strands after a rope has been opened.

lay hold—Grasp or seize a rope.

lead—Direction of a rope.

line—Common name for all kinds of cordage, often in preference to calling it rope.

long-jawed—Stretched rope that has lost much of its twist.

make fast—Secure a rope, usually by knotting it.

Manila—The name given to rope made from abaca fiber, obtained chiefly from Manila. One of the best yacht ropes before the coming of synthetic fibers.

marl—Secure with a series of half hitches.

marline spike—A metal spike used for opening rope strands.

marry—Bring two ropes ends together, particularly when the separated strands are fitted between each other ready for splicing.

mesh—The opening in a net.

mesh stick—Gauge for regulating the size of mesh in a net.

messenger—A light line used to heave a heavier one or an extra line used around a capstan.

middle a rope—Fold a rope into two equal parts.

moor—Tie up to a dock or bank. Secure by bow and stern to buoys or anchors.

mouse—To use light line across a hook to prevent rope in it from coming out. The weight used to lower a line through a hollow mast.

nettles or knettles—Yarns rubbed into small parts to make fine lines from the end of a rope for plaiting or pointing.

nip—A sharp turn in a rope. A grip on a rope. The point in the knot where parts grip each other.

noose—A loop around its own standing part. It will daw tight when handled, as in a lariat or lasso.

norman—Bar across the top of bitts or a samson post.

oakum—Yarns picked from old rope. Once used for caulking.

overhaul—Separate the blocks of a tackle, ready for another pull.

palm—A leather strap to fit over the hand with a hole for the thumb with a metal pad for pushing a sail needle.

painter—Short rope attached to the bow of a small boat for mooring and towing it.

parbuckle—Arrangement of rope ends around an object for lifting it.

parcel—Protect a rope by binding it with cloth, like a bandage, before covering it with serving.

part—Break.

pay out—Allow to run out, under control.

plait—Interweave parts as in making sinnet, usually for decoration.

play—Extra amount to allow for adjustment or shrinkage.

point—Decorative cone-shaped end to rope which may help in reeving through blocks and holes.

pricker—A pointed steel tool like a marline spike, but with a handle.

purchase—An arrangement of blocks in a tackle. Gives a mechanical advantage.

quilting—Rope mats used for protection or covering.

rack—Seize ropes together.

racking turns—Seizings or lashings made in a figure-eight manner.

ratline—Lines across shrouds to form steps. Small three-strand line.

reef points—Means of reefing a sail by gathering up surplus fabric. The reef points hang on each side of the sail and are joined with reef knots around the sail, thus giving the knot its name.

reeve—Pass a rope through a space, particularly through a block.

render—Ease off or slacken.

ride—One turn on a capstan or in a lashing mounting over another.

riding turns—Extra turns over a lower layer, as in some seizings.

robands—The bands to secure the luff of a sail. Actually rope bands and pronounced robbins.

rope—Traditionally any cordage over 1-inch circumference, but loosely applied to most types of line.

rigging—Collective name for all of a ship's ropes, with those that support called standing rigging and those that move called running rigging.

round up—Take up slack, particularly in a tackle.

round turn—Line completely encircling an object.

rubber—Wood or bone tool for rubbing down canvas seams.

send—Sailor's preferred term. Send down means to lower. Send aloft is to hoist or raise.

seizing—A lashing of small line around ropes.

serving—Turns of small line around heavier ropes as protection, usually over worming and parcelling.

serving board or mallet—Levering tool for putting on tight serving.

set up—Tighten, as when tensioning rigging.

sheave—The pulley wheel over which a rope is put in a block.

shroud-laid-rope—Four-strand rope laid up right-handedly.

shrouds—The supporting side stays from a mast to the rail or gunwale.

sisal—Fibers of the henequin plant once used for one of the cheaper types of natural rope.

sinnet—Braided cordage, usually for decorative purposes. May also be spelled sennit or called plaiting.

slack away—Ease off or let out rope.

sling—Rope around an object for hoisting it.

slip knot—Any knot that can be released by pulling an end.

snub—Check a line by passing a turn around a post or in a similar manner.

soft laid—Loosely twisted rope.

span—A rope fast at the ends, intended to be hauled at its center.

spill—Undo, usually accidentally.

splice—Joining the end of a rope to its own standing part or to another rope by interweaving its strands.

small stuff—Sailor's name for any cordage less than 1-inch circumference.

snarl—Tangled lines.

spunyarn—Small line loosely twisted and often made from old rope.

standing part—The main part of a rope, away from the ends.

start—Slack off a little to ease strain.

stay—Any item of standing rigging.

stick—Tuck, as when entering strands in a splice.

stop—Seize or lash, usually temporarily.

strand—The part of a rope made up of yarns twisted one way, then the strands are twisted together the other way to make the rope.

stranded rope—Rope made of strands to distinguish it from braided rope. Traditionally rope with a damaged strand.

strap or strop—Rope around a block or a sling.

swallow—The gap between the cheeks of a block.

swift—Set up rigging.

swig—Pull on the center of an already taut rope to gain a little more. It is taken up at a cleat or belaying pin as the pull is released.

tabling—Wide hem at the edge of a sail to which the boltrope is sewn.

tackle—An arrangement of blocks and ropes to provide a purchase. Pronounced tayckle.

tackline—Short length of line put between signal flags. The line used at the tack of some fore-and-aft sails for hauling it forward.

take a turn—Put a turn on a cleat or belaying pin.

taper—Reduce the size of a rope strand by scraping away some of the fibers.

thimble—Round or heart-shaped metal or plastic fitting, grooved for rope spliced around it. It protects the eye of a rope when attached to a metal fitting.

thoroughfoot—Tangled tackle due to the blocks and fall twisting.

thread—Yarn or very small line that make up strands of rope. Fine line used for sewing with a needle.

throat seizing—Used to lash an eye in a rope. Temporarily hold a thimble ready for eye splicing.

thrums—Short pieces of small stuff used to make up chafing gear.

tie—The common term for making a knot, but a seaman avoids its use, preferring to bend, hitch or make fast with.

tier—One level of turns in a coil of rope.

toggle—Small pin, usually wood, with a groove at its center, around which a rope is spliced. The toggle in one rope may engage with an eye in its other end or another rope. Also any wooden peg thrust into a knot for security or quick release.

trice—Haul up and tenon.

trim—Adjust ropes as required for them to be correct.

truss—Bind or lash.

turn—One round of rope on a solid object. To take a turn is to belay completely.

twice-laid rope—Rope made from yarns from other rope.

unbend—Untie, cast off, let loose.

unlay—Open rope to separate the strands.

unreeve—Remove the rope from blocks.

vang—Rope to control or trim the gaff of a fore-and-aft sail.

veer—Allow a rope to run out gradually.

veer and haul—Adjust a spar by letting out one rope and hauling in another.

warp—A large rope used to move a vessel. Also the action of doing so.

whip—Bind the end of a rope to prevent it from unlaying.

with the lay—Coiling clockwise.

worming—Filling the spaces between strands with small stuff to make the exterior cylindrical ready for parcelling.

worm, parcel and serve—The complete protective treatment when the rope is wormed, then parcelled with cloth and the whole covered with a tight serving.

yarn—Fibers twisted together as the first step in forming a rope.

yoke lines—Ropes from the yoke on a rudder used for steering a small boat.

Additional Reading

The following books contain additional information that should be of use to anyone wishing to learn more about particular aspects of ropework:

The Ashley Book of Knots by Clifford W. Ashley (Doubleday, Doran). First published in 1945. A large and comprehensive book of ropework.

Encyclopedia of Knots and Fancy Rope Work by Raoul Graumont and John Hensel (Cornell Maritime Press). First published in 1945. Almost as large as the Ashley book, but with more emphasis on decorative rope work. Mostly illustrated with photographs.

The Art of Knotting and Splicing by Cyrus Lawrence Day (Dodd, Mead). First published in 1947. Selected practical knots and historical information.

Knots, Splices and Fancy Work by Charles L. Spencer (Brown, Son & Ferguson, Glasgow). First published in 1934. General coverage of knotting with detailed instructions on fancywork.

The Harrison Book of Knots by P. O. Harrison (Brown, Son & Ferguson, Glasgow). First published in 1964. Fancy knotting, some history and full coverage of bell ropes.

Knotting and Splicing Ropes and Cordage by Paul N. Hasluck (Cassell, London, Toronto). First published in 1904 and many later editions. Interesting historically.

Netmaking by Percy W. Blandford (Brown, Son & Ferguson, Glasgow). First published in 1941 and later editions. All aspects of making nets.

Note—Many publications by Brown, Son & Ferguson and other British publishers can be obtained from International Marine Publishing Company, Camden, Maine.

Index

A CATALOG OF SELECTED
DOVER BOOKS
IN ALL FIELDS OF INTEREST

A CATALOG OF SELECTED DOVER
BOOKS IN ALL FIELDS OF INTEREST

CONCERNING THE SPIRITUAL IN ART, Wassily Kandinsky. Pioneering work by father of abstract art. Thoughts on color theory, nature of art. Analysis of earlier masters. 12 illustrations. 80pp. of text. 5⅜ x 8½.　　　0-486-23411-8

CELTIC ART: The Methods of Construction, George Bain. Simple geometric techniques for making Celtic interlacements, spirals, Kells-type initials, animals, humans, etc. Over 500 illustrations. 160pp. 9 x 12. (Available in U.S. only.)　　　0-486-22923-8

AN ATLAS OF ANATOMY FOR ARTISTS, Fritz Schider. Most thorough reference work on art anatomy in the world. Hundreds of illustrations, including selections from works by Vesalius, Leonardo, Goya, Ingres, Michelangelo, others. 593 illustrations. 192pp. 7⅛ x 10¼.　　　0-486-20241-0

CELTIC HAND STROKE-BY-STROKE (Irish Half-Uncial from "The Book of Kells"): An Arthur Baker Calligraphy Manual, Arthur Baker. Complete guide to creating each letter of the alphabet in distinctive Celtic manner. Covers hand position, strokes, pens, inks, paper, more. Illustrated. 48pp. 8¼ x 11.　　　0-486-24336-2

EASY ORIGAMI, John Montroll. Charming collection of 32 projects (hat, cup, pelican, piano, swan, many more) specially designed for the novice origami hobbyist. Clearly illustrated easy-to-follow instructions insure that even beginning papercrafters will achieve successful results. 48pp. 8¼ x 11.　　　0-486-27298-2

BLOOMINGDALE'S ILLUSTRATED 1886 CATALOG: Fashions, Dry Goods and Housewares, Bloomingdale Brothers. Famed merchants' extremely rare catalog depicting about 1,700 products: clothing, housewares, firearms, dry goods, jewelry, more. Invaluable for dating, identifying vintage items. Also, copyright-free graphics for artists, designers. Co-published with Henry Ford Museum & Greenfield Village. 160pp. 8¼ x 11.　　　0-486-25780-0

THE ART OF WORLDLY WISDOM, Baltasar Gracian. "Think with the few and speak with the many," "Friends are a second existence," and "Be able to forget" are among this 1637 volume's 300 pithy maxims. A perfect source of mental and spiritual refreshment, it can be opened at random and appreciated either in brief or at length. 128pp. 5⅜ x 8½.　　　0-486-44034-6

JOHNSON'S DICTIONARY: A Modern Selection, Samuel Johnson (E. L. McAdam and George Milne, eds.). This modern version reduces the original 1755 edition's 2,300 pages of definitions and literary examples to a more manageable length, retaining the verbal pleasure and historical curiosity of the original. 480pp. 5³⁄₁₆ x 8¼.　　　0-486-44089-3

ADVENTURES OF HUCKLEBERRY FINN, Mark Twain, Illustrated by E. W. Kemble. A work of eternal richness and complexity, a source of ongoing critical debate, and a literary landmark, Twain's 1885 masterpiece about a barefoot boy's journey of self-discovery has enthralled readers around the world. This handsome clothbound reproduction of the first edition features all 174 of the original black-and-white illustrations. 368pp. 5⅜ x 8½.　　　0-486-44322-1

STICKLEY CRAFTSMAN FURNITURE CATALOGS, Gustav Stickley and L. & J. G. Stickley. Beautiful, functional furniture in two authentic catalogs from 1910. 594 illustrations, including 277 photos, show settles, rockers, armchairs, reclining chairs, bookcases, desks, tables. 183pp. 6½ x 9¼. 0-486-23838-5

AMERICAN LOCOMOTIVES IN HISTORIC PHOTOGRAPHS: 1858 to 1949, Ron Ziel (ed.). A rare collection of 126 meticulously detailed official photographs, called "builder portraits," of American locomotives that majestically chronicle the rise of steam locomotive power in America. Introduction. Detailed captions. xi+ 129pp. 9 x 12. 0-486-27393-8

AMERICA'S LIGHTHOUSES: An Illustrated History, Francis Ross Holland, Jr. Delightfully written, profusely illustrated fact-filled survey of over 200 American lighthouses since 1716. History, anecdotes, technological advances, more. 240pp. 8 x 10¾. 0-486-25576-X

TOWARDS A NEW ARCHITECTURE, Le Corbusier. Pioneering manifesto by founder of "International School." Technical and aesthetic theories, views of industry, economics, relation of form to function, "mass-production split" and much more. Profusely illustrated. 320pp. 6⅛ x 9¼. (Available in U.S. only.) 0-486-25023-7

HOW THE OTHER HALF LIVES, Jacob Riis. Famous journalistic record, exposing poverty and degradation of New York slums around 1900, by major social reformer. 100 striking and influential photographs. 233pp. 10 x 7⅞. 0-486-22012-5

FRUIT KEY AND TWIG KEY TO TREES AND SHRUBS, William M. Harlow. One of the handiest and most widely used identification aids. Fruit key covers 120 deciduous and evergreen species; twig key 160 deciduous species. Easily used. Over 300 photographs. 126pp. 5⅜ x 8½. 0-486-20511-8

COMMON BIRD SONGS, Dr. Donald J. Borror. Songs of 60 most common U.S. birds: robins, sparrows, cardinals, bluejays, finches, more–arranged in order of increasing complexity. Up to 9 variations of songs of each species.
Cassette and manual 0-486-99911-4

ORCHIDS AS HOUSE PLANTS, Rebecca Tyson Northen. Grow cattleyas and many other kinds of orchids–in a window, in a case, or under artificial light. 63 illustrations. 148pp. 5⅜ x 8½. 0-486-23261-1

MONSTER MAZES, Dave Phillips. Masterful mazes at four levels of difficulty. Avoid deadly perils and evil creatures to find magical treasures. Solutions for all 32 exciting illustrated puzzles. 48pp. 8¼ x 11. 0-486-26005-4

MOZART'S DON GIOVANNI (DOVER OPERA LIBRETTO SERIES), Wolfgang Amadeus Mozart. Introduced and translated by Ellen H. Bleiler. Standard Italian libretto, with complete English translation. Convenient and thoroughly portable–an ideal companion for reading along with a recording or the performance itself. Introduction. List of characters. Plot summary. 121pp. 5¼ x 8½. 0-486-24944-1

FRANK LLOYD WRIGHT'S DANA HOUSE, Donald Hoffmann. Pictorial essay of residential masterpiece with over 160 interior and exterior photos, plans, elevations, sketches and studies. 128pp. 9¼ x 10¾. 0-486-29120-0

THE CLARINET AND CLARINET PLAYING, David Pino. Lively, comprehensive work features suggestions about technique, musicianship, and musical interpretation, as well as guidelines for teaching, making your own reeds, and preparing for public performance. Includes an intriguing look at clarinet history. "A godsend," *The Clarinet,* Journal of the International Clarinet Society. Appendixes. 7 illus. 320pp. 5⅜ x 8½. 0-486-40270-3

HOLLYWOOD GLAMOR PORTRAITS, John Kobal (ed.). 145 photos from 1926-49. Harlow, Gable, Bogart, Bacall; 94 stars in all. Full background on photographers, technical aspects. 160pp. 8⅜ x 11¼. 0-486-23352-9

THE RAVEN AND OTHER FAVORITE POEMS, Edgar Allan Poe. Over 40 of the author's most memorable poems: "The Bells," "Ulalume," "Israfel," "To Helen," "The Conqueror Worm," "Eldorado," "Annabel Lee," many more. Alphabetic lists of titles and first lines. 64pp. 5³⁄₁₆ x 8¼. 0-486-26685-0

PERSONAL MEMOIRS OF U. S. GRANT, Ulysses Simpson Grant. Intelligent, deeply moving firsthand account of Civil War campaigns, considered by many the finest military memoirs ever written. Includes letters, historic photographs, maps and more. 528pp. 6⅛ x 9¼. 0-486-28587-1

ANCIENT EGYPTIAN MATERIALS AND INDUSTRIES, A. Lucas and J. Harris. Fascinating, comprehensive, thoroughly documented text describes this ancient civilization's vast resources and the processes that incorporated them in daily life, including the use of animal products, building materials, cosmetics, perfumes and incense, fibers, glazed ware, glass and its manufacture, materials used in the mummification process, and much more. 544pp. 6¹⁄₈ x 9¹⁄₄. (Available in U.S. only.) 0-486-40446-3

RUSSIAN STORIES/RUSSKIE RASSKAZY: A Dual-Language Book, edited by Gleb Struve. Twelve tales by such masters as Chekhov, Tolstoy, Dostoevsky, Pushkin, others. Excellent word-for-word English translations on facing pages, plus teaching and study aids, Russian/English vocabulary, biographical/critical introductions, more. 416pp. 5⅜ x 8½. 0-486-26244-8

PHILADELPHIA THEN AND NOW: 60 Sites Photographed in the Past and Present, Kenneth Finkel and Susan Oyama. Rare photographs of City Hall, Logan Square, Independence Hall, Betsy Ross House, other landmarks juxtaposed with contemporary views. Captures changing face of historic city. Introduction. Captions. 128pp. 8¼ x 11. 0-486-25790-8

NORTH AMERICAN INDIAN LIFE: Customs and Traditions of 23 Tribes, Elsie Clews Parsons (ed.). 27 fictionalized essays by noted anthropologists examine religion, customs, government, additional facets of life among the Winnebago, Crow, Zuni, Eskimo, other tribes. 480pp. 6⅛ x 9¼. 0-486-27377-6

TECHNICAL MANUAL AND DICTIONARY OF CLASSICAL BALLET, Gail Grant. Defines, explains, comments on steps, movements, poses and concepts. 15-page pictorial section. Basic book for student, viewer. 127pp. 5⅜ x 8½.
0-486-21843-0

THE MALE AND FEMALE FIGURE IN MOTION: 60 Classic Photographic Sequences, Eadweard Muybridge. 60 true-action photographs of men and women walking, running, climbing, bending, turning, etc., reproduced from rare 19th-century masterpiece. vi + 121pp. 9 x 12. 0-486-24745-7

ANIMALS: 1,419 Copyright-Free Illustrations of Mammals, Birds, Fish, Insects, etc., Jim Harter (ed.). Clear wood engravings present, in extremely lifelike poses, over 1,000 species of animals. One of the most extensive pictorial sourcebooks of its kind. Captions. Index. 284pp. 9 x 12.   0-486-23766-4

1001 QUESTIONS ANSWERED ABOUT THE SEASHORE, N. J. Berrill and Jacquelyn Berrill. Queries answered about dolphins, sea snails, sponges, starfish, fishes, shore birds, many others. Covers appearance, breeding, growth, feeding, much more. 305pp. 5¼ x 8¼.   0-486-23366-9

ATTRACTING BIRDS TO YOUR YARD, William J. Weber. Easy-to-follow guide offers advice on how to attract the greatest diversity of birds: birdhouses, feeders, water and waterers, much more. 96pp. 5³⁄₁₆ x 8¼.   0-486-28927-3

MEDICINAL AND OTHER USES OF NORTH AMERICAN PLANTS: A Historical Survey with Special Reference to the Eastern Indian Tribes, Charlotte Erichsen-Brown. Chronological historical citations document 500 years of usage of plants, trees, shrubs native to eastern Canada, northeastern U.S. Also complete identifying information. 343 illustrations. 544pp. 6½ x 9¼.   0-486-25951-X

STORYBOOK MAZES, Dave Phillips. 23 stories and mazes on two-page spreads: Wizard of Oz, Treasure Island, Robin Hood, etc. Solutions. 64pp. 8¼ x 11.
                                    0-486-23628-5

AMERICAN NEGRO SONGS: 230 Folk Songs and Spirituals, Religious and Secular, John W. Work. This authoritative study traces the African influences of songs sung and played by black Americans at work, in church, and as entertainment. The author discusses the lyric significance of such songs as "Swing Low, Sweet Chariot," "John Henry," and others and offers the words and music for 230 songs. Bibliography. Index of Song Titles. 272pp. 6½ x 9¼.   0-486-40271-1

MOVIE-STAR PORTRAITS OF THE FORTIES, John Kobal (ed.). 163 glamor, studio photos of 106 stars of the 1940s: Rita Hayworth, Ava Gardner, Marlon Brando, Clark Gable, many more. 176pp. 8⅜ x 11¼.   0-486-23546-7

YEKL and THE IMPORTED BRIDEGROOM AND OTHER STORIES OF YIDDISH NEW YORK, Abraham Cahan. Film Hester Street based on *Yekl* (1896). Novel, other stories among first about Jewish immigrants on N.Y.'s East Side. 240pp. 5⅜ x 8½.   0-486-22427-9

SELECTED POEMS, Walt Whitman. Generous sampling from *Leaves of Grass.* Twenty-four poems include "I Hear America Singing," "Song of the Open Road," "I Sing the Body Electric," "When Lilacs Last in the Dooryard Bloom'd," "O Captain! My Captain!"–all reprinted from an authoritative edition. Lists of titles and first lines. 128pp. 5³⁄₁₆ x 8¼.   0-486-26878-0

SONGS OF EXPERIENCE: Facsimile Reproduction with 26 Plates in Full Color, William Blake. 26 full-color plates from a rare 1826 edition. Includes "The Tyger," "London," "Holy Thursday," and other poems. Printed text of poems. 48pp. 5¼ x 7.
                                    0-486-24636-1

THE BEST TALES OF HOFFMANN, E. T. A. Hoffmann. 10 of Hoffmann's most important stories: "Nutcracker and the King of Mice," "The Golden Flowerpot," etc. 458pp. 5⅜ x 8½.   0-486-21793-0

THE BOOK OF TEA, Kakuzo Okakura. Minor classic of the Orient: entertaining, charming explanation, interpretation of traditional Japanese culture in terms of tea ceremony. 94pp. 5⅜ x 8½.   0-486-20070-1

CATALOG OF DOVER BOOKS

FRENCH STORIES/CONTES FRANÇAIS: A Dual-Language Book, Wallace Fowlie. Ten stories by French masters, Voltaire to Camus: "Micromegas" by Voltaire; "The Atheist's Mass" by Balzac; "Minuet" by de Maupassant; "The Guest" by Camus, six more. Excellent English translations on facing pages. Also French-English vocabulary list, exercises, more. 352pp. 5⅜ x 8½. 0-486-26443-2

CHICAGO AT THE TURN OF THE CENTURY IN PHOTOGRAPHS: 122 Historic Views from the Collections of the Chicago Historical Society, Larry A. Viskochil. Rare large-format prints offer detailed views of City Hall, State Street, the Loop, Hull House, Union Station, many other landmarks, circa 1904-1913. Introduction. Captions. Maps. 144pp. 9⅜ x 12¼. 0-486-24656-6

OLD BROOKLYN IN EARLY PHOTOGRAPHS, 1865-1929, William Lee Younger. Luna Park, Gravesend race track, construction of Grand Army Plaza, moving of Hotel Brighton, etc. 157 previously unpublished photographs. 165pp. 8⅞ x 11¾. 0-486-23587-4

THE MYTHS OF THE NORTH AMERICAN INDIANS, Lewis Spence. Rich anthology of the myths and legends of the Algonquins, Iroquois, Pawnees and Sioux, prefaced by an extensive historical and ethnological commentary. 36 illustrations. 480pp. 5⅜ x 8½. 0-486-25967-6

AN ENCYCLOPEDIA OF BATTLES: Accounts of Over 1,560 Battles from 1479 B.C. to the Present, David Eggenberger. Essential details of every major battle in recorded history from the first battle of Megiddo in 1479 B.C. to Grenada in 1984. List of Battle Maps. New Appendix covering the years 1967-1984. Index. 99 illustrations. 544pp. 6½ x 9¼. 0-486-24913-1

SAILING ALONE AROUND THE WORLD, Captain Joshua Slocum. First man to sail around the world, alone, in small boat. One of great feats of seamanship told in delightful manner. 67 illustrations. 294pp. 5⅜ x 8½. 0-486-20326-3

ANARCHISM AND OTHER ESSAYS, Emma Goldman. Powerful, penetrating, prophetic essays on direct action, role of minorities, prison reform, puritan hypocrisy, violence, etc. 271pp. 5⅜ x 8½. 0-486-22484-8

MYTHS OF THE HINDUS AND BUDDHISTS, Ananda K. Coomaraswamy and Sister Nivedita. Great stories of the epics; deeds of Krishna, Shiva, taken from puranas, Vedas, folk tales; etc. 32 illustrations. 400pp. 5⅜ x 8½. 0-486-21759-0

MY BONDAGE AND MY FREEDOM, Frederick Douglass. Born a slave, Douglass became outspoken force in antislavery movement. The best of Douglass' autobiographies. Graphic description of slave life. 464pp. 5⅜ x 8½. 0-486-22457-0

FOLLOWING THE EQUATOR: A Journey Around the World, Mark Twain. Fascinating humorous account of 1897 voyage to Hawaii, Australia, India, New Zealand, etc. Ironic, bemused reports on peoples, customs, climate, flora and fauna, politics, much more. 197 illustrations. 720pp. 5⅜ x 8½. 0-486-26113-1

THE PEOPLE CALLED SHAKERS, Edward D. Andrews. Definitive study of Shakers: origins, beliefs, practices, dances, social organization, furniture and crafts, etc. 33 illustrations. 351pp. 5⅜ x 8½. 0-486-21081-2

THE MYTHS OF GREECE AND ROME, H. A. Guerber. A classic of mythology, generously illustrated, long prized for its simple, graphic, accurate retelling of the principal myths of Greece and Rome, and for its commentary on their origins and significance. With 64 illustrations by Michelangelo, Raphael, Titian, Rubens, Canova, Bernini and others. 480pp. 5⅜ x 8½. 0-486-27584-1